A MAGAZINE OF HER OWN?

The woman's magazine has had a central place in popular print throughout the twentieth century, but the history of the form has been almost completely neglected. How did it become so important? When and how did it develop its familiar elements – the agony aunt, the fashion plate, the repeated promise to transform the reader and fulfil her desires? Did it empower or disempower these readers as they sought to be gendered and sexual 'women'?

A Magazine of Her Own? addresses a range of such questions as it charts the history of the British woman's magazine through the nineteenth century. It is simultaneously a chronological story, a set of detailed case studies, and an intervention into recent debates about gender and sexuality in popular reading. Margaret Beetham argues that the magazine as a form has been shaped by its association with women as readers but also and crucially that the meaning of femininities – whether of the domestic woman, the fashionable lady or the romancing girl – have been made in and through the magazine.

The range of Beetham's original scholarship will make this book valuable to scholars but it is also clearly, accessibly written. It is of interest across a range of scholarly disciplines, including women's studies, media and cultural studies, literature and history. It will also appeal more widely to any reader interested in the history of women and of popular reading.

Margaret Beetham teaches in the Department of English and History at the Manchester Metropolitan University, where she is Course Leader in the Women's Studies MA programme. She is a co-author of *Women's Worlds: Ideology, Femininity and the Woman's Magazine* (1991).

A MAGAZINE OF HER OWN?

Domesticity and desire
in the woman's magazine,
1800–1914

Margaret Beetham

London and New York

First published 1996
by Routledge
11 New Fetter Lane, London EC4P 4EE

Simultaneously published in the USA and Canada
by Routledge
29 West 35th Street, New York, NY 10001

Routledge is an International Thomson Publishing company

Typeset in Garamond by Harper Phototypesetters Limited, Northampton
Printed and bound in Great Britain by Biddles Ltd, Guildford and Kings Lynn

British Library Cataloguing in Publication Data
A catalogue record for this book is available from the British Library

Library of Congress Cataloguing in Publication Data
Beetham, Margaret
A magazine of her own? : domesticity and desire in the woman's magazine,
1800–1914/Margaret Beetham.
p. cm.
Includes biographical references and index.
1. Women's periodicals–Great Britain–History. 2. e-uk. I. Title
PN5124.W6B44   1996
052' . 082–dc20

ISBN 0–415–04920–2 (hbk)
ISBN 0–415–14112–5 (pbk)

CONTENTS

CONTENTS

FIGURES

PREFACE

As a clever middle-class girl I was taught that I should despise women's magazines as silly if not pernicious. When I grew up and became a feminist activist and academic, I still had mentors who argued that such reading perpetuated my ideological oppression as a woman (Friedan 1965; Greer 1971). Then in the mid-1980s as popular culture began to be rescued for progressive politics I, like other feminists, began to explore the illicit pleasures of these magazines and our hate–love relationship with their endlessly repeated promises of transformation (Winship 1987). In the 1990s these ambiguities still remain unresolved and 'post-feminist' Naomi Wolf describes such magazines as simultaneously oppressive of women and the only chance for a female form of mass culture (Wolf 1990: 548–85).

All these critics stressed the importance in late twentieth-century culture of the 'women's interest magazine', a category which includes a third of British periodicals (Mintel 1986). There is some exciting recent writing on these contemporary magazines and their cultural significance (McCracken 1993; Winship 1987). There is no similar body of work on how they came to occupy their crucial place in popular reading and in the contested meanings of our femininity. Yet these titles, their characteristics and their cultural significance are the products of a specific cultural and material history. Understanding that history should enable us to locate ourselves politically and theoretically as late twentieth-century readers.

Cynthia White's *Women's Magazines, 1693–1968* opened up the field of study in 1970 and there have been useful studies of particular magazines or short periods since (Adburgham 1972; Shevelow 1989). Four of us jointly wrote a brief history which, like White's book, traced the form from its beginning to today (Ballaster *et al.* 1991). However, there is still a notable absence of historical research and writing on women's magazines and, as I have discovered to my cost, such work is very difficult, both in methodological and practical terms. Theoretical work on periodicals as popular texts is still relatively undeveloped despite their importance. Where it exists it is in cultural and media studies and in relation to late twentieth-century texts. The practical problems of this historical research are also daunting, mainly because of the sheer mass of material involved.

This book seeks to continue the task of making good the absence of history from both popular and scholarly accounts of women's magazines. I have taken a wide sweep. My subject is popular women's journals from the whole nineteenth century. In that period the mass press, the first of the mass media, came into existence in Britain and the woman's magazine evolved both its characteristic format and its crucial place in popular publishing. However, rather than attempt another descriptive general history, my method here is the case study in which I read and analyse particular magazines as representative or significant. This method will, I hope, both provide detailed historical knowledge and carry forward the debate about how to read texts of this kind and what they mean for our gender politics.

I define the 'woman's magazine' by its explicitly positioning its readers as 'women'. I therefore bring together the history of a particular publishing tradition and an analysis of the way 'woman' has been defined in and through that tradition. I privilege the concept 'woman' not because I think all women are united by their biology or by some essential womanliness but because historically the category has been used to locate and regulate women – as indeed it still is. The magazines which are my subject were and are part of that process; they not only defined readers as 'women', they sought to bring into being the women they addressed. The 'womanliness' the magazines sought to produce was always contradictory and entangled with other differences – especially those of class, nation and religion. Its relationship to the lives of the historical women – and men – who edited, wrote and read these magazines was likewise fractured and difficult to chart. Yet the concept 'woman' retained its political and ideological power across these contradictions.[1]

This book is, therefore, rooted in historical and bibliographical research and uses that research to tell a story. However, it also addresses the theoretical questions about the place of popular print in the cultural politics of gender. It is interdisciplinary and draws on a range of debates within literary and cultural studies and contemporary feminism to read some important but neglected texts.

What follows is simultaneously a chronological narrative, a set of case studies in textual analysis and an argument about the use of contemporary theory. Its range is wide both theoretically and historically. I make no claims, however, to be exhaustive. Though I deal with more than a century of popular print, this is by no means the whole history of the magazine for women (see Ballaster *et al.* 1991). I have used an eclectic range of theories about the relationship between texts and readers as gendered, sexual and embodied selves.

You may, if you wish, read this book as we read the magazines which are its subject, going to the chapters which you think look most interesting, skipping, reading from back to front. Each chapter should make sense on its own. However, I hope you will read it as I designed it to be read, from the beginning through to the end. As a chronological story and a set of arguments, this way of reading makes better sense. However, as I argue throughout, it is always up to readers to consent to or resist the writer's designs upon them, and so it is here.

ACKNOWLEDGEMENTS

This book has been a long time in the making and I have often wondered why I embarked upon it at all. In the course of its somewhat tortuous development I have incurred more debts both intellectual and personal than I can fully acknowledge here. Janet Batsleer, Laurel Brake, Elspeth Graham, Lynette Hunter and Linda Walker read chapters and commented on them in ways I found both stimulating and supportive. Helen Beetham discussed the whole with me and suggested cuts and amendments which helped shape the final draft, as well as typing a full bibliographical Appendix, which we were not in the end able to include. Brian Maidment encouraged me with ideas and volumes from his library. Erica Burman helped clarify my thinking on the final chapter. I have been sustained throughout by a network of women colleagues and friends to whom I owe much; thankyou Pat, Janet, Erica, Karen, Joanna, Carole, Peta, Elspeth and Miriam. David Beetham has been a constant enabler and support through the switchback ride of writing this book. To him and to my daughters, Helen and Kate, I can only hope the appearance of the book is some consolation as well as a token of my love and gratitude.

I am grateful also to my department and to its head, Colin Buckley, for a sabbatical term in the summer of 1994, which enabled me to complete the final draft. Thanks to the librarians and keepers of the various places where I did research: Birmingham City Library, the British Library, Colindale, the Brotherton Library of Leeds University, Manchester Central Library and Gallery of English Costume whose keeper allowed me to use their Archive, and above all thanks to staff of my own library at the Manchester Metropolitan University. I have given papers based on the material here at a number of seminars and conferences where discussion has helped me clarify my ideas.

I am grateful to Manchester City Art Gallery for permission to reproduce material from: the *Lady's Magazine* for 1780, *La Belle Assemblée* for 1806, three advertisements from *Queen* and material from *Home Chat*. Thanks also to the Manchester Metropolitan University for permission to use material from the *Family Friend*, the *Englishwoman's Domestic Magazine* and *Queen*.

It is usual to end with a disclaimer and I would not want to accuse any of my friends and colleagues of being responsible for what follows. I am, however, mainly aware of the impossibility of writing anything on one's own – just as I argue that the texts I discuss must always be read in terms of their relationships to each other and to other texts.

LIST OF
PERIODICAL ABBREVIATIONS

BA	*La Belle Assemblée*
BM	*Le Beau Monde*
BMM	*British Mothers' Magazine*
CLM	*Christian Lady's Magazine*
CR	*Contemporary Review*
E&M	*Exchange and Mart*
EDM	*Englishwoman's Domestic Magazine*
EWJ	*English Woman's Journal*
EWR	*Englishwoman's Review*
Fam.Mag.	*Family Magazine*
FF	*Family Friend*
Fem. F.	*Female's Friend*
F.Econ.	*Family Economist*
FR	*Fortnightly Review*
G.	*Gentlewoman*
GOP	*Girls' Own Paper*
H&H	*Hearth and Home*
HC	*Home Chat*
HHW	*Household Words*
Id.	*Idler*
Ld.	*Ladies*
L.	*The Lady*
LM	*Lady's Museum*
LM&M	*Lady's Magazine and Museum*
L.Mag.	*Lady's Magazine*
LN	*Lady's Newspaper*
LR	*Lady's Realm*
MM	*Mother's Magazine*
MP	*Monthly Packet*
MW	*My Weekly*
Myra	*Myra's Journal*
NMBA	*New Monthly Belle Assemblée*

19th C.	*Nineteenth Century*
Q.	*Queen*
Sat.	*Saturday Review*
W.	*Woman*
W. at H.	*Woman at Home*
WL	*Woman's Life*
WR	*Westminster Review*
Wo. R.	*Woman's Realm*
YE	*Young Englishwoman*
YW	*Young Woman*

1

INTRODUCTION

In the 1930s I sent for a dress pattern, costing 4/11 [25p]. I made it up and wore it during my honey moon. In 1943, I sent for a cut-out pink satin night-dress – very glamorous. I wore this after the birth of my second daughter. The cost then was 10/- [50p]. Now when I've read your magazine I pass it to my daughter-in-law, who gives it to her mother and aunt. Quite good value, wouldn't you say?

(Mrs A.F. Smith, Kent, letter to *Woman* 13 Feb. 1988, 7)

Last week I invited my girl friend to my house for a romantic dinner at which I intended to ask her hand in marriage. I had planned the meal weeks previously but, alas, I forgot one of the major ingredients. Frantically I turned to a copy of *Bella* that my girl friend had left behind. I came across a recipe for sweet-and-sour bacon chops for which I had all the ingredients. The meal was tremendous and my girl friend was impressed. She also agreed to my proposal. I can't thank you enough.

(Tony Docherty, letter to *Bella*, 10 Feb. 1990)

Throughout its history, the woman's magazine has defined its readers 'as women'. It has taken their gender as axiomatic. Yet that femininity is always represented in the magazines as fractured, not least because it is simultaneously assumed as given and as still to be achieved. Becoming the woman you are is a difficult project for which the magazine has characteristically provided recipes, patterns, narratives and models of the self. Mrs Smith of Kent explained that it was precisely this for which she had valued it over many years. *Woman* had provided patterns for her to follow as she negotiated the complexities of an identity which encompassed sexual woman, frugal housekeeper and mother. The glamorous nightdress she bought through the magazine enabled her to become a desirable woman without abandoning her role as good housekeeper. For the magazine has historically offered not only to pattern the reader's gendered identity but to address her desire.

This femininity has been addressed in and through a form which is itself fractured and heterogeneous. The magazine has developed in the two centuries of its history as a miscellany, that is a form marked by variety of tone and constituent parts. The relationship between the two elements in the term 'woman's magazine' has been and is dynamic. The magazine evolved as it did because from its inception it was a genre which addressed 'the feminine', but 'femininity' has also been

1

informed by the development of print, particularly the magazine. The history of their relationship has been marked by continuity but also by discontinuity and by the constant re-working of the 'same' elements whose meanings are radically unstable. Mrs Smith's letter, with its public revelation of her intimate life, was in a tradition which had been re-worked during 200 years of feminine journalism.

Her letter earned her £5 and the 'good value' she identified in the magazine was economic rather than ideological or psychological. Magazines are commodities, products of the print industry. They have also become a crucial site for the advertising and sale of other commodities, whether nightgowns or convenience foods. Magazines are, therefore, deeply involved in capitalist production and consumption as well as circulating in the cultural economy of collective meanings and constructing an identity for the individual reader as gendered and sexual being. The woman's magazine works at the intersection of these different economies – of money, public discourse and individual desire – and it is there I situate the history I trace in the rest of this book.

Unlike earlier historians of the women's press, therefore, I do not read the magazines of the last century exclusively as instruments of a pervasive domestic ideology and a regime of sexual repression (Adburgham 1972; White 1970). This reading was embedded in a view of the period which has since been challenged by historians from a range of positions, including feminists (Barret-Ducrocq 1991; Bland 1995; Foucault 1981; Gay 1984; Shires 1992; Smart 1992). It has also been challenged by the theorising of post-structuralists, notably Foucault, whose theorising of the relationship of discourses to knowledge and power, problematic though it is for feminists, provides some useful tools here (Foucault 1981). In particular his argument that power is productive and not simply repressive throws light on the complex relationships enacted in women's magazines between readers, writers and editors.

Mrs Smith's letter suggests the power of the magazine's discourses of femininity but it also shows her capacity to exploit them. The magazine itself becomes, for her, a medium of exchange among a community of women, a process which circumvents the economic aims of its producers and reasserts an alternative set of values. Perhaps she is even exploiting her knowledge of the assumptions of the letters page to earn herself £5. Certainly she knows how to play the part of 'Mrs Smith', the average woman to whom the magazine is addressed.

Readers may be relatively less powerful than writers but they can still accept or resist meanings the writer produces. Writers are powerful in relation to language and the reader but less so in relation to the editor, the publisher or the advertiser. Editorial power is itself limited, discursively and economically, by pressure from advertisers and from readers. Moreover the balance of power between these different groups varies historically and is constantly in process. In the woman's magazine, gender and sexuality – yet other complex sets of power relationships – are caught up in these dynamics. Popular print is too complex a phenomenon to be understood in the simplistic terms of 'patriarchy' or of 'class', and theories of gender which construct women only as victims of repression are theoretically and politically suspect.

To collapse power absolutely into discourse, however, is likewise to oversimplify and to lose sight of the material and political history in which struggles over meaning take place. This means recognising that as commodities magazines are only available to those with the necessary levels of literacy, income, leisure and space for reading. It also means that as texts, magazines enact relations between groups which are very differently situated in the social and cultural structures of power. In the complicated negotiations over meaning which characterise popular print, some groups have more power than others to make their meanings 'stick' (Cameron 1986; Thompson 1984). In the rest of this book, readings of specific magazines are situated in unequal power relationships, particularly – but not exclusively – those of gender.

The asymmetry of gender is clearly evident in Tony Docherty's letter to *Bella* which forms the other epigraph to this chapter. Throughout its history men have entered the woman's magazine as readers, writers and editors. It may be that by doing so, they learn to read 'as women'. Certainly, the magazine provided Tony Docherty with that crucial recipe and with a narrative of romantic encounter. But his reading gave him access not to being a woman but to the feminine world of the domestic and to female sexuality, which he appropriated 'as a man'. The language of this letter with such phrases as asking her hand in marriage suggests that this appropriation may be ironic, even parodic. Nevertheless the point remains.

Like the nineteenth-century middle-class home, the woman's magazine evolved during the last century as a 'feminised space'. It was defined by the woman who was at its centre and by its difference from the masculine world of politics and economics. But whereas the middle-class woman could not enter the public world of work or politics, the middle-class man could and did come home at night to be revived and humanised by his immersion in the domestic world of the feminine. The equation of the feminine with the human – or at least the humane – is only one aspect of the complexity of gender dynamics which the popular magazine enacts. It did not necessarily empower women. The feminised world of the magazine whose history I trace is constantly entered and appropriated by historical men (Modleski 1991). The asymmetry of gender difference therefore recurs throughout this book and is fundamental to its project. It would be impossible to write a comparable history of magazines which defined men in terms of their masculinity.[1]

However, the woman's magazine like other 'feminised spaces', including women's studies courses, hen parties and girls' schools, also has a radical potential. Like them it may become a different kind of feminised space, one in which it is possible to challenge oppressive and repressive models of the feminine. As the following pages show, the potential mismatch between 'femininity' and historical women could be a source of power for those women, though in the context of gender inequalities this was rarely the case.

FEMININITY AND THE TEXT

This book arises at the intersection of two interdisciplinary academic projects, women's studies and cultural studies and I have drawn on methods and theoretical approaches evolved in both. Two key concepts which recur throughout the book, therefore, are 'femininity' and the 'text'. Its implicit argument is that the meaning of both these terms and the relationship between them which is my subject must be situated historically. Indeed I want to resist the academic pressures to separate 'theory' and conceptualising from historical practice, analysis and narrative. Nevertheless a brief account of how I use these two key terms may clarify the argument and method of what follows.

In addressing 'women', the magazines I discuss assumed the tidy coincidence of gender and sexuality with the embodied self. These categories are utterly entangled in our culture and their relationship is constantly assumed as given. In the late twentieth century, feminist, gay and lesbian, and queer theorists and activists have argued that the mapping of femininity (that is appropriate social behaviour) onto female heterosexual desire, and of both onto biological femaleness, far from being natural is only accomplished by powerful social, linguistic and psychological forces.[2] Moreover, that task is never fully accomplished. Early critiques of social construction which suggested that gender was imposed on a more basic sexuality and that the body at least was natural have themselves been subjected to the criticism that they deny the extent to which sexuality is an effect of discourse and the female body a product of the social expectations of femininity (see esp. Butler 1990, 1993).

Throughout this book I assume not only that the meaning of femininity was and is radically unstable but that its relationship to sexuality and the female body had to be constantly re-worked. I do not assume that the magazines imposed a socially constructed femininity on a natural sexuality or on already existing bodies, but rather that the meaning of these terms was dynamically related. Nor did this go on simply in the realm of discourse. The female body was materially shaped by the corsets, medicines and hairstyles which the magazines recommended. And these recommendations were themselves the products of economic as well as ideological imperatives, the need for the magazines simultaneously to insist upon femininity and to attract advertising from the makers of corsets and medicines.

At certain moments the radical instability of these categories and the slippages between them became obvious, as happened in the 1890s (see Ch. 8). However, that instability was endemic throughout the nineteenth century. Indeed, I would argue that the magazine as a form assumed the place it did in women's reading in part because it addressed this problem. It sought to bring into being the woman it addressed as gendered, sexual and embodied. The naturalness of this complex identity had to be insisted upon again and again precisely because it was so slippery, and for this the magazine which comes out regularly weekly or monthly over time is the ideal form.

Across these instabilities there were certain constants. The first of these is that 'woman' was always positioned as other to and deviant from a norm assumed to be masculine/male. The second was that this involved not just difference but also power and the third that the meaning of these categories was always worked out within particular material histories. This is crucial also for my second key concept, that of the text.

In defining the magazine as a text I am drawing on the Barthesian definition of the text as a 'methodological field and site of interdisciplinary study' (see Pykett 1990:12). I read the magazine neither as reflecting nineteenth-century culture nor as a place in which the ruling class or group imposed its ideology directly on subordinate groups. Nor do I understand the magazine as producing experience as an effect. The magazine as 'text' interacts with the culture which produced it and which it produces. It is a place where meanings are contested and made. For the way we make sense of our lives as individuals and social groups involves constant negotiations in which there is no single determinant (Cameron 1985: 170). This process also characterises the making of meaning in the magazine.

There are, however, structures and power relations which shape those negotiations in the magazine as in the wider culture. The texts I discuss were structured by the technologies of print and paper-making, which produced them as material objects, and by the economics of the publishing industry, which produced them as commodities. Crucially, also, the periodical press was a literary formation. The magazine developed its own generic and linguistic conventions and its sub-divisions, each with their own discourses and practice. Increasingly, also, it developed a set of visual conventions and techniques through use of illustration. These economic, technological and literary or visual formations were caught up also with the social formations and power inequalities of gender, class and nationality. Together these structured but did not determine the way readers and writers used the magazine to make sense of their society and of their lives. Above all this was a dynamic process and not static, as the metaphor of structures may suggest. Just as the meaning of femininity was always being re-made, so was the meaning and the form of the magazine and its conventions.

METHODOLOGY

Defining the magazine as text shapes the methodology of this book. Textual reading depends on close attention to particularities. This book is, therefore, organised around case studies in which I offer close readings of particular magazines. I chose these as representative or significant after extensive sampling of the hundreds of titles I identified in an extensive bibliographical search.[3] The case study method has also provided a way of dealing with the sheer mass of material involved in a study of this scale. Such a method may more accurately be described as inter-textual than textual analysis, since it is impossible to decide what constitutes a single text when one is dealing with a serial which came out weekly for years. Each number of a magazine only makes sense as part of a field of other texts as well as a field of power relations.

Literary and social historians are used to turning to periodicals for evidence about the past. However, they have rarely treated them as texts in themselves, using them instead as repositories from which they can remove 'facts', expressions of ideas and ideology, or fictional work in prose and poetry. There are notable exceptions to this, scholars on whose work I have drawn heavily.[4] However, I have found most useful methodologically the work by feminists writing about contemporary serial forms for women, particularly Janice Winship's work on magazines and Tani Modleski's on soap opera (McRobbie 1978a and b; Modleski 1984; Winship 1987).

Treating the magazine as a text involved me also in considering the way it developed as a form over a period of time. Despite its importance in print culture, literary scholars have not considered the periodical as a genre with its own history. Yet, like the realist novel, the magazine was a form with recognisable conventions which were re-worked over the years and should be studied along a span of time. I have, therefore, combined the case study with the chronological narrative. The case studies represent particular moments in the development of the genre over the period of more than a century and they are organised more or less chronologically. This enables me to discuss the continuities and discontinuities in the magazine's development and to relate them to the making and re-making of gender definitions through time.

It is not, however, a simple chronology. Rather, I have used the case studies to construct an argument about periodisation. The book is divided into four sections but effectively I divide the century into three periods, so the last two sections of the book deal with the most important period – the 1880s and 1890s. The emergence of a strand of magazines specifically targeted at women was complicated and slow. In the first section of the book, which deals with the period from 1800 to 1850, I chart this process. The second section uses the Beeton's magazines which flourished between the 1850s and 1870s to discuss the consolidation of that tradition in both middle- and upper-class reading. In the third and fourth sections I discuss how a diverse women's press became established at the centre of popular publishing. Throughout, the development of the magazine as a text is intertwined with the changing meaning of womanhood. In the rest of this chapter I set out some of the ways this relationship is explored in the book which follows.

THE ENGLISH WOMAN OF THE MIDDLE CLASS

The woman's magazine came into existence during the late eighteenth and early nineteenth century when the press and gender relations were both caught up in the revolution which made Britain the first industrialised and urban society. Historians have long since noted the emergence from that revolution of group identities understood in terms of 'class'. It is only recently that feminist historians like Catherine Hall and Leonore Davidoff have argued that middle-class identities were constructed on the ground of gender difference and took one of two forms, that of the masculine breadwinner or the domestic woman (Davidoff and Hall

1987). Nancy Armstrong's more radical argument concerns the textual production of the domestic woman in conduct books and novels (Armstrong 1985).

Women's magazines were produced by and produced these politics of classed
gender or gendered class. Because material conditions made regular purchase of
even relatively cheap printed matter beyond the reach of working women, most
magazines targeted the middle class and offered explicitly bourgeois models of
feminine behaviour. Throughout the century, femininity was represented as
hidden in the privacy of the home and in the female heart, analogous sites for the
exercise of virtuous self-control.

Yet this powerful discourse was constantly disrupted by others, particularly the
discourse which vested femininity in appearance and located gender difference in
the 'natural' difference of the body. The female body both as the mark of difference and as an erotic surface was always inscribed within the domestic. The
biological difference of sex was marked culturally by dress. For most of the century
men's and women's clothes were exaggeratedly different, not least because the
curves of the female figure were emphasised through the use of corsets. The
clothed female body represented in the fashion-plate became a staple of the periodical genre and the corset reappears again and again as a motif in this history.

The definition of femininity in terms of physical appearance alone was associated with an outmoded, aristocratic ideal but the biological and social necessity of
female beauty proved a concept highly resistant to bourgeois moralising. In the
discourses of dress, and especially in the illustrations, it persisted in middle-class
magazines throughout the century and emerged in the 1880s and 1890s as a revitalised aristocratic model of femininity.

Since the nineteenth century defined itself as a class society, the relationship
between class and gender definitions were often specifically spelt out in the magazines. The identification of femininity with 'Englishness', whiteness or
Christianity by contrast only became explicit at particular moments. However,
like those of class, these identifications were consistently assumed and constantly
re-worked. The association of 'true' femininity with the English middle-class
woman, articulated in domestic literature like Sarah Ellis's *Women of England*
series of the 1830s and 1840s, entered deeply into the tradition of women's magazines (Ellis 1839, 1842). It combined with the evangelical tradition embodied in
various mothers' magazines which made an analogous identification of femininity
with Christianity. All these fed into the more explicit nationalism and racism of
the 1880s and 1890s when England's imperial role was widely discussed.

Women's magazines, unlike newspapers, were not published in provincial
centres outside London. My research in one such centre, Manchester, has revealed
no magazines addressed specifically to women and a number which assumed that
regional identity was inherently masculine (Beetham 1985). Throughout the
century, therefore, women's magazines produced an exclusively metropolitan
version of femininity. By the 1880s and 1890s women's magazines were read
across the empire but the identity offered in the magazines bound readers firmly
into the culture of the capital. Even 'provincial' readers in Britain were at the

7

margin of the magazines' world, a problem only emphasised when magazines arranged agents to shop in London for goods they recommended.

FEMININITY AS CONSUMPTION

The move from reading to shopping became increasingly central to the genre. The magazines positioned women both as purchasers and readers of texts, although the two were not necessarily the same person. Mrs Smith, like many other purchasers, circulated her magazine around her family. In the nineteenth century, when magazines were relatively more expensive, the ratio of readers to purchasers was even higher than today (Altick 1957: 322–3; Mintel 1986). The magazine bought by an upper middle-class woman might be read by her daughters, her servants and her friends, then swapped for another through the exchange pages of the first magazine before being thrown out or sent to a second-hand book shop.

For the woman purchaser, one commodity – the magazine – gave entry into a world of commodities. In the nineteenth century, the feminine role of providing for the household became increasingly defined as shopping, as well as – or instead of – making. This representation of woman as domestic provider then came to overlap with other rather different ways in which femininity was linked to consumption, and contrasted with the (implicitly masculine) world of production.

In the 1880s and 1890s the definition of women as 'shoppers' became central to the magazines' advice columns. Commodities were increasingly represented as essential to the work of being feminine. Shopping itself was changing, especially with the development of urban department stores which made the display of commodities important both inside the shop and in their plate-glass windows (Adburgham 1964; Bowlby 1985). The woman shopper was defined both by the activity of looking – whether through plate-glass windows or at newspaper advertisements – and by how she looked herself. The definition of femininity in terms of appearance thus returned in the 1890s linked primarily not to the display of the aristocratic lady but to that of bourgeois commodity culture.

By the end of the century, women's magazines across the market were carrying as many pages of advertising as of editorial copy and were relying on advertising revenue at least as much as direct sales. The importance of commodities for the feminine was established not only for 'the lady' but for a mass readership. Femininity in the 1890s magazines appeared both in the body constructed through the purchase of certain commodities – the dress, the hair-piece, the ointment – and in the domestic scene (or *mise-en-scène*) which likewise depended on skilful shopping for and deployment of commodities. There was, therefore, a dynamic relationship between this re-making of femininity and the material basis of the magazines in advertising revenue.

INTRODUCTION
THE PERIODICAL AS COMMODITY

The generic term 'periodical' includes all serial forms of print: newspaper, journal, review and magazine. The importance of class as a determinant of the development of the periodical press was recognised by contemporaries and by later scholars (Altick 1957; Wiener 1969). However, the place of gender in that history has been relatively neglected. Yet the first periodicals aimed to include 'the fair sex' as readers or even as writers and, like the novel with which its early history was so entwined, the periodical has at particular moments been understood as a feminine or feminised form (Ballaster *et al.* 1991; Shevelow 1989). The development of a strand of magazines which named women specifically as target readers must be understood within that general history.

The reasons why the magazine rather than the newspaper became associated with femininity are taken up in what follows. However, all periodical forms share certain important qualities, chiefly their relationship to time: the 'periodicity' which gives the genre its name and distinguishes it from other kinds of print. This feature is crucial both economically and discursively.

Ironically, given that I am considering examples from the last century, the periodical is above all an ephemeral form, produced for a particular day, week or month. Its claims to truth and importance are always contingent, as is clear from the date which is prominently displayed (sometimes on every page). This affects its material form as well as its meaning. Because they are designed to be thrown away, most periodicals are physically more fragile than books, produced on cheap paper and without stiff covers.

Nineteenth-century readers who could afford it had their periodicals bound in volume form, a practice which ensured that millions of issues have been preserved and has made possible books like this. However, the low status of popular magazines for women mean few libraries hold copies, let alone complete runs, and the practice of stripping out covers and advertisements before binding into volume form makes even these copies largely incomplete. Because of the convention of anonymous or pseudonymous journalism, which only began to give way at the end of the century, it is also often difficult to discover the identity or even the gender of different writers and editors. The contingent claims for truth of the individual periodical, therefore, inform its history, too.[5]

However, its relationship to time has also been the source of the periodical's immense vitality as a form. Though each number is rooted in a particular historical moment, the series of which it is a part may continue for years, decades or even centuries. Of course the continuation of a title does not necessarily mean a periodical remains 'the same'. The *Queen* magazine was launched in the 1860s and continues to appear in the 1990s after amalgamating with *Harper's Bazaar*. It is clearly not now the same magazine as Mr and Mrs Beeton's original. Nevertheless there are powerful pressures towards continuity in periodicals – not least the need to be recognised and bought by regular readers – and *Harper's and Queen* is still an up-market publication with an emphasis on fashion. This capacity to re-make itself, each number the same and yet different, characterises the form.

These qualities ensured that as nineteenth-century Britain became a literate society, periodicals became central to popular as well as elite reading. The *Waterloo Directory* (Wolff *et al.* 1976) lists 29,000 titles for the period 1824–1900 and it remains incomplete. I compiled a list of nearly 1,000 titles for this book, some of which came out weekly over decades. Daunting though it may be to scholars, however, the volume and variety of this material is testimony to the vitality of the form.

As a commodity, the periodical was the first to have its sell-by date stamped on it. This allowed producers to control precisely when their material became obsolete but it also put pressure on them to make production and distribution efficient. Throughout the century, new technologies of print and picture reproduction, paper-making and distribution were all pioneered in periodical publishing where speed and regularity were essential.

The periodical was, therefore, crucially involved in the development of the nineteenth-century economy. Changes in finance (the appearance in the 1890s of large companies financed from public flotation on the Stock Exchange), the development of the professions – including journalism – the new technologies of communication and transport like the railways and the telegraph, were all involved in the development of the press. The magazines analysed in this book were, through their crucial role in advertising, also locked ever more firmly into the capitalist economy. Not only were periodicals themselves commodities, they helped to create a commodity culture.

THE WOMAN AS READER

Though she might not have been a purchaser, the woman addressed by the magazine was always a reader. The importance of gender in the culture of print was taken up in much nineteenth-century debate on reading (Flint 1993). Because reading became identified as an activity carried on in the privacy of the home, the middle-class woman who was the hub of that domestic world became central also to the activity of reading. Her leisure was the signifier of her gender and it was her leisure which was the necessary condition for the emergence not only of the novel but also of other forms of print such as the family magazine (Watt 1957).

Yet women, like the working class, were assumed to read differently from the middle-class male norm and there was much anxiety over appropriate reading matter for them.[6] Concern was concentrated in particular on the possible access of young women to sexual knowledge, since sexual ignorance was essential to true femininity. The axiom that women read mainly fiction heightened this anxiety, in part because of the lingering belief that fiction was inferior to biography, history or science because it was not 'true', but also because fiction dealt with sexuality, though in the legitimated form of romance. The figure of the reader as a young girl in need of protection from illicit knowledge thus dominated the production of fiction, the policy of libraries and debates about reading until the 1890s (Flint 1993; Grierst 1970: 120–55; Moore 1885). Women's magazines addressed this ambiguous figure of the woman reader as both limit to and centre of the reading public.

Untangling the relation between these debates about female reading and historical readers is a task beset by difficulties, particularly in relation to magazines. There is a dearth of specific information about who historically read these texts and how. In the absence of independent auditing of magazine circulations in the nineteenth century, global circulation figures are usually drawn from the unreliable versions given by proprietors and editors. All this makes it difficult to discuss the question of readers' engagement. Although I argue that cultural meanings, including those of gender, were negotiated in these magazines, I have had to rely on the texts themselves to provide evidence for this. Unlike cultural critics of the contemporary I am not able to interview readers directly and therefore am in danger of assuming that I can construct the historical reader from the text. In particular, by focusing on how the texts produce meaning I may seem to deny readers any possibility of resisting or re-making those meanings.

In dealing with this problem, I have drawn on the recent debate in critical theory over the concept of reading 'as a woman' (Culler 1982; Fuss 1989; Jacobus 1986; Mills 1994). The argument that women have often been taught to read 'as men' and the counter-argument that men can learn to read 'as women' can too easily deny the material and ideological conditions in which women learn to become 'women', that is learn to take on their gender. In particular it can too easily write out the asymmetry of power relations in which masculinity is the norm. Nevertheless, the separation between the reader constructed or positioned by the text and the historical reader, which is central to this debate, is a necessary and useful one.

Since gender is not natural or stable, there is – as I have suggested – always the potential for a space to open up between the historical woman reader and the way the text defines her femininity. It is in that space that the 'resisting reader', in Judith Fetterley's phrase, may come into being (Fetterley 1978). Any text can be read in this way, but, as I argue in the next section, the magazine as a form empowers its readers in specific ways which encourage the possibility of diverse readings. The evidence for the resistance of nineteenth-century readers is sometimes directly evidenced but has also to be inferred from the way the dominant definitions of femininity had constantly to be reasserted, a process which the chronological sweep of the book makes clear. However, I would argue that the possibility of a resistant reading depends on the political and social context in which the reader is placed.

I am also aware that I am a historical reader and my readings, too, are contingent upon the context of late twentieth-century feminist politics and academic debate in which I am situated. I attempt to read these relatively neglected texts in terms which recognise the historical distance between their production and my reading. However, I also read with an awareness of the continuities between these texts and contemporary constructions of femininity and today's magazines for women.

POWER AND READING: THE PERIODICAL TEXT

The key element in reading the periodical is its double relationship to time.[7] Each number of a periodical is both of its moment and of a series, different from and yet the same as those which have gone before. The economic imperative is to be consistent enough to maintain a readership, and this is achieved by a number of devices, including general format, mix of ingredients and price. Most important of all, however, the individual periodical works by positioning its readers in a particular way, as 'Tories' or 'interested in sport' or 'women'. This is something more than market targeting: it affects the contents, the price, the style and the tone in which readers are addressed. It must be more or less consistent both within one number and across the series in order to reinforce and to reassure readers of the identity being offered to them. We are very familiar with this from contemporary media where a woman's magazine can describe its readers by its own title as 'Cosmo Girls'.

This positioning of the reader may be described as ideological, as inserting or 'interpellating' individuals into social identities which already exist and which offer them ways of making sense of the world (Althusser 1971). If the reader accepts the position of 'woman' offered by the magazine, she takes on both the role and the character which it defines as womanly. As I have suggested, I want to resist this way of describing how the periodical works, not least because as a genre it has another equally important characteristic which militates against this argument.

For the periodical is also marked by a radical heterogeneity. It refused, and still refuses, a single authorial voice, for example. When one prodigiously energetic writer was rumoured to have written a whole number single-handed, this had to be denied (Colby 1970: 199). It also mixes media and genres. While the review and the academic journal may consist almost entirely of one kind of writing, the more successful periodical forms like the magazine and newspaper are the least homogeneous. The periodical is generically as well as physically more liable to disintegrate than the book. Its typical contents – narratives, poems, pictures, competitions and even jokes – are forms which have a more substantial cultural presence outside the periodical. Even that most periodical of genres, the article, was and is quite likely to be collected and appear in volume format. All this suggests a fractured rather than a rigidly coherent form.

As I have suggested, this diversity empowers readers of periodicals in particular ways. First, they are empowered as consumers who can decide whether to continue to buy the periodical or not. Regular buyers are essential for the periodical's survival and they may influence the shape of their magazines by their consumer choices. Second, they have power as readers because they can to a unique degree construct their own text from the printed version. We do not read a magazine straight through from front to back as we do a novel. The form invites us to flip through, read in any order, omit some sections altogether and read others carefully. Finally, periodical readers are constantly being invited to become writers. Eighteenth- and early nineteenth-century magazines relied on readers to provide a good deal of copy. As professionalisation transformed the press, the role of readers-turned-writers was confined to the letters pages but these were and still are an important element of the form. We are all potential Mrs Smiths when we read magazines, just as we are all potentially resisting readers.

The magazine is the most mixed and various of all periodical forms. In the examples I discuss, the 'interpellation' of the reader into the role which the magazine defines is therefore fractured by the way the form works to empower the reader. In this respect one might argue that the form is inherently subversive, or even inherently 'feminine'.

THE PERIODICAL AS A FEMININE FORM?

The argument that the periodical is 'feminine' takes various forms. The first draws broadly on Julia Kristeva's distinction between 'men's time', which is linear, and 'women's time', which is less bound by clock and calendar and more attuned to bodily and psychic processes (Kristeva 1986: 188–213, esp. 191–3). Mattelart (1986) uses the idea that women's perception of time is cyclical to argue that serial or periodical forms, like soap operas and magazines, chime better with women's experience than men's. As such they are of particular importance to women though they are not highly valued in male dominated culture.

Another analogous but rather different argument describes serial forms like soap opera as 'feminine' not because they are cyclical but because they resist closure. They thus correspond to an account of feminine psychology as more open than the masculine, less marked by rigid ego boundaries and less dependent on a single orgasm or closure for its pleasure. Magazines may not be examples of *écriture féminine* but their qualities of fragmentation and openness seem to suggest that such publications are by their very nature potentially subversive of masculine cultural norms (Modleski 1982).

These ideas of the consonance between the form of the magazine and femininity are interesting but do not take account of the double-faced quality of the periodical. As well as being part of a continuum, magazines are also of their particular moment; the series is open-ended and fluid but each number is contained. Such arguments are also unsatisfactory insofar as they pose an essential femininity divorced from historical uses and meanings and, above all, from the way that in our culture serials provide a specific structure of regulation in terms of the calendar and the clock.

The historical development of the periodical as part of capitalist expansion in nineteenth-century Britain was tied in with the development of new ways of organising work and leisure under the pressure of industrialisation. Increasingly mechanised work practices and the growth of the factory system meant that work time had to be regulated and controlled in a way which also shaped time away from work (Thompson 1967; Whipp 1987). The Sunday papers, bought by nineteenth-century working-class men to mark their one day of rest in the week, were a symptom of a wider process whereby leisure and entertainment become regulated. The weekly or monthly magazine still provides a deep structure which ties entertainment and individual pleasure into the calendar and the demands of industrial society. Far from seeing serial forms as having been historically in tension with the dominant 'masculine' values and power structures, then, I see them as consonant with and reinforcing those structures.

Besides, a brief study of such periodical forms as the major intellectual reviews, academic journals or even newspapers shows that historically men have been in control of these forms, and to describe them as simply as feminine raises again those questions about the relation of femininity to the experience of women. I would, therefore resist accounts of these forms simply in terms of their 'femininity' or their potential for subversion.

At the same time, those qualities of fluidity and openness to the future which characterise serial forms do make them attractive to the powerless. As readers, we recognise the feeling that, however disappointing this number of our favourite magazine may be, it holds out the promise of future satisfaction. There will be another number, next week or month. We may describe this as a kind of addiction but this openness to the future also carries an implicit utopianism which makes it attractive to all those dissatisfied with the current social order (Jameson 1979; see also Modleski 1982: 107).

Here again, the form is deeply contradictory, simultaneously rooting its readers in the present while pointing them to the future. The history of the woman's magazine shows clearly how this formal relationship to time resonates with the construction of femininity in our culture. The promise of self-transformation is endemic in the form. The modern magazine's promise that this week's number will cure your fat thighs problem is symptomatic of the way the regular appearance of the magazine has been harnessed to the work of femininity. Dissatisfaction with the social self is recognised but endlessly displaced. However, it is only by looking at particular uses of these forms in history that we can see how they relate not only to masculinity and femininity, but to men and women as writers and readers.

Part I

THE MAKING OF THE MAGAZINE, 1800–50

2

THE 'FAIR SEX'
AND THE MAGAZINE:
THE EARLY LADIES' JOURNALS

[*Lady's Magazine* is] a production mainly feminine.
('Address to the Public', *Lady's Magazine* XI 1780: 4)

I have heard some of my own sex lament that they were debarred from the privileges and pleasures which males freely enjoy; but in the very outset of my intended labours, I wish to caution them against indulging such ideas . . . . A woman entirely beloved by her husband . . . is the happiest of human beings.
('The Old Woman', *Lady's Monthly Museum* I 1798: 29)

In 1798 a new magazine, the *Lady's Monthly Museum or Polite Repository of Amusement and Instruction* (hereafter *Lady's Museum*) was launched by 'A Society of Ladies'. They claimed it was 'an assemblage of whatever can please the fancy, interest the mind and exalt the character of the British Fair' (*LM* I 1798: 1). This magazine flourished with only minor changes until 1832. Then it merged with an even older title, the *Lady's Magazine* (1770–1832) and then with another well-established rival, *La Belle Assemblée* (1806–32), to produce a combined title which lasted until 1847. These three journals were aristocratic not popular but, separately and together, they established the woman's magazine as the genre we recognise today.

The idea of a journal for ladies was not new in 1798. In 1709 Steele had launched the first number of the *Tatler* for a readership he defined as 'publick spirited men' and 'the Fair Sex, in Honour of whom I have invented the title of this Paper' (quoted in Shevelow 1989: 93). This installed gender as crucial to the definition of the periodical and its reading public. Moreover, it opened up a specifically feminised space within the genre, even though this remained secondary to the masculinised space of the 'publick spirited' male.

Throughout the eighteenth century, periodicals had continued to 'fair sex it', in Swift's words (Shevelow 1989: 1). Women were addressed specifically as readers but they were also active as writers and editors. 'Womanliness' or femininity was installed as a crucial topic for discussion. Thus women were simultaneously positioned as consumers and producers of these texts and as objects of their analysis (Adburgham 1972; Ballaster *et al.* 1991; Shevelow 1989).

The meaning of this feminised space was ambiguous, however. Steele's double-edged compliment dismissed women's interest as 'tattle' while it made the figure of the 'Tatler' stand for the whole readership. Women were thus positioned as marginal, but that marginality enabled them to represent metonymically the whole class of those with leisure for reading and conversation at whom the new periodical press was aimed. The position of the feminine in the periodical, therefore, could not be understood solely in terms of relative powerlessness, but as providing a vantage point from which to view and judge the world of 'publick spirited' men and their politics.

Throughout the eighteenth and into the early nineteenth century the possibility of such a feminine vantage point was explored across a range of periodicals, from those with a general readership like the *Tatler* to those like the *Lady's Magazine* specifically for 'the fair sex'. In her history of the women's magazines Cynthia White argued that there was 'a sudden reversal of the trend which promised [women] wider participation in social affairs' and that a monolithic and utterly repressive domestic ideology came to characterise the woman's magazine from the 1820s onwards. This view has been widely accepted (Adburgham 1972; Braithwaite and Barrell 1988; Shevelow 1989). White quotes the editor of the *Lady's Magazine* who in 1825 lamented:

> The times are changed . . . women have completely abandoned attempts to shine in the political horizon and now seek only to exercise their virtues in domestic retirement . . . . Writers . . . proclaim the mental as well as the bodily inferiority of the weaker sex.
>
> (*L.Mag.* 1825: 64, quoted in White 1970: 39)

However, the change which White describes was neither sudden nor absolute. Throughout the late eighteenth and early nineteenth centuries the concept of 'the lady' was in flux between an older aristocratic definition and a new set of values associated with the bourgeois family. These meanings coexisted in tension with each other. In magazines like the *Lady's Museum* attacks on women's claims for male 'privileges and pleasures' appeared side by side with eloquent statements of these claims (*LM* I 1798: 1; IV 1801: 115). The piece White quotes was a polemical intervention into a debate about femininity in which the dominance of the domestic ideal was still contested and incomplete. What is clear is, first, that in defining themselves the new 'lady's magazines' also set out to define their readers. Reading the magazine both produced femininity and was its signifier. Second, the magazines assumed gender as a crucial marker of the identity they defined. The new meaning of 'the lady' which they struggled to create constantly reduced the status and class connotations of the term to an aspect of gender.

In the first section of the book I chart the establishment and development of the woman's magazine during the first half of the nineteenth century. Though a distinct women's press only gradually emerged, the name 'magazine', its character as a mixed periodical and even the particular elements which still persist in the 'woman's magazine' today were all put into place during this period. These processes were caught up with struggles over the meaning of 'the lady', which I take up in this chapter. In the next two chapters I focus on the way the magazines produced and were produced by that struggle and how it was enacted around various female identities: the Queen, the woman journalist, the Beauty and the Christian Mother.

THE MULTI-AUTHORED TEXT: READERS AND WRITERS

The *Lady's Magazine* and the *Lady's Museum* established the magazine as *the* periodical form for women and developed the basic pattern it still retains. Two characteristics distinguished the magazine from the various other periodical forms current at the time. Unlike the essay-serial, it mixed genres and had a variety of authorial voices but unlike that other mixed periodical form, the newspaper, it carried no 'news'. Both these were significant for its role as women's reading.

The term 'magazine', which meant a store-house, only gradually came to be preferred over such alternatives as 'repository' and 'museum'. The *Gentleman's Magazine* was important in this process and its address to a specifically masculine readership also produced a series of counter-attempts to provide for 'the sex excluded' from these 'repositories' (*L.Mag.* XI 1780: 4). What these various names had in common was the identification of variety – both of authorial voice and of constitutive elements – as the crucial characteristic of the genre.

The difficulty of sustaining a single-authored serial for any length of time must have contributed to the evolution of the multi-authored text. Even the prodigiously energetic Mrs Trimmer gave up producing the *Family Magazine* (1788–9) after eighteen months, 'finding it very inconvenient to conduct a periodical work' in this way (*Fam.Mag.* III 1789: 38). Multiple authorship and variety of voice thus became the norm in serials for ladies as well as those for a general readership.

One feature of this variety was extensive contribution from readers. Though the *Lady's Museum* boasted that it drew on 'ladies of established reputation in literary circles', it relied heavily on readers to provide copy (*LM* I 1798: 1). In this, as in much else, it followed the example of the *Lady's Magazine* as did *La Belle Assemblée* when it began. As journalism was not yet established as a profession, and indeed the whole concept of 'profession' was in the making, the boundary between 'literary ladies' and 'readers' remained unclear. It is therefore impossible to tell what proportion of each paper's copy originated with readers, but it seems to have been substantial.

'Notes to Correspondents' were extensive:

> We have to return our thanks to many of our early Friends and Patrons of our work, some of whose Communications will be found in the present Number . . . thanks to our constant friend J.M. of Kingsland, to R.C. of Surrey Street, to Sabina and to Philemon . . .
>
> ('To Correspondents', *BA* I 1806: unnumbered, facing 1)

And often they were severe:

Lest any of our correspondents whose favours do not appear should think themselves slighted, we beg leave to say, that Laura's Ode is read and not approved; we are sorry that the name Sappho did not introduce some better poetry; the Acrostic and Anagram from Kensington are written in such an illegible hand that we could not submit ourselves to the drudgery of deciphering them . . . . The poems entitled The Village Maniac, the Ode, – Glory, Love, etc. etc. are infinitely too long and too dull; Salutary Hints on Juvenile Performers is rejected; the Eastern Essay is hyperbolical bombast. The Indian Tale shall appear in our next . . .

(ibid.)

The practice of anonymity meant that readers' names never appeared. They were not paid and even had to cover the cost of postage (Hunter 1977: 105). Nevertheless, a surprising number were so eager to see their work in print that they risked both expense and editorial censure, and magazines routinely complained that 'both with manuscripts and books our table has been groaning' (*LM&M* VII 1835: unnumbered).

These early magazines, then, positioned readers as members of a reading/ writing community rather than simply as consumers. Unlike the street, and also unlike the middle-class work-place or the recently founded literary and philosophical societies and private libraries, the magazine was a communal space in which the fair sex felt welcome. It extended the reader's community beyond the domestic circle to which she was increasingly confined – not least, ironically, by the discourses of the magazine itself.

There were obvious advantages to proprietors in using unpaid contributors as writers. The advantages to editors were more mixed. There was no shortage of copy but controlling it was difficult, and the serial nature of the form demanded that contributions come in with a regularity that not all readers were able to maintain. 'Notes to Contributors' often mention late copy or beseech contributors to end their readers' suspense by sending the next instalment. The *Lady's Magazine* had a great deal of trouble over a translation of Rousseau's *Emile*. When polite requests to 'be punctual' proved ineffective, the editor's temper finally snapped:

The translator of Rousseau's Emile will excuse us for taking the liberty desiring either an immediate supply, an excuse for the suspense or leaving continue the remainder of the work ourselves, as it was always our principal to gratify not to torture curiosity.

(*L.Mag.* XI 1780: 283)

The question of how we in the late twentieth century read such texts must take account of this dynamic. The publication of *Emile*, though presumably with editorial approval, cannot necessarily be read as an indication of coherent editorial policy on women's education (see Parker 1984: 37). The magazines were contradictory. Yet across the plurality of voices there was a shared assumption that the project of the magazine was both to address 'the lady' and to define who she was.

This becomes clear over the issue of male contributors. The practice of anonymity made it as difficult for contemporaries as it is for modern scholars to discover the gender of writers (Ballaster *et al.* 1991: 71). Jean Hunter's research on the *Lady's Magazine* suggests that, despite claims that it was for and by ladies, the proportion of female contributors in its early years was never more than two-thirds and sank as low as a fifth (Hunter 1977: 109). This may mark a tension between the policy of inviting readers to write and the growing professionalisation of journalism, which meant it was increasingly a male preserve.

This contradiction was addressed by the editor of the *Lady's Museum* in 1813, who rejected a contribution from a male correspondent explaining:

> Although our Museum boasts of many subscribers of the male sex, we certainly expect that the production of correspondents shall have some reference to the female character and pursuits.
>
> (*LM* N.S. IV 1813: 120)

The crucial issue was thus not men or women but the 'female character'. Men who wrote for or read the magazine were presumed to write or read 'as women'. This enabled the magazine to keep its male subscribers, to accept contributions from men, even to employ men as editors, as long as they located themselves in relation to the feminine. For the woman reader, of course, that location demanded that she not only 'have reference to the female character', but embody it. She had not only to read but also to live 'like a woman' (see pp. 10–11).

THE MAGAZINE AND GENERIC VARIETY

Variety of authorial voice was only one aspect of the genre established by the ladies' magazines: variety of elements was even more important. Indeed many of the elements which were to make up the woman's magazine formula were already in place by 1800: the illustrated life, fiction in serial and short-story form, poetry, reviews and illustrated 'modes'. Notably absent was practical advice on cooking, dress-making or child-rearing. Visually these magazines must soon have begun to look old-fashioned, as they were printed across the page like a book rather than in the double columns which became the usual magazine format by the 1830s. They also lacked the profusion of illustration which was to become a feature of women's magazines by the end of the century. Still, illustration, especially the fashion-plate, was already an essential part of the genre by the 1790s and there were two copper-plate 'embellishments' in each issue of the *Lady's Museum*.

It was the 'usual custom' to begin with 'a portrait and memoir' of 'a notable woman', 'a female distinguished by the splendour of her rank or the lustre of her talents' (*LM* I.S. II 1820: 121; *LM* N.S. VII 1818: 121). The tone of these brief lives was moralising rather than gossipy. They were the forerunners of the exemplary biographies that became so popular in the Victorian period, when *Clever Girls and How They Became Famous Women* or *Heroines of the Household* were given as prizes for School and Sunday School attendance (Author of . . . n.d.; Johnson n.d.).

However, the genre of the exemplary female life was not yet clearly established. The *Lady's Museum*'s first subject, Hannah More – author and founder of the Religious Tract Society – was certainly a model woman. Less obviously so was the actress Mary Robinson, who had quit the stage for her lover, or the various other beauties who featured purely because of their aristocratic blood (*LM* I 1798: 1; *LM* III 1781: 1; Adburgham 1972: 175). Even more startling was the *Lady's Museum* announcement that it had

> taken particular pains and gone to some expense to procure a faithful likeness and some authentic particulars of the life of [Mary Ashford, who had been the victim of a violent rape and murder], a sweet flower, so early and so cruelly blighted.
>
> (*LM* VII 1818: 121–6)

This disruption of the usual high moral tone was indicative both of the fractured nature of the magazine and of the femininity it addressed.

Fiction also played a crucial role in creating both the genre and the meaning of its gendered readership. More than any other magazine genre, fiction developed across a range of publication modes: periodical, part-issue, multi- and single-volume. Through all these, the link between popular fiction and femininity persisted from the eighteenth into the nineteenth century.[1] It is not surprising, then, to find fiction occupying a substantial proportion of space in these magazines.

Most of these stories were what one reader called 'larmoyanty love-tales', centred around a female protagonist, but not all were of this type (Cruse 1930: 192). The most famous series in the *Lady's Magazine* was Miss Mitford's 'Our Village', which appeared from 1819, establishing the fame of the author and 'the fortune of the lucky periodical' (Adburgham 1972: 232; Cruse 1930: 193). Nevertheless, 'love and marriage' dominated periodical fiction (*LM* I 1798: 298). Even when set in foreign lands it assumed a universal femininity marked by the desire to be desired, and by the inevitable suffering this involved.[2] Magazine stories therefore dealt with the paradox, familiar from gothic fiction, that love was central to femininity but attaining it was fraught with disaster and danger.

In order to help in this endemic difficulty, the *Lady's Museum* invited readers to confide in the 'Old Woman', a forerunner of the modern agony aunt. The tradition of the female confidante stretched back to 1693 when the *Ladies' Mercury* had invited 'All questions relating to love' to be sent to 'the Ladies' Society' at the 'Latine Coffee House in Ave-Mary-Lanes' (Ballaster *et al.* 1991: 47). The *Lady's Museum*'s immediate model, once again, was the *Lady's Magazine*. Here 'The Matron' – also called 'Mrs Grey' – claimed to be:

> duly qualified to make my monthly appearance in the Lady's Magazine while I am able to hold pen, being in my grand climacteric and having been

deeply engaged in numberless scenes variegated and opposite, serious and comic, cheerful and afflicting.

(*LM* V 1774: 33)

The Old Woman, too, offered to advise readers from the vantage point of her age and experience. Unlike the later agony aunt, however, her tone was bracing rather than sympathetic.

If a miss scarcely entered her teens asks my advice respecting a lover or inveighs against her mother . . .; if a wife, forgetting her duty to her husband, attempts to engage me in her favour when she is disposed to bid defiance to his lawful commands, I surely cannot show myself more their friend than by conveying to oblivion the folly of the one, and the worthlessness of the other.

(*LM* XIV 1805: 79)

These articles usually consisted of generalised moralising. The Old Woman's series was not, like later advice columns, a correspondence page in which readers could directly discuss the difficulties of love, family relationships or appearance. The large number of letters which the Old Woman claimed to receive were rarely reproduced and where they were their function was not to produce the authentic voice of the reader but to stand for a representative or symbolic correspondent: 'Miss Madcap' or 'Biddy Willing' (*LM* I 1798: 289; White 1970: 37).

Nevertheless these articles, and the occasional series by Mrs Hofland called 'A Bachelor's Recollections' which replaced them in the 1830s, had an important role in the magazine. The Old Woman's persona as the defender of women's moral influence represented the most persistent pressure in the magazine to define femininity exclusively in domestic terms. She consistently told readers to 'confin[e] yourselves to your domestic duties, where alone you are calculated truly to shine' (*LM* I.S. II 1805: 193).

These exhortations were necessary precisely because the model of femininity to which she constantly returned was a transgressive one, that of the 'miss . . . ask[ing] advice respecting a lover' and the 'wife forgetting her duty to her husband'. A letter from Drama Place, Play Street to 'My Old Quiz' began:

What signify all your grave lectures about prudence and propriety and dress and nonsense? No person of *taste* minds your antiquated morality and your obsolete notions. You do not, indeed, old mother, seem to have the most distant idea of gentility and high life, or you would never take upon you, as you do, to censure modes and customs which are sanctioned by the highest characters in the kingdom and therefore must be right . . .

(*LM* XIV 1805: 83)

and so on for a page and a half.

Whether invented by the Old Woman or the actual work of a young Miss, this letter produced an alternative femininity within the discourse of domestic morality. This alternative was powerful not just because of the energy of the writing but because it related to those changes in the definition of the female self which were at stake in the culture. It was also echoed in other parts of the magazine – notably the treatment of dress, theatre-going and fashionable life which I discuss later in this chapter.

APPROPRIATE KNOWLEDGE:
INSTRUCTION AND NEWS

The early nineteenth-century magazine offered both amusement and instruction. It was 'An Entertaining Companion for the Fair Sex' but also sought to fulfil the role of guide to conduct which was already established as central to female reading (Armstrong 1985). The *Lady's Magazine* had made this explicit with its claim to guide readers from the 'Temple of Folly' (see Figure 2.1). In the new century this didactic strain became more explicit. The *Lady's Museum*, subtitled 'the Polite Repository of Amusement and Instruction', claimed 'to inform the minds and refine the manners of the rising generation' (*LM* I 1798: 1).

The regular collapse of entertainment into instruction was to mark the women's magazine for the next two centuries, a constant reminder of the instability of femininity. Woman was 'the sex' in eighteenth-century terminology, the signifier of natural sexual difference. Yet historical women were always having to be told how to be feminine. In the early nineteenth century this problem was caught up in the particular historical struggle to define 'the lady' who was the magazine reader. Whereas 'amusement' assumed this lady already existed and sought to address her pleasure, 'instruction' assumed that the reader was not yet the lady she ought to be and sought to make good the lack.

These different objectives did not run neatly between the magazine's different genres. The fiction did not simply offer 'amusement' and the articles 'instruction'. There was a more complex relationship between the ideal of instruction and the constituent genres, most of which – in any case – had their own conventions and histories which extended beyond the magazine into other modes of publication.

In this mix of genres, one kind of instruction which was notably absent was regular information about current politics though these magazines did sometimes carry brief 'Epitomes of Public Affairs'. It was precisely the absence of 'news' which came to distinguish the magazine from that other mixed kind of periodical, the newspaper. The evolution of this distinction was shaped by battles over access to politics in which class rather than gender was the issue. The category 'news' was contested throughout the period between 1712 and the 1850s, during which successive governments imposed a stamp duty on newspapers explicitly in order to limit public debate. The development of the periodical without news, therefore, was partly a political response and partly a shrewd commercial strategy devised by the new press entrepreneurs to avoid payment of the tax (Hollis 1970; Wiener 1969). By the time stamp duty was finally lifted in the 1840s, allowing a huge

Figure 2.1 The Genius of the *Lady's Magazine* leading its votaries
from Folly (*L.Mag.* XI 1780: 4) © Manchester City Art Galleries

expansion of the newspaper press, the magazine was already firmly established as an attractive genre in its own right.

The stamp duty was part of a wider government strategy of taxing print. These 'taxes on knowledge', as the radicals called them, which included duty on paper, rag and advertisements, continued to inflate the price of all printed media until the last tax – on paper – was lifted in 1861.

Magazines for women, like improving magazines for the working class, developed in the economic and ideological nexus of the 'taxes on knowledge'. Economically, they continued to be relatively expensive, even though they avoided the specific tax on newspapers. Ideologically, the gender dimension of access to 'news' was more nebulous than that of class. However, the periodical without 'news' emerged as an appropriate medium for the domestic woman.

This did not mean newspapers explicitly defined their readership as male, nor that women never read newspapers, though perhaps few went as far as Bronte's fictional character Shirley who played out her masculine role by reading even the financial pages (Bronte 1849). Like the male reader of the woman's magazine, the woman might read the same pages but differently. In 1848 the *Family Friend*, under the heading 'Hints to Wives' advised women rather than complain about their husbands reading the newspaper: 'read it yourself so that you can talk to him about it' (*FF* I 1848–9: 119). Nevertheless, the absence of 'news' from women's magazines became institutional, along with the definition of femininity as incompatible with engagement in public affairs.

All periodicals in the era of the taxes on knowledge were likely to be shared by several readers. Newspaper reading, even after the launch of the *Daily Telegraph* in the 1850s, was associated with public coffee houses, clubs and reading rooms (Lee 1976: 36–37). Ladies' magazines, too, had multiple readers. Charlotte Bronte read the back copies of the *Lady's Magazine* which her aunt brought with her to Howarth in the 1820s, and the arrangement whereby two school-girls clubbed together to buy the *Lady's Museum* in 1806 was almost certainly repeated across the country (Cruse 1930: 193; *LM* VI 1806: 78). However, this sharing was private. It was enacted in the middle-class home where current copies of the magazines were displayed on the drawing room table and lent to visitors and friends (*LM&M* VI 1835: inside front cover).

The location of these magazines in the domestic home was enacted also in their physical dimensions. A tradition of pocket-books and almanacs for women continued from the eighteenth century into the 1820s and 1830s and included yet another *Lady's Museum*, but the magazines which gradually replaced these were too substantial to be easily carried in a pocket. They were 16 × 25 cm (6½ × 10 inches) to 14 × 20 cm (5½ × 8 inches) and contained 60 or even 84 pages of text.

DEFINING 'THE LADY': DOMESTICITY AND DUTY

In 1792 Mary Wollstonecraft had argued the claims of a universal womanhood in *The Vindication of the Rights of Woman*. These magazines, however, although they assumed gender as a ground of identity, did not use the word 'woman' in their titles. Of fifty 'female' titles published between 1800 and 1850, twenty-seven included the word 'lady' but none included 'woman'.[3] The relationship between 'woman' and 'lady' both in and beyond the magazine title returns again and again throughout this history. When the magazines discussed in this chapter claimed to be 'addressed particularly to the ladies' they assumed the primacy of gender, but the term still carried connotations of high status.

This is evident from their price. *La Belle Assemblée*, the dearest at 3s. (15p), was roughly equivalent to a daily wage for the highest-paid skilled worker in affluent London (Cole 1946: 80, 206). The *Lady's Magazine* maintained its price at 6d. for several decades but the drift in the new century was upwards. The *Lady's Museum* cost 1s. (5p) in 1806 and 1s. 6d. (7½p) in 1813, while the combined title was 2s. 6d. (12½p) in the 1830s.

The *Lady's Museum* made explicit from the start that it defined femininity in class-specific terms. In an article, 'On the Duties of Women in the Superior Class of Society', strategically placed in the first number, it offered its readers three roles; as wives, mothers and mistresses or 'heads of families' (*LM* I 1798: 34).[4] The duty of wives was 'the disposal of that part of the husband's revenue which is consumed by the family'; of mothers to be 'responsible for the religion and moral education of their children'; and of mistresses to control the 'moral conduct of female domestics' (ibid.).

The qualities of this lady were thus both gender- and class-specific. As distinct from men of the 'superior class', she was concerned only with the family's consumption and not at all with productive or paid work. This gendered division of labour distinguished 'the lady' both from the bourgeois man and from the working-class woman – specifically the female domestic. Like children, female domestics were always the object, and never the subject, of this benevolent femininity. The servant was also a potentially sexual being, which the lady was not, despite being 'a wife'. The displacement of the mistress's sexuality onto other subordinate female figures whom she had to control was a recurrent rhetorical strategy in the magazines.

Their dominant discourse was of an abstract morality. Although she was expected to oversee her household and to control the family expenditure, the magazines offered the lady little specific guidance on such matters. *La Belle Assemblée* in its first year promised a series to deal, not with 'the lower, more practical part of cookery', but with marketing, 'the ornament of the table and the general management of the family' (*BA* I 1806: 41). However, its appearance was extremely erratic and it rapidly disappeared altogether, perhaps because the contributor failed with the copy, but also because when copy did appear the editor did not give it space (*BA* I 1806: facing 121). Although they all carried advertisements inside the covers, as many as 14 pages in the *Lady's Museum* of the 1830s, in the body of the text the magazines did not recognise woman's power or responsibility for family buying, except for her own and her daughters' clothes.

As well as being class-specific, the femininity of these magazines was that of the

'British Fair'. The place of the lady in national society was directly analogous to her role in the family and was confined to the exercise of her influence over husband and sons. The moral worth of the nation, like that of the family, was nevertheless her responsibility. At its launch the *Lady's Museum* declared that 'Female worth is a distinguishing feature in the character of a virtuous nation' (*LM* I 1798: 1).

Like the elision of femininity with beauty and blondness in the tag 'the Fair Sex', the nationalist sentiment in the idea of the lady was usually implicit. When it did become explicit, it was often as a counter-example to the women of post-revolutionary and Napoleonic France. The Old Woman rallied her 'Fair Countrywomen, Englishwomen! Daughters of Britain! descendants of a free-born and virtuous race and hopes of your land!' to exert their influence 'against the prevailing spirit of innovation' emanating from across the channel (*LM* I.S. II 1820: 193). This meant resisting extravagance and teaching children that 'the traitor to his king is the traitor to his God', advice which returned the reader firmly to the family and domestic management.

EDUCATING THE DAUGHTERS

Despite the narrow range of their activities, the moral power attributed to women was such that enormous anxiety was generated by the possibility of their failure. The claim that magazines would 'make the daughters of the present age wiser and better' articulated this endemic anxiety (*LM* I 1798: 1). The *Lady's Museum* typically boasted that it provided reading 'the chastest matron may peruse' and added:

> No Mother, Guardian, or Mistress of Female Seminaries will ever need to examine its contents previously to their putting it in the hands of their Daughters, Wards or Pupils.
>
> (*LM* XIV 1805: 'Preface')

In part this was a marketing strategy. Individual schoolgirls could rarely afford the magazines but those who taught them – either at home or in the burgeoning numbers of schools for middle-class girls – had the necessary shillings if they could be persuaded to part with them. However, magazines were able to sell themselves in this way only because of the widespread anxiety about young women's access to knowledge, which had been the subject of books by Erasmus Darwin, the Edgeworths and Hannah More. The magazine's general offer to provide instruction thus focused upon the education of the girl.

In this debate about girls' education the difference of gender was taken as axiomatic. What was at issue was how to make girls into fit mates for men. In seeking to make their daughters 'wiser and better', the magazines increasingly collapsed the first into the second: they offered moral wisdom rather than intellectual stimulation. Articles on botany and history were commonly geared to what were perceived to be feminine interests and everything became grist to the moralising mill. Thus, the 'Spirit of History' became a lesson in how 'great events result from minute causes' (*LM* I.S. II 1820: 198).

The argument that intellectual activity was incompatible with women's moral role was openly articulated in the magazine in the 1830s. Like Mrs Ellis, her contemporary, Mrs Hofland made the case that 'highly educated women are uneducated wives', that 'the preponderance of knowledge as well as power is on the side of the male part of creation' and that where 'occasionally' a woman might 'have more a talent or more experience . . .' she should use them to help her husband (*LM&M* VI 1832: 32, 317). In the early years of the century, however, anxiety about female access to knowledge was primarily about the control of female sexuality, displaced here not onto domestic servants but onto 'the daughters, wards and pupils' in the lady's care.

The 'Preface' to the *Lady's Museum* makes clear that the construction of a suitable knowledge for daughters depended on their sexual ignorance. The matron, who was herself 'chaste', at least knew what her daughter ought not to know. Sexual knowledge was therefore a constant threat, excluded from the magazine only by the constant vigilance of its producers, who were in turn kept under scrutiny by the implied purchasers, the 'Mother, Guardian and Mistress of Female Seminaries'. Thus, although the daughter was constructed in opposition to the adult woman, it was she and not the matron who came to stand for the entire readership. The infantilised reader produced by these magazines was to dominate the writing and circulating of fiction throughout the century. The transgressive daughter not only had a place in the text, she was assumed to be its reader.

The figure of the daughter embodied the possibility of resistance to the construction of femininity as moral management. However, she should not be read simply in terms of repression or as the mad woman in the domestic attic who has been the subject of so much fruitful discussion by feminist critics (Gilbert and Gubar 1979). Her youth and ignorance meant that the threat she posed could be relatively easily contained, as she in turn became a wife and a 'chaste matron'. The magazines regulated her progress towards this state while at the same time representing its desirability in terms of financial and sexual adulthood and of access to woman's only legitimate source of power. The potential for 'the revolt of the daughters' was not therefore realised until the 1890s (see Ch. 9). And domesticity was not identified as a cause of women's disempowerment until the twentieth century.

The empowering of women as 'chaste matrons' was central to the formation of the middle class as distinct from the old aristocracy, who were represented as sexually lax. In the struggle to define 'the lady', however, certain elements of the old aristocratic femininity persisted into the new formations of gender and publishing, in particular in relation to leisure and dress. Both were rooted in the material privilege which made possible the life of 'the lady', whether aristocratic or middle class. Rather than withering away in the new century, these elements became incorporated into the discourses of the magazines and their femininity.

DEFINING THE LADY: LEISURE

The meaning of leisure in modern societies brings together issues of economic power, class, gender and the sources of pleasure. All these impinge upon the creation of the woman's magazine as leisure reading and the creation of the leisured woman who read it. The purchase of an expensive magazine on a regular basis and the time and space in which to read it assume material prosperity, but the magazine was involved in a gendering of the concept of leisure which gave a new meaning to that material privilege and in turn created new forms of wealth production, not least in the publishing industry.

Since the middle-class woman was distinguished from the middle-class man by her exclusion from 'work', leisure – always a marker of class – 'became also a marker of gender' (Shevelow, 1989: 55). The discourse of leisure therefore existed as an alternative to that of morality in defining the domestic space, but one which united rather than divided the middle class and the aristocracy. The leisured woman from either class had time for pleasure and 'improvement of mind'. The article on women 'in the superior class of society' which opened the *Lady's Museum* had named 'an interest in poetry, music and paintings' as the woman's duties in 'second place' to her duties as wife, mother and mistress (*LM* I 1798: 34).

Reading was an appropriate activity for the woman of leisure, as were music, conversation and embroidery – a strictly non-functional kind of sewing. The ladies' magazines, like the early novels, were produced by and for this leisure time. But they also produced it in its characteristic forms. They included embroidery patterns, music reviews and sometimes sheet music, poetry, notices of theatres and above all reading matter, provided both directly and through the reviews of other books which occupied a substantial number of their pages.

These activities were the signifier of the wealth and status a woman enjoyed, not in her own right but by virtue of her husband. Her cultural capital was the mark of his economic capital. However, although it was the work of the husband which enabled her to be 'a lady', the content of 'leisure' (music, painting, reading) did not insist upon her role as a relative creature. Male readers argued in the magazine that the informed wife was necessary for 'domestic happiness, social harmony and universal respect' (*BA* II 1806: 73), but the possibility remained that a woman might read not only to make herself a fit companion for her husband but also for her own pleasure. Painting, embroidery and music could become more than genteel accomplishments – an opportunity for the woman to exercise her creativity and talent.

Even in the mid-1830s, when the domestic ideology seemed firmly in place, magazines provided access to a range of potentially challenging and serious reading. In 1835, ten years after the watershed identified by Cynthia White, the *Lady's Magazine and Museum* ran 22 pages of book reviews in one month (October) including: Peter Gaskell's *Prospects of Industry*, Andrew Ure's *Philosophy of Manufactures*, John Clare's *Rural Muse*, a biography of *The Young Queen*, Sir James Mackintosh's *History of England*, Emma Roberts on characteristics of

Hindostan and numerous other books and periodicals (*LM&M* I.S. Enlarged, VII 1835: 225ff). The leisured lady had access to political economy and the best of contemporary poetry if she desired.

This model of femininity, which retained the pattern of aristocratic leisure, did not fit easily with the ideal of the lady as moral agent. It disrupted debates on girls' education where the value of 'accomplishments' continued to be disputed throughout the century.

DRESS AND FASHION

Even more difficult to accommodate within the domestic ideal was another aspect of aristocratic discourse which entered the woman's magazine during these decades, namely fashion. In the 1790s a number of publications devoted to fashion began to appear, including the *Gallery of Fashion* in 1794 and the *Magazine of Female Fashions of London and Paris* in 1798. These spurred the *Lady's Magazine* to be more systematic about its fashion coverage and ensured that from its start the *Lady's Museum* included each month a 'Cabinet of Fashion' with engravings (Adburgham 1972: 204–17). Dress and appearance thus entered the magazine as 'fashion', with reports of what was being worn by court ladies in London and in Paris. This set of associations was to become a staple of women's magazines for the next 200 years and has entered deeply into the ideology of gender. But in the early nineteenth century, the link between femininity and 'fashion' in this sense of dress was still in the process of being forged (see Craik 1994: ix–xii).

During the Regency period the meaning of dress and appearance in aristocratic society was in a state of flux. On the one hand the new middle class, and particularly the evangelical movement, leaned towards a sober and functional style of dress. As trousers gradually replaced breeches as the standard form of masculine dress, male attire became the mark not of specific status or job but of business in general, and therefore of bourgeois masculinity. On the other hand display in dress – like leisure – ceased to signify aristocratic status alone and became a mark of femininity (Wilson 1985: 34).

There was resistance to this trend from within the aristocracy. The Dandies, led by George Brummel, produced a new version of masculine dress and a lifestyle in which appearance became an end in itself – the signifier neither of class or gender but an excess which refused these definitions. But such a refusal was itself read in gendered terms; according to Barbey: 'For dandies as for women, to seem is to be' (Gagnier 1986: 80).

The dandy disappeared after the Regency, rejected by bourgeois Victorians who saw him as an anachronism like Dickens's Mr Turveydrop (Dickens 1853). Dark trousers and jacket became the uniform of middle-class men, except for the army's red so beloved of silly girls in contemporary novels. However, the idea of dandyism remained attractive to rebels against the culture of the sober-suited bourgeoisie, especially the working-class 'swells' (Walkowitz 1994: 43–4). At the end of the century Oscar Wilde famously mobilised this tradition of deviant masculine dress as a marker of resistance (Gagnier 1986).

By contrast, the creation of a self through dress and appearance moved to the centre of feminine identity. Woman's dress did not signify the productive labour of making commodities but rather the labour of self-production. This process is well illustrated in a publishing squabble which took place in 1806. The appearance of *La Belle Assemblée or Bell's Court and Fashionable Magazine addressed particularly to the Ladies* in February of that year has rightly been described as a landmark in women's magazine publishing (Adburgham 1972: 219). It was produced by John Bell, proprietor of a circulating library and publisher of the successful *Morning Post*.

This shrewd businessman recognised the growing importance of the ladies' magazine market and *La Belle Assemblée* offered the leisured lady 'light entertainment and elegant amusement' according to the now familiar formula, with a particular emphasis on fiction (to which it devoted roughly a quarter of its pages), poetry and book news and, in the 1820s, a supplement, the 'Literary and Scientific Intelligencer'. What distinguished this magazine from its rivals, however, was the quality of its production and its coverage of 'fashion'. It was beautifully produced, in a large size (royal octavo), with a high quality engraved portrait and a double-page engraving of the latest fashions, which were also available coloured (which meant by hand) (see Figure 2.2).

Nine months later, in November 1806, a rival publication was launched by Bell's son, John Browne Bell. *Le Beau Monde or Literary and Fashionable Magazine* imitated *La Belle Assemblée* but instead of being addressed exclusively to the ladies it gave the concept of 'the fashionable' a masculine connotation. Where *La Belle Assemblée*'s first portrait was of the Queen, and its fashion-plates and dress descriptions were of women, *Le Beau Monde*'s first portrait was of the King and its plates showed fashionable 'gentlemen' as well as furniture and carriages. However, fashion and femininity were no longer so readily separable. Almost immediately *Le Beau Monde* was forced to include news and illustrations of female dress since 'Many of the distinguished fashionables of this country have expressed their desire that this magazine should be embellished with ladies' fashions as well as gentlemen's' (*BM* I (ii) 1806: unnumbered page opp. 1). No readers demanded men's fashions in *La Belle Assemblée*.

The competition between the two generations of Bells is more than a story of familial rivalry. It marks a moment when the definition of a particular kind of reading public and a particular idea of femininity were crystallising. *Le Beau Monde* was not a success. Bell senior's magazine, by contrast, went on in various forms until 1847. Its fashion coverage remained a major selling point, especially in the period when that section was run by Mrs M.A. Bell, famous as the proprietor of the Magazin de Modes and inventor of the Circassion Corset, both of which she vigorously promoted (Adburgham 1972: 226).

La Belle Assemblée established quality engravings and detailed advice on dress as crucial elements of the lady's magazine, and those who could not match it were

Spring Fashions for 1806.

Taken from the Walking Dresses in Kensington Garden 1 June 1806.

Printed exclusively for La Belle Assemblée or Bells Court & fashionable Magazine July 1.1806.

Figure 2.2 Fashion-plate, *La Belle Assemblée* (June 1806) © Manchester City Art Galleries

forced onto the defensive. ('Preface', *LM&M* IV 1813: unnumbered). It therefore consolidated the tradition of elegantly produced fashion magazines for an all-female readership which has culminated in today's glossies. The story of women's magazines in the rest of the century is the story of how 'fashion', now completely feminised, engaged a wider and wider circle of women readers. Mrs Bell's corset was only the first of many similar garments which promised readers their own desirable, natural-but-always-to-be-improved female body.

However, the discourse of fashion brought with it into the magazine other elements of its aristocratic inheritance which were difficult to accommodate within the middle-class discourse of the domestic. These included its direct references to an unpopular court, its pro-French tendencies and its stress on extravagance. Fashion was determined by what was worn at court, on Rotten Row and in the other aristocratic meeting places of London and of Paris. *La Belle Assemblée* by its very name invoked such meeting places and referred to the 'modes' of the French as well as the English aristocracy. This was in sharp contrast to the scene of domestic reading and the anti-French sentiment assumed elsewhere in lady's magazines.

Quality engravings not only increased the actual cost of the fashion magazine, they assumed a life devoted to conspicuous rather than careful consumption (see *BM* I (i) 1806: 61). *La Belle Assemblée* was unique among nineteenth-century periodicals in offering a special supplement of advertisements which could be bound and kept as 'a record of the commercial and fashionable concerns of the present time' ('Advertisement Notice', *BA* I (ix) 1806: unnumbered). This contrasted with the Old Woman's call for the Free-born British Fair to resist the French by careful control of family expenditure.

Above all, fashion represented a femininity located in appearance and display, old aristocratic values which – however revised – contradicted the bourgeois ideal of a femininity hidden in the domestic home and the female heart. Fashion not only stressed the physical body. It was associated with an aristocracy and court notorious for sexual promiscuity. *La Belle Assemblée* recognised that in this new era sexual licence – even sexual 'tattle' – was no longer appropriate to the lady; it was becoming the mark of a specifically masculine upper class. *Le Beau Monde* could include in its 'Varieties' stories of sexual adventure, like that of a fashionable nobleman 'of dash and style' who has left 'his fair helpmate for another object . . . who more resembles Martha Gunn the washerwoman' (*BM* I (ii) 1806: 116). It could even include a letter complaining that 'certain ladies' had been banned from the theatre (*BM* III (xviii) 1808: 85–6). *La Belle Assemblée* carried no such titillating items for its female readership. Nevertheless, fashion brought the potentially sexual female body into the centre of the lady's magazine.

These contradictions persisted in the magazine as in the wider culture. Other lady's journals which sprang up in the first thirty years of the nineteenth century enacted the same tension between fashionable leisure and the duties of moral management. They, too, juxtaposed engravings of fashion with complaints that 'more attention [is] paid to the . . . fashion of the times than to the virtues of the heart . . .' (*BA* II (i) 1806: 73).

It was the domestic scene of reading which produced coherence from the magazine's diversity, at least according to one male reader who looked back on it nostalgically from prison:

> . . . from the varied stores of tale, essay and anecdote which your pages furnish we have all derived recreation and amusement; especially when, the weary labours of the day being terminated, and seated almost in 'Imperial Pride' in my easy chair, my pretty Jane has, alternatively with her not less lively sister Julia, cheated the otherwise dull and lingering hours of winter evenings, by reading aloud the Ladies' Museum to their mother and myself.
>
> ('A Constant Reader', Letter from Kingsbench Prison,
> *LM* XXIII 1826: 247)

This scene of reading – a version of the domestic as Pastoral Idyll – produced the heterogeneous magazine as uniformly amusing, just as it united the family which was differentiated by generation and by gender. This account cannot admit the possibility that Jane might secretly read like Miss Madcap or Julia be another Florence Nightingale for whom reading aloud in the family circle was a form of torture, the psychological equivalent of force-feeding (Strachey 1978: 402; Gagnier 1991). However it does allow that the members of the family read the same magazine differently. It also represented that family as under threat, both externally – from the weary world of work and the impending imprisonment of the breadwinner – and internally – from the boredom of the domestic winter.

Against the threats of deviant femininity and material and psychological failure, the magazines returned again and again to situate the woman reader in the idealised middle-class family. In the late eighteenth and early nineteenth century that ideal was – with difficulty – being put into place.

3

THE QUEEN, THE BEAUTY
AND THE WOMAN WRITER

The Belle, the Belle, the Monthly Belle,
That does its thousands quickly sell ...
Where every week does Modish shew
What bonnets are worn what caps are 'the go'
(*New Monthly Belle Assemblée* I 1834: 1)

THE ANOMALY OF A QUEEN ON THE THRONE

So much was invested in the idealised domestic woman. She was the ground on which the social and political system was understood and regulated and, in her biological difference, she guaranteed that such a system was natural. In 1832, when the Reform Act extended the vote to middle-class men, the legal exclusion of women from politics drew little comment. One of the radical papers of 1832, the *Isis* – a sixpenny weekly publication – was 'edited by a lady'. But Eliza Sharples was an exceptional 'lady' and, insofar as it named a female editor, this was an exceptional political paper. By the 1840s, even the Chartists' demand for 'universal' voting rights meant *male* suffrage. The designation of public politics as a masculine realm spanned the entire class spectrum, and its separation from the feminised private had become axiomatic across legal, political, economic and domestic space. It structured popular print in the 1830s and 1840s. Yet that separation was not monolithic but marked by exceptions which constantly threatened its designation as natural.

The most overt of these was Victoria's presence on the throne. Her accession in 1837 produced what Caroline Norton called the 'grotesque anomaly' of a country 'governed by a female sovereign' in which gender alone was sufficient grounds for exclusion from legal and political existence (quoted in Poovey 1989: 6). The Queen was indeed a potentially disruptive figure and the meaning of her power an important locus of debate across the spectrum of popular genres (Homans 1993). Women's publications like the *Christian Lady's Magazine* devoted considerable space to the meaning of her accession for women (*CLM* X 1838: 11–12, 68–9, 405–6). This evangelical magazine was unusual in that it consistently offered articles on 'important public events' in a form which it jokingly described as 'Politics made easy or every woman her own representative' (*CLM* I 1834: 74). But this

36

formulation itself reveals the difficulty of thinking 'woman' as a political group or class, requiring representation. Even the *Christian Lady's Magazine* deplored those who set themselves up as 'political agitators, political economists or what not' instead of seeking to exert their influence as mothers and wives (*CLM* I 1834: 74).

Given the power of these discourses, it is not surprising that Victoria was represented and represented herself – especially after her marriage – in terms of the domestic and the familial, as wife, mother and widow.[1] Mrs Ellis encapsulated this in *Wives of England; their relative Duties, Domestic Influence and Social Obligations* which she dedicated, with her permission, to the Queen 'in whose exalted station the social virtues of domestic life present the brightest example to her country-women and the truest presage of her empire's glory' (Ellis 1843: title page). Victoria became, ironically, a symbol of the naturalness of domestic femininity.

However, inscribed within the domestic was another set of meanings attached to the Queen, which did not disappear but continued to circulate, particularly in the ladies' magazines. For Victoria as monarch was centre of the court and there-fore at the heart of fashionable life. Even in the years immediately before her acces-sion, when popular support for the monarchy was at its lowest, the court retained its social importance. For aristocratic young women, presentation here was the doorway to the fashionable world and to marriageable femininity. In the ladies' magazines, court news and fashion coverage, inextricably linked, still provided crucial copy, like the printed lists of all those presented at court, together with brief descriptions of their dresses (110 on one occasion) (*LM&M* VI 1835: 360–5).

Print entrepreneurs and those who advertised in their papers still competed for royal patronage. The Duchess of Kent, Victoria's mother, gave her personal patronage to at least two magazines – the *Lady's Magazine and Museum* in the 1830s and the *New Monthly Belle Assemblée* in the 1840s. This was apparently still valuable enough to generate a dispute between the editor and proprietors of the *Lady's Magazine and Museum* when the editor, Mr Glenny, tried to take her patronage to a rival *Royal Lady's Magazine*, which he was about to launch (*LM&M* VIII 1836: inside front cover). Advertisers also habitually pictured coronets or royal coats of arms with the names of their products and used royal recommenda-tions as a selling point.[2]

Such patronage died out as press entrepreneurs moved to selling cheaper papers in greater numbers. Nevertheless, this alternative symbolism of royalty and the court remained. The anomalous figure of the female monarch – both model mother and courtly lady – was re-worked in women's magazines throughout Victoria's reign.

THE BEAUTY AND THE FASHIONABLE

The older ladies' magazines and their versions of the courtly lady were in decline, however. In 1832 the *Lady's Magazine* and the *Lady's Museum* merged and *La Belle Assemblée* was relaunched as the *Court Magazine and Belle Assemblée* with Caroline

Norton as editor (Perkins 1910: 46). After her departure two years later the magazine slid gradually downhill, first going into parallel publication and then merging with the joint *Lady's Magazine and Museum* (1838) until the combined title ceased publication in 1847. The disappearance of these three long-standing periodicals marked, as Cynthia White has said, the end of a press era (White 1970: 41). Periodical reading for the upper-class lady did not simply dwindle away in the 1830s and 1840s, however. It diversified into new publishing forms, re-making the idea of 'the lady' for the next generation. Through them all the idea of 'the Beauty' and the importance of fashion persisted, not as abstract ideas but enacted in the materiality of print and made possible by the technologies of engraving, printing and distribution.

Among the genres important in these processes of re-making the lady were the keepsakes and annuals, sometimes called 'Books of Beauties'. These gift-books, which became popular in the 1830s, offered high quality engravings accompanied by poetry and short prose pieces from well-known authors and 'fashionables'. They were a departure from the tradition of annual publications, pocket-books, diaries and almanacs which had appeared since the early eighteenth century, often explicitly addressed to ladies. The *Ladies' Diary or Complete Almanack*, for example, ran from 1704 to 1840, offering 'for the use and diversion of the FAIR SEX' a calendar, information about fairs and sessions, rhyming enigmas, mathematical problems and brainteasers. Even after its merger with the *Gentleman's Diary* in 1841 it continued to keep alive – in however small a way – the idea that ladies as well as gentlemen might enjoy intellectual puzzles. Like all 'pocket-books' it was small (duodecimo) though not cheap (stitched copies cost 2*s.* 3*d.* in the 1820s).

The new annuals were the opposite of this in every way. Designed for the drawing-room table, they were famous as 'gorgeous inanities called Books of Beauties' or in Wordsworth's words 'greedy receptacles of trash'; a judgement which did not prevent him contributing to one (Adburgham 1972: 236; Cruse 1930: 269). They exemplified the best in contemporary book production, printed on good quality paper and bound in hard covers with steel engravings of high quality. But critics like Thackeray complained that, once the picture had been chosen:

> Miss Landon, Miss Mitford or my Lady Blessington writes a song upon the opposite page about a water-lily, chilly, stilly, shivering beside a streamlet, plighted, blighted love-benighted, falsehood sharper than a gimlet . . . and so on. The poetry is quite worthy of the picture and a little sham sentiment is employed to illustrate a little sham art.
>
> (quoted in Cruse 1930: 280)

These keepsakes were not addressed to an exclusively female readership nor were the engravings exclusively of female subjects. They remain important for this study, however. First, as Thackeray satirically pointed out, they were often edited by women and featured women writers, a point I return to later in the chapter.

Second, they aimed for the same drawing-room readership as the magazines. The keepsakes were in competition with the bound annual forms of periodicals such as *La Belle Assemblée* and the two influenced each other. In 1827, for example, *La Belle Assemblée* had suggested that its monthly 'embellishments' offered readers 'A Gallery of Britain's nobility in the form of engravings' (*BA* N.S. XXXII 1827: 89). Heath advertised his *Gallery of British Engravings* in the *Lady's Magazine and Museum* in the 1830s (*LM&M* VI 1835). The *New Monthly Belle Assemblée* in the 1840s carried steel engravings of 'Beauties', each, as in the annuals, accompanied by a poem (*NMBA* XXI 1844).

Through their engravings and embellishments these annuals, together with the magazines, consolidated a publishing tradition in which the clothed or draped female figure was reproduced as 'the Beauty'. This reproduced the discourse of the female body in ways which challenged that of the domestic woman. Its alternative femininity was defined in terms both of visibility and the materiality of the page, made possible by technology.

Firstly, 'the Beauty' was a visual re-working of the verbal tag 'the Fair Sex'. The pleasure of looking was well understood by print entrepreneurs of the time from sellers of broadsides upwards. In ladies' magazines that pleasure was specifically linked to femininity and to reproductions of the clothed female body. These engravings or embellishments located femininity as object in a sexual dynamic where the gaze was assumed to be male. Like the fiction, which constructed female desire as the desire to be desired, the engravings constructed the desirable woman in terms of being looked at.[3]

Second, this visible beauty was inseparable from the printed page and was produced by the technologies of print production. What Walter Benjamin called the means of 'mechanical reproduction' did not simply extend old meanings of aristocratic beauty to a wider social group; they ensured that new meanings were produced through the processes of reproduction and circulation of images (Benjamin 1968). In the 1841 edition of *Heath's Book of Beauty*, edited by the Countess of Blessington, Charles Heath included sixteen steel engravings of court ladies, beginning with a picture of 'Her Majesty on her Nuptial Day'. The Queen was represented here neither as female sovereign nor as domestic woman but as 'Beauty', as surface rather than depth. The meaning of both genre and gender was created in the visual quality of the engraving and the tactile quality of the paper.

The Beauty took various forms each of them informed by this dynamic. The first of these was the aristocratic beauty as named contemporary – 'Lady Seymour', the 'Duchess of Beaufort' or even 'Her Majesty'. Since embellishments were sold separately and could be detached from the magazine, print technology moved the portrait of the aristocratic lady from the wall of her home into different contexts where its meaning was radically altered. It might even re-appear decorating the mean lodgings of young clerks, like Dickens's Mr Guppy and his friends in *Bleak House* (Dickens 1853). Reproduction in a magazine or book transformed the portrait of the lady from a sign of individual status and wealth into an object for public consumption.

Another version of the beauty had a mythical or typical title – 'Zuleika' or 'Lesbia' (*NMBA* XXI 1844: unnumbered, opp. 129, 383). These recalled the high-art tradition of female beauty which legitimated the reproduction of draped rather than clothed female figures. As with the aristocratic lady, the reproduction and dissemination of these figures altered their meaning. These processes brought the eroticised female body into public print as art. These plates thus produced beauty simultaneously as evidence of the viewer's taste, as the defining aspect of 'the sex' and as the distinctive quality of particular individuals. This last contradiction is still evident in their late twentieth-century descendants, magazine cover girls.

The most pervasive version of this body in the magazines was that which dissolved 'the Beauty' into her clothes. Fashion, as I suggested in the last chapter, had come to define the feminine. In their fashion-plates the magazines brought the model of the aristocratic beauty into relationship with the language of dress, through the device of 'embellishment'. Here again the reproduction and circulation of the visible image gave it a new cultural significance. The reader could take the illustration of the 'mode' to her dress-maker to be copied, changing its meaning once again as she worked to reproduce herself in terms of the fashionable image.

This construction outlasted the craze for books of beauties and shaped periodicals for women throughout the rest of the century. In the 1830s and 1840s a number of new magazines for ladies, like the *Ladies' Cabinet of Fashion, Music and Romance* (1832–70) were launched, following the already established pattern. As well as these general monthlies, a number of new fashion-centred magazines were launched to follow on the success of journals like *Ackerman's Repository* (1809–29) and the *Ladies' Fashionable Repository* (1809–95).[4] All of these assumed that fashion was a necessary ingredient in the ladies' magazine.

Even more significantly, alongside these expensive monthlies a series of penny weeklies sprang up to take fashion to a very different group of readers. Once again 1832 was a turning point, as there seems to have been a rush of them in that year. Most were short-lived but the *Maids', Wives' and Widows' Penny Magazine and Gazette of Fashion* (1832–3) had a longer history under its energetic editor, Mrs Baron Wilson. It began as a rather cheeky penny-halfpenny imitation of the up-market journals and made this explicit the following year when it changed its title to the *Weekly Belle Assemblée* (1833–4). Its price drifted up to tuppence and a year later it became a monthly, now called the *New Monthly Belle Assemblée* (1834–70). Increasingly difficult to distinguish from the other new ladies' journals, by 1852 its contents were identical with the *Ladies' Cabinet* and the *Ladies' Companion* in a publishing manoeuvre like that of the three veteran journals which they imitated and outlasted.

The details of this publishing history demonstrate the uneven progress of fashion from the pages of the expensive journals into popular reading for women. In the 1850s a new kind of journal was to establish fashion as central to middle-class women's journals, while publishers of general and family magazines also coded 'fashion' along with fiction as markers of the feminine (see Chs 5 and 6; Altick 1957: 361). Fashion in the *Lady's Magazine and Museum* was still linked to its gossipy 'Paris Chit-chat' and 'London Chit-chat' about the doings of the aristocracy. This together with the priority accorded to French fashion was to be reworked in the second half of the century (see Ch. 7).

THE PATHOLOGICAL FEMALE BODY

The ladies' magazines used their address to the upper classes in their bid for advertising:

> So many thousands peruse the Lady's Magazine and Museum . . . that its advertising pages are rendered superior to almost any other medium not only for the great majority of literary and musical works which issue from the press but also for the lighter subjects which interest the fashionable world, all of which depend so much for their popularity on the patronage of the Fair Sex.
>
> (*LM&M* VI 1835: endpapers)

Advertising was relatively unimportant as a source of magazine finance in this era. Still taxed, it was confined to the endpapers or pages inside the covers which were stripped out when the volumes were bound. Such advertising as I have been able to find, however, suggests that advertisers largely shared the publishers' assumptions about the magazine reader. The lady was leisured, fashionable, and the manager of her household including her children and domestics. Advertisements for servants and governesses were therefore juxtaposed with announcements for books and music – always a staple of magazine advertising – and advertisements for the millinery, corsets and hair and teeth products needed to maintain the lady's appearance (ibid.).

These last advertisements, however, produced the female body in a very different way from the embellishments and plates. Here it was not a beautifully finished surface but a body constantly under threat, constantly having to be recreated with corsets, hair colouring and other invisible aids. More seriously, it was a body requiring Royal Cough Lozenges, stomach pills, vegetable syrups and books on 'the Diseases of Females' if it was not to slide into incipient pathology (ibid.). The dispensers of quack medicines were among the first to realise the potential for advertising in the modern media (Richards 1990: 168ff). Their construction of the female body as inevitably sick resonated with more 'scientific' medical discourses of the period which also linked 'femininity' and 'disease'. In the ladies' magazines this imperfect – even diseased – female body existed at the margins, in tension with the idealised beauty of the embellishments but constantly underscoring the difficulty of achieving a 'natural' femininity.

The female body, whether represented by 'the Beauty' or pathologised by the advertisers, was rarely allowed to disrupt the domestic ideal in the magazines.

Their staple articles and fiction continually returned the woman reader to her familial duties, which encompassed an appropriate attention to her appearance and her dress. Occasionally, however, that potential for disruption was manifest. A didactic story embedded in one of Mrs Hofland's 'A Bachelor's Recollections' brought together the claim for political rights, the idea of fashion and the inherent pathology of the female body in a moral tale. It concerned a young woman who read that dangerous volume, *The Rights of Woman* (Wollstonecraft 1792), and learned to follow her desires instead of obeying her husband. She insisted first on going to a hunt when pregnant and then attending a ball wearing the 'height of the mode', a low-cut gown made transparent by being wetted. Inevitably, within the logic of these narratives, she dies (*LM&M* VIII 1836: 168–72).

This exemplary tale made explicit those problems of women's 'rights' and the nature of sexual difference which the magazines more often addressed obliquely. Though juxtaposed with the illustrated 'modes', it made the choice of fashion literally death-dealing. At issue here was not only gender but also sexuality, the danger of woman following her own desire rather than her husband's. That danger was represented as a choice between a female sexuality defined by appearance and one defined by wifely obedience and maternity. So powerful was this opposition that it pulled into its orbit the whole debate around women's rights. Wollstonecraft's *The Rights of Woman* was represented as

> a book containing many good points but capable of misconstruction [which if the heroine had read] at thirty, when as a wife and mother she knew the tendency of human affairs [would have done no harm].
>
> (ibid.)

Wisdom for women thus depended entirely on acceptance of the demands of matrimony and maternity. In these states women's rights were transformed into responsibilities for others and a willing acceptance that 'the preponderance of knowledge as well as power is . . . on the side of the male part of creation' (Mrs Hofland in *LM&M* VI 1835: 317). Mrs Hofland, like the Old Woman earlier in the century, had to insist regularly that such inequalities were natural in order to contain the anomalous femininities evident in the same number of the magazine.

THE WOMAN WRITER AS ANOMALY

In naming the anomaly of Victoria, Caroline Norton herself embodied another anomalous female figure: the woman writer. Her challenge to the domestic woman lay not in her embodiment as beauty but in her challenge to the exclusive right of the male part of creation to knowledge and economic activity. Writing for publication was one of the few ways in which middle-class women could make money without losing their status. This depended on the construction of reading as an essentially domestic activity, of writing as a task which could be undertaken at home, and of certain genres – notably fiction and improving or domestic articles – as potentially feminine in character. Individual women of energy and talent, like Sarah Ellis, were thus able to earn a living in the public sphere, frequently by producing works which located women's power exclusively in the private and domestic. This was not simply hypocritical, though there was an opportunist element in Sarah Ellis's business dealings (Ellis 1893: 138). It was one way of dealing with the woman writer's position as 'a singular anomaly' in the masculine world of publishing (Colby 1970).

Since its inception the periodical had involved women as writers and editors, and women were often highly visible in the new press. Three notable editors – Christian Johnstone, Mary Howitt and Eliza Cook – produced improving magazines. Eliza Cook, already well known as a poet and journalist, owned and edited the magazine which carried her name. Mary Howitt was a translator and author of children's and adult fiction, a prolific journalist (including contributions to the *Lady's Magazine and Museum*) and joint editor with her husband, William, of *Howitts' Journal.* Caroline Norton wrote for every kind of journal from *La Belle Assemblée* to the *Family Herald.* The annuals and Books of Beauty were often associated with aristocratic literary pretensions and edited by society hostesses, like the Countess of Blessington, but middle-class women journalists also edited annuals, as did the poet, L.E. Landon (L.E.L.), Mary Howitt and even Sarah Strickney (later Mrs Ellis) (Lee 1955: 80–3; Ellis 1893: 55).

Where magazines had offered reader participation as a benefit they now advertised the attractions of familiar names. In the 1830s and 1840s the *Lady's Magazine and Museum* by-lined regular writers like Mrs Hofland and Camilla Toulmin and posted the names of well-known women contributors on their cover (see *LM&M* VI 1835: back cover). Behind the scenes there were struggles over how far the magazines should continue to rely on unpaid readers' contributions ('Notices', *LM&M* VI 1835). These were dramatised in an editorial row in 1834 between the Lady Caroline Norton, who was editor of the *Court Magazine and Belle Assemblée*, and her proprietor, Bell, over his insistence that the cost of the 'literary portion' be kept under 9–10 guineas, relying on 'gratis performance' for the rest (Perkins 1910: 55, 59).

The periodical press thus enabled the development of journalism as a profession and provided a space in which some women could earn their living 'like men'. The growth and professionalisation of the press did not, however, produce a coherent discursive position for these women to occupy. Women writers – with few exceptions – were less successful than their male counterparts both materially and culturally. Their 'lack of education, lack of opportunity, lack of status and lack of property combined to narrow their literary horizons' (Cross 1985: 203; Mumm 1990). Named women writers were outnumbered by men, even in the ladies' magazines. The nineteenth-century creation of professions – whether journalism, medicine or engineering – was always predicated upon the exclusion of women and others deemed unsuitable for the job. The presence of women in journalism threatened its status as a profession.

Nor was this all. Because she usually turned to writing out of economic necessity, the woman journalist challenged that fundamental division between public and private which rested on the presumption that a man provided financially for his wife (Mumm 1990). Christian Johnstone, an outstanding editor of *Tait's Edinburgh Magazine* between 1834 and 1846, 'was never given the fame she deserved' perhaps because – as she herself put it – 'the woman who turns her talents to any profitable use is, in some occult sense, I own I do not comprehend it – but she is in our Society *degraded*' (Houghton 1966–87: 479–80).

The disruptive potential of the woman journalist remained repressed throughout the mid-Victorian period but she would return to haunt the women's magazine later in the century.

4

FAMILY AND MOTHERS' MAGAZINES: THE 1830s AND 1840s

Domestic Economy, Education, Sanitary Reform, Cottage Gardening, also Social Sketches, Moral Tales, Family Secrets and Valuable Household Recipes.

(*Family Economist* I 1848: contents list)

My maternal readers, the sentiment of our motto is the *mighty power of maternal influence for good or evil.* Ponder it deeply and unceasingly.

(*Mother's Magazine* 1846–7 unnumbered volume: 181, emphasis in original)

―――――――――

THE GROWTH OF THE POPULAR PRESS

The 1830s and 1840s were years of enormous expansion in the periodical press, indeed some scholars would argue that the first mass magazine appeared in the 1840s and that in these decades the modern press began.[1] Here, too, 1832 was a turning point, for in that year appeared three cheap papers without news whose success laid the foundations for the 'journalism for the middle class . . . in the approaching Victorian era' (Altick 1957: 332). They were *Chambers's Edinburgh Journal*, the *Penny Magazine* and the *Saturday Magazine.* These differed in appearance, formula and commercial strategy but they all cost a penny, sold in their tens or even hundreds of thousands and aimed to provide 'wholesome' reading for the working man (Altick 1957: 335; Bennett 1982).

The discovery of a potentially vast readership for cheap papers combined with developments in distribution – particularly as the railway boom got under way – to revolutionise the periodical press in the 1830s and 1840s. From 1836 the Taxes on Knowledge began to be reduced. Illiteracy and material poverty still meant that these projects of 'pervading the whole society' had limited success. Nevertheless, these magazines, even if read by the lower middle class and skilled artisans, represented an extraordinary democratisation of print (Altick 1957: 335; Mitchell 1981: 2; Vincent 1989: esp. 228ff; Wiener 1969).

The role of women readers in that process was, in a familiar anomaly, both central and marginal, even deviant. The new readership was defined in class rather than gender terms and *Chambers's* and the *Penny* assumed the masculine as the unarticulated norm, though they may have been read by women as they were by the middle class. However, to separate class from gender definitions is to fail to acknowledge how closely these were entangled. The new journals located their readership in the privatised sphere of the woman-centred family which middle-class discourse had defined. According to one argument against the Taxes on Knowledge, it was better that the 'poor man should have his newspaper in his cottage than that he should be sent to a public house to read it' (quoted in Vincent 1989: 235). Even the newspaper read in the privacy of the home, could encourage domestic virtues rather than the disorderly and political feelings likely to erupt in a reading scene which was public, masculine and working class. How much more conducive to those virtues were magazines called the *Family Economist*, the *Family Friend* or the *Magazine of Domestic Economy*.

The 'family' journal was the most significant development of the 1840s and it came to dominate Victorian popular publishing. These papers not only included 'woman' in their readership, they assumed that her domestic management provided the scene of reading. The *Family Friend* was relatively dear at tuppence but still claimed a readership of 50,000 after its first year and sales of its bound volumes of more than 75,000 (*FF* I 1848–9: iii; II 1849–50: i). Its frontispiece, with its scenes of family reading and of women sketching and sewing, made clear that the domestic was both its subject and its destination (Figure 4.1). Offering a mean between religious and sensationalist publications, its varied diet of fiction, poetry, popularised science and practical advice offered something for each member of the family (*FF* I 1848–9: iii).

The *Family Friend*, like the ladies' magazine, linked femininity to fiction-reading and needlework but it rooted these activities in practical domestic management. Recipes were provided by 'a medical gentleman' after testing by his wife (*FF* II 1850: iv). Advice on garden and household management featured not only in the articles but in the 'Answers to Correspondents' which became a major feature of such magazines, dealing with everything from removing rust to making bread, 'popping the question' and juggling as indoor exercise for women (Appendix, *FF* II 1849–50: 10).

The *Family Economist*, launched in the same year as the *Family Friend*, produced a different version of domestic management. As a penny monthly, it sought to extend a proper 'Family Economy' beyond the middle class to those 'too poor or indifferent to spare even a penny for themselves', on whose behalf readers were urged to 'buy a dozen or two [copies] each month and distribute gratuitously to your poorer friends' (*F.Econ.* I 1848: 217).

Addressed explicitly to the 'industrious' class by their social superiors, it assumed that their improvement would be achieved through domestic manage-ment rather than the acquisition of 'useful knowledge' by individual (male) readers. The magazine therefore offered a model of gender difference which tran-scended class division. Aphorisms such as 'No man ever prospered without the co-operation of his wife' typified both its style and ideology (*F.Econ.* I 1848: 76).

Figure 4.1 Frontispiece of the *Family Friend* (II 1849–50)

47

Although such journals extended the discourse of the domestic in ways which shaped popular print for the rest of the century, they did not make gender their defining category. They were not 'women's magazines'.[2] A better case could be made for a quite different kind of 'family' journal. The *Family Herald* (1842–1939) and the *London Journal* (1845–1912) were penny weekly miscellanies offering entertainment rather than self-education, and their staple was fiction. They were the most widely read publications in Britain, the *Family Herald* claiming 125,000 circulation in 1849 (to *Chambers's* 60,000–70,000) and the two journals jointly selling 750,000 copies a week by the mid-1850s. No need here for the dispensing of gratuitous copies to the poor.

These journals, as Sally Mitchell has shown, catered for women as distinct from ladies, and almost certainly had a high proportion of female readers (Dalziel 1957: 21–32; Mitchell 1981: 1–21). Their fiction, especially the serialised novels, focused on love and romance, often in upper-class settings, sometimes involving seduction and betrayal but always in the end endorsing sexual morality and female moral responsibility (Mitchell 1981: 16–18 and passim). Their 'Answers to Correspondents' dealt more realistically with health, beauty, and personal relations – the stuff of domestic femininity – as well as with legal and factual enquiries.

These too, however, were 'family' rather than women's magazines. The great expansion of print in the 1830s and 1840s produced no cheap magazines aimed specifically at women. The tradition of the expensive ladies' journal continued and publications for specific groups of 'mothers' or 'Christian ladies' began to appear (see Ch. 5). But for most publishers maximising sales meant providing 'something for everyone' and they targeted a family readership presumed to be united in its tastes, if differentiated by gender and generation (Mitchell 1981: 1). The magazine – diverse and relatively cheap – was the ideal form for this.

'The woman reader' remained central to the discursive practices of publishing but she was still assumed to read differently, even deviantly, from the norm. Middle-class anxieties about female reading centred on the popularity of fiction journals such as the *Family Herald*, and the working-class woman was regarded as doubly deviant from the male middle-class norm and tainted by her love of escapist fiction. However, most women had less time or space for reading than their men and were likely to be less literate (Vincent 1989: 24–5). The scene of domestic reading remained for most of them unrealisable.

CHRISTIAN LADIES AND MOTHERS

There was, however, one important serial publishing tradition which specifically addressed the woman reader, deliberately excluding the aristocratic lady. Serious and deeply religious, these magazines stressed women's spiritual and moral responsibilities as Christians. Appearance, of either the woman herself or the magazine she read, was a trivial distraction from the substance or the soul. The *Christian Lady's Friend and Family Repository* only lasted a year (1832–3) but the

Christian Lady's Magazine (1834–49) ran for fifteen years, during which time a series of magazines addressed to Christian Mothers appeared, most lasting for several years and one considerably longer.[3]

These 1830s and 1840s magazines were in the evangelical tradition with its immediate roots in the religious revival of the late eighteenth and early nineteenth century. Nineteenth-century American culture was dominated by the relationship between evangelical Christianity, femininity and popular publishing, a relationship in which *Godey's Lady's Book* played a key part (Douglas 1977). There was no single magazine in Britain which played a role like *Godey's* in America, but the cultural similarities extended beyond a common language and certain common publications. In Britain 'serious Christianity' was central to the creation of a distinct middle class, not least in its differentiation of gender. The diffusion of evangelical beliefs through respectable society meant that 'church-going, family worship, the observance of the Sabbath, and an interest in religious literature' had come to characterise the middle class by the time of the 1851 Religious Census (Davidoff and Hall 1987: 76ff).

For women, evangelical Christianity offered a contradictory position. Before God all were equally sinful and equally able to be saved. The problem of selfhood was simple and stark:

> Why was I made to hear his voice
> And enter while there's room,
> While thousands make a wretched choice
> And rather starve than come?
> <div align="right">(<i>MM</i> 1840: 37–8)</div>

However, men and women were not equal within the family or wider society; the husband was the head over the wife and her superior in judgement if not in spiritual grace. Moreover, hierarchies of respectability militated against the radical demands of equality before God. In the world beyond Britain, which evangelicals reached through a growing network of missionary societies, the heathen too were both potentially equal and yet radically other and inferior. Evangelicalism stressed self-examination and self-awareness, yet the identity of the self caught in these contradictions was uncertain, even threatened. The magazines I discuss in this section negotiated what it meant to be a 'Christian Lady' or a 'British Mother' in this tangle of sameness and difference.

As a religion of the book, evangelicalism made reading central to its practice. The development of the cheap press owed much to the energy and skill of evangelicals, particularly of women. Charlotte Elizabeth Tonna, founder editor of the *Christian Lady's Magazine* in 1834, stood in a line of committed women which included Hannah More and Sarah Trimmer, the pioneers of improving literature for the 'lower classes'.

Sarah Trimmer had, among her other activities, produced and edited the *Family Magazine*, whose aims were spelt out in its cumbersome sub-title: 'A Repository of Religious Instruction and Rational Amusement designed to counteract the pernicious Tendency of Immoral Books etc. which have circulated of late Years among the Inferior classes of People'. Hannah More had recognised the potential of the broadside format to carry religious and social messages, and her work through the series of Cheap Repository Tracts in particular shaped popular publishing for decades.

More had been particularly concerned to define the role of Christian women 'of rank and fortune' in the crisis of English society caused (she believed) by the revolution in France. Writing on 'Female Education', she assured 'women of the higher class' that their most important talent, 'one which they can scarcely rate too highly . . . is influence' (More 1834: 11). Though she did not herself start or edit a magazine for women, Hannah More's 'influence' on women's reading spread beyond publications specifically aligned with serious Christianity including the ladies' magazines, which were pervaded by a watered down evangelicalism.

Hannah More's influence was also specifically invoked in these journals. The *Lady's Monthly Museum* had made her the subject of its first biography and portrait (*LM* I 1798: 1ff). In a now familiar paradox, this represented her simultaneously as role model of achieving woman and messenger of women's limitations. But it also signalled her importance in the project of providing reading for ladies – however fractured that project proved to be. The short-lived *Female Preceptor* (1813), a lady's magazine specifically dedicated to More, claimed to address the 'rationally devout . . . women of rank and fortune' with its mixture of fashion news, poetry, and essays 'Chiefly of the Duties of the Female Sex' (White 1970: 38).

In contrast to these, many Christian magazines of the 1830s and 1840s attacked aristocratic lack of seriousness and stressed the 'immense consequences . . . involved in a habit of extravagance, whether in dress, equipage or pleasure!' (*MM* 1838–9: 176). They located their devout readership clearly in the middle or lower-middle class. Some were designed to be shared around members of a church or local group (*MM* 1840: 187). I had access to bound volumes of the *Mother's Magazine* from the collection of the Mechanics Institution Library in Levenshulme, Manchester, with the names of borrowers on a label pasted inside the front cover.[4] Clearly improving magazines, like tracts or the exemplary biographies given as school prizes, circulated widely through informal and formal educational networks. These extended well beyond the middle-class girls' boarding schools at which the *Lady's Museum* had aimed.

The question of who actually bought these magazines and the extent of overlap between purchaser and reader is, as always, complex. Certainly some were designed to be bought and then given away or passed on to a quite different readership. This practice had been pioneered by More and the Religious Tract Society and continued throughout the century. In 1869, the up-market *Queen* praised the New Series *Mother's Friend* because 'it promises to be even more fitted for the use of the poor and of their friends who would make them good, wise and happy' (*Q.* XLV 1869: 27). Yet at 1 *d.* the magazine was accessible to middle-class women who wanted to read it for themselves, and the evidence of reader participation which I discuss in a moment suggests they were an active and engaged readership.

Although produced to be sold – even if the buyer subsequently passed it on – the *Mothers' Magazine* made few concessions to appearance to tempt prospective purchasers. It was a similar size to the *Lady's Museum* (8 × 5½ inches), printed across the page rather than in columns, unillustrated and sober – even boring – in its lay-out. Just as *La Belle Assemblée* matched its medium to its message about the importance of looks for women, so this sober journal defined feminine beauty entirely in spiritual terms. Unlike the ladies' magazines, even the *Female Preceptor*, these journals carried no articles on fashion or dress. Indeed they shared a general belief that ever since Eve cut her first fig leaf, 'dress [was] the memorial of our primal sin' (*BMM* XI 1855: 120).

THE *CHRISTIAN LADY'S MAGAZINE*

The first and most lively of these journals was the *Christian Lady's Magazine*. Charlotte Elizabeth Tonna, who often signed herself simply Charlotte Elizabeth, was its first editor and a major contributor throughout.[5] She set out to create readers who were 'active, intelligent, useful Christian wom[en]' (*CLM* I 1836: 327). Small in size (6½ × 4 inches), her magazine offered a varied diet of poetry, letters, book reviews and articles on geology, history and what it called 'religious reading' as well as politics. While conceding that certain topics were to be avoided as 'better adapted to periodicals of a more masculine stamp', Tonna insisted that 'It is not in the interests of the one half of the species that the other half should be kept in a state of mental degradation' (*CLM* I 1836: i, 396).

Abstract declarations that women should not be mentally degraded were easily made; negotiating the specific boundaries of women's proper knowledge was far more difficult. The editor in its first number acknowledged that

> few qualities come under our consideration as Christian females more weighty in their relative importance or more difficult to answer by a precise definition than the extent to which it is both lawful and expedient for us publicly to 'intermeddle with all wisdom'.
>
> (*CLM* I 1836: 3)

The issue here was 'spiritual matters' in which Tonna argued both that women 'were not excluded' from knowledge and that 'a boundary is assigned' (ibid.). She drew the boundaries relatively generously.

In negotiating the area of legitimate political knowledge, the *Christian Lady* was similarly inclusive. Introducing a series of articles on politics, the question 'What in the world have you to do with politics?' was answered 'What is there so droll in a woman's endeavouring to collect the heads of a few important public events for the consideration of her own sex?' The response 'Why nothing to be sure, if that is all your aim' safely excluded the kind of illegitimate knowledge which involved 'women leaving their assigned sphere' to become 'political agitators, political economists or whatnot' (*CLM* I 1836: 74).

Under this rubric, the series on politics in the first volume included discussions of the slave trade, Ireland, the factory system, and political economy and taxation (*CLM* I 1836: 73–6, 78, 154–60, 439–48). No wonder one writer, signing herself an 'Old Blue Stocking' wrote enthusiastically:

> What an age is the present! Ladies writing upon theology, science, meta-physics, and ladies, too, their readers. Yet these very ladies leave behind none of their sex as mothers, wives, guides of their houses, followers of every good work. Time was when a Lady's Magazine was only a miscellany of fashion and foppery . . . so much was the mental culture of the female sex an object of dread to the lords of creation . . . . Surely, then this is an age of improve-ment. Welcome the march of intellect!
>
> (*CLM* I 1836: 25–6)

Despite the march of intellect, Tonna had constantly to defend the political content of her magazine. She insisted that 'a female demagogue is, next after a female infidel, the greatest outrage on the divine author', but argued that as 'mothers, wives and guides of their houses' women had a responsibility to use their influence for the common good (*CLM* I 1836: 160; see also 249–56).

However, the line between political agitation and exerting influence was not always so clear cut. In the later 1830s, the magazine offered a radical critique of conditions of the new industrial working class with a concern for their material poverty as much as the spiritual neglect in which they lived. Tonna used the maga-zine to publish fictional accounts in prose and verse of the plight of women and children in the factories of Britain. The number which hailed Victoria's accession carried an article on children in factories called 'English Slavery' and a poem called 'The Factory Girl's Last Day' which ended:

> That night a chariot passed her
> While on the ground she lay;
> The daughters of her master
> An evening visit pay;
> Their tender hearts were sighing
> As negro wrongs were told,
> While the white slave lay dying
> Who gained their father's gold.
> (*CLM* X 1838: 67)

Unlike the poem 'The Death of the Factory Child' – commissioned from the working-class poet J.C. Prince for the radical unstamped *Fleet Papers* in 1841, this powerful poem was clearly situated in a debate among women of the middle class about their political responsibility (Maidment 1987: 111–19). The magazine's position was that, as evangelical women had been in the forefront of the campaign against slavery, so they must turn their attention to the slavery on their doorsteps. Factory workers were linked to them both by the spiritual ties of sisterhood in Christ and by the economics of profit.

In 1839, when Tonna was no longer editor, the magazine began publishing a series of her novelettes subsequently collected in volume form as the *Wrongs of Woman*, a title with an ironic reference – conscious or not – to the very un-evangelical Wollstonecraft (Kovacevic 1975: 94–5, 303–12). *Helen Fleetwood*, serialised between 1839 and 1840, was according to Kovacevic 'the first English novel to be entirely concerned with the lives of industrial workers' (1975: 303). Certainly Tonna and her magazine pioneered the use of fiction to debate 'the Condition of England' question, as it came to be known.

This was remarkable not least because the magazine had originally refused to 'indulge in fictitious narratives'. It shared the evangelical belief that novels were harmful, particularly to young women, in whom imagination was active and judgement weak (*CLM* I 1836: 328). As one writer in the *Mother's Magazine* put it briskly, 'If you want to become weak-headed, nervous and good for nothing, read novels' (*MM* 1840: 65). But both the *Christian Lady* and the *Mother's Magazine* allowed 'fictions of the allegorical and parabolic kind . . . as sanctioned by Scripture': 'Those . . . which give just representation of life, without the accompaniment of a love story, may, to a limited extent, be allowed' (*MM* 1840–41: 53–6, 65–70, 89–91). Such 'Instructive Tales' were part of the evangelical tradition developed by Mrs Trimmer and Hannah More.

Tonna herself was a skilled story-teller and well aware of the importance of feeling as against the 'abstract idea of a suffering family' if her readership were to be moved to act (Kovacevic 1975: 305). Her *Wrongs of Woman* stories drew on Blue Books and other documentary evidence but used considerable narrative skill to involve the reader. In 'The Little Pin Headers' Tonna invited the middle-class woman to understand her own complicity in the factory system, for which pin-making had become the metonym. Her story focuses on the children, appealing to Christian concern and maternal feeling and concluding with an impassioned attack upon the system as 'a crime against God and our brethren'. Her final plea for readers to work towards Sunday Schools for the poor comes as something of an anti-climax (Kovacevic 1975: 313ff). What is significant, however, is that this magazine consistently argued not only that Christian women must be politically informed, but that they had a duty to intervene in economic and public affairs – even if the solutions within their power seemed inadequate to the task.

A faint echo of this argument was sometimes heard in the *Lady's Magazine and Museum*, despite its claim that 'to obtrude the angry strife of party politics on the attention of cultivated and elegant-minded women is a barbarism we never commit' (*LM&M* VII 1835: 146). The world of politics inevitably intruded into the feminine world, just as politicians, business men and merchants came home in the evening to feminine conversation. That disclaimer, in fact, introduced an article on 'Infant Schools' which urged the 'Ladies of Great Britain' to concern themselves with educational provision; for

> when any measure is proposed likely to be adopted by our legislature which
> is likely to soften the temper and improve the morals of the ignorant and
> oft times suffering, lower classes where can it better look for support and

approbation than among the mothers, wives, and daughters of our land who enjoy the affluence and know the blessings of education?

(ibid.)

Lacking Tonna's religious concern, this article appealed specifically to the *maternal* in its readers, arguing that it was precisely those qualities excluded from the masculine public domain which were now needed to redeem it.

MOTHERS' MAGAZINES

In the other evangelical magazines which were launched in the 1830s and 1840s, this idea of Christian motherhood moved to centre stage. The *Mother's Magazine* drew the boundaries of legitimate knowledge and activity far more tightly than the *Christian Lady* and the magazine itself was less fractured in terms of genre and discourse. Readers were addressed specifically as 'mothers' and the idea of motherhood was assumed both as grounds of identity and as an ideal to which the reader must constantly aspire. Motherhood in this discourse meant 'training up the child in the way he should go', that is in Christian faith.

The magazine consisted largely of articles and meditations on the spiritual life together with instructive tales, poems and accounts of maternal experiences. Much of the writing was informed by the rhetoric of the pulpit, taking the form of textual expositions or direct addresses to the reader. However the autobiographical letter or story was another staple form which sometimes provided lively accounts of family life. The mother who fears her child has stolen money from her purse, or 'Little John', a 2-year-old locked in by himself for some misdemeanour who boasted how 'I cried when I was in the other room', are represented in realist detail (*MM* 1840–1: 120–1, 133–6).

The *Mother's Magazine* concerned itself exclusively with the moral and spiritual aspects of mothering; there was nothing on cookery, needlework or the practicalities of sickbed nursing. It offered its readers a definition of their womanly role which turned on scrupulous attention to the minutiae of family life, especially the bringing up of children marked by original sin. The acceptance of the corruption of unredeemed nature was central to the magazine, as to all evangelical faith. Mothers must monitor their own and their family's inner lives constantly. To modern readers the attitude to children seems uncompromising, with tales of 3-year-old deathbed conversions and of 8-month babies trained to obedience (*MM* 1842–3: 173, 175–6). Although smacks were administered, punishment was principally psychological and 'the entire end of punishment' was a Foucauldian internalisation of the discipline, so that 'the child appears not only humbled and gentle in spirit but affectionate towards [the disciplining parent]' (*MM* 1840–1: 121; Foucault 1979).

The maternal identity which the magazine produced for its readers therefore depended upon self-examination and self-regulation. The spiritual autobiography was sufficiently well established by this time to offer a model for producing the experiences of motherhood in writing. Certain kinds of scene recur in these mini-autobiographies, for example the child's deathbed (*MM* 1840–1: 43). At one level these can be read as realistic representations of women readers' common experience. High infant mortality rates meant that many would have lost children, and the language of faith embodied in the magazine provided a way of coming to terms with this. However, these recurrent deathbed scenes also represented that nearness of the spiritual which invested the smallest household tasks with meaning.

The life of unremitting spiritual labour which the magazine offered mothers was mitigated by three things. First, a high level of emotional intensity was created by the use of biblical language and the rhetoric of exhortation developed in evangelical pulpits. The centrality of feeling to the religious experience was a general feature of evangelicalism but here it was given a particular emphasis by the characterisation of women as more given to emotion than men (and perhaps, therefore, of deeper religious faith). Second, the magazine assured women that they were important, and that the hidden, private life of the family was valued in the eyes of God. The role of mothers was constantly held up as perhaps the most weighty task given to Christians. Third, the woman at home was promised support and companionship – both that of God and that of an earthly community of other women.

This earthly community was central to the magazines. It included but went beyond that dependence on contributions from readers which had characterised the early ladies' magazines. The *Mother's Magazine* was originally an American publication of the 'Maternal Associations' of the evangelical churches. Its British counterpart published by James Paul in London, was 'reprinted from the American Edition' and consisted largely of American material. The indigenous *British Mothers' Journal* was similarly aimed at 'Maternal Meetings'.

These were local groups of women who met to share their experience as Christian mothers. Reports of meetings were included in each volume, as were contributions from members. These associations gave women a collective presence in the church and the wider society, where they pursued their mission in philanthropy, in Sunday Schools, in tract distribution and even in work among 'fallen women' (Rendall 1987: 82, 259–60). They were never as well established in Britain as in America, and women were less openly involved in moral reform outside the home. Nevertheless, the specifically British mothers' magazines which developed during the 1850s and 1860s did address such questions as 'the formation of Mothers' Meetings among the Poorest and Lowest Classes' and the provision of ragged schools (*BMM* XI 1855: 42–4).

For readers, the magazine itself was both enabler and signifier of a community of mothers, putting women in touch with each other, giving them a space in which to share their experience, and offering support. Each number included letters and accounts of meetings not only from New York, Boston and Philadelphia, Dorchester and Dover, but from missionaries in Hawaii, Ceylon and elsewhere across the world (*MM* 1841–2: 12, 35, 183). The insistent reproduction of mothering in the magazines, however, not only carried strong class overtones. It assumed a Protestant faith and practice which carried a racial dimension. In the *Mother's Magazine* the overseas letters were from the white missionaries. The maternal association in Jaffna, Ceylon (six members when it was founded in 1821, eight in 1840), welcomed the magazine as a way of keeping in touch with their sisters at home when they were 'far away among the heathen' (*MM* 1841–2: 13–14); 'the heathen' were clearly excluded from the motherhood addressed by the magazines.

Yet the discourse of evangelical Christianity involved a world mission and a universalised model of female nature. That model was a double one. Woman was a fallen creature, given to vices of triviality and love of dress (which the aristocratic were particularly prone to), but she also possessed natural feelings of maternity which made her more susceptible to religion. The difficulties of negotiating these complexities in the magazines were compounded by the hierarchies of class and race. In 1836, for example, the Reverend Jackson, a missionary in Burma, wrote that he had made his Burmese female converts give up their ornaments and jewels because the chief obstacle to the Gospel was 'that principle of vanity, that love of dress and display . . . that has in every age and in all countries been a ruling passion of the fair sex' (*CLMV* 1836: 61). In the correspondence this provoked, at least one reader felt he had been 'over-zealous' and the editor invoked New Testament compassion against the missionary's Old Testament judgement (ibid.: 222–7).

For Eve was both the cause of the fall and the 'mother of all living'. Mother love was 'natural' and the 'unconverted mother', however poor or heathen, could be converted into a 'Christian Mother' on the strength of that love (see *MM* 1846–7 'Three Qualifications for a Mother': 136–7; and 1840–1, 'The Unconverted Mother': 117). This definition of maternity demanded the complete refusal of femininity as appearance. The beautified body was that of the fallen (aristocratic) woman. The truly female body was not biologically defined but redeemed the biological role of child-bearing by transforming maternity into language, into a disciplinary discourse (Foucault 1979).

Part II

THE BEETONS:
THE DOMESTIC ENGLISH
WOMAN AND THE LADY,
1850–80

5

THE BEETONS AND
THE *ENGLISHWOMAN'S DOMESTIC*
MAGAZINE, 1852–60

The ENGLISHWOMAN'S DOMESTIC MAGAZINE will doubtless be
found an encouraging friend to those of our countrywomen already initiated
in the secret of making 'home happy' and to the uninitiated . . . we shall offer
hints and advice by which they may overcome every difficulty . . .
(*Englishwoman's Domestic Magazine* I 1852: 1)

The Case of Albert: NETTIE writes: I am induced . . . to address Albert,
since he has in your last number so kindly favoured us with a description of
himself and made us acquainted with that *he* considers his beau ideal of a
wife. Now I must tell Albert first of all a *terrible* little secret . . . – Oh Albert
. . . I am (I must say so) very very untidy. Can Albert ever exist with an untidy
wife but one who promises faithfully to endeavour all she can to improve
herself in this particular. NETTIE never mends her stockings and cannot
undertake to keep either boxes or drawers tidy but . . . is of a *most* 'amiable,
loving and affectionate' disposition and would be very useful to ALBERT
and *try* to keep *his* gloves mended and his buttons on.
('Cupid's Letter Bag', *Englishwoman's Domestic Magazine* III 1854–5: 96)

The *Englishwoman's Domestic Magazine* (hereafter *EDM*) launched in 1852,
marked a watershed between the exclusive ladies' magazines and the popular
women's domestic journals which were to become the staple of the genre from the
1890s. It assumed that women wanted fiction and fashion but it also dealt with
the dailiness of readers' lives. Unlike the mothers' magazines, however, it secularised those lives, offering the way to domestic happiness rather than salvation.

It was an immediate success. By 1857 it claimed a circulation of 50,000 readers
(Preface, *EDM* VI 1857). The *Daily Telegraph*'s assertion that it had 'in one year
gained a greater number of patrons than any other magazine in the Empire',
though impossible to verify, indicates the standing of the magazine among the
middle classes (Spain 1956: 69). Ten years later the *Standard,* another middle-
class paper, reported that 'We have the authority of materfamilias for saying that
the house would go to sixes and sevens if the *Englishwoman's Domestic Magazine*
failed to make its appearance' (in Spain 1956: 131). Some of this success was due
to Beeton's 'bold' experiments in selling. He offered various prizes, notably a 15

59

guinea gold watch which could be claimed on presentation of a year's worth of coupons (*EDM* I 1853: 352). Whatever the inducements, however, Beeton created in the *EDM* a magazine aimed specifically at women which established and maintained a substantial new readership. It was a propitious moment for such a venture: 1852 was the year after the Great Exhibition, Chartism had been defeated and a period of political stability and economic growth, the 'Age of Capital', the 'Age of Equipoise' was under way (Best 1982: 19–23, 250–1; Hobsbawm 1975). These next twenty-five years were a time of relative economic growth and intellectual confidence in which the middle class consolidated its power.

The Samuel Beeton who launched the *EDM* represented that class archetype, the mid-Victorian entrepreneur. He understood and grasped the new opportunities presented by the market in print. His first publishing venture had been a series of reprints which he took over from Vizitelly and marketed under the catchy – if tautological – title, 'Readable Books'. This included one of the first English reprints of Harriet Beecher Stowe's *Uncle Tom's Cabin*, the success of which may well have provided the capital for his other ventures, including three magazines for women and two for boys, the Beeton dictionaries and guides, and Isabella's *Beeton's Book of Household Management*, which made 'Mrs Beeton' famous (Driver 1989: 101–2; Freeman 1977: 216–17). Beeton embodied the crucial ideological formula of the 'self-made man' which linked masculinity to capitalist enterprise and was given its clearest articulation in Samuel Smiles's 1859 volume, *Self Help*.

However, British society was neither economically nor discursively monolithic. Even the boom decades of the 1850s and 1860s were marked at a national level by the uncertainties of the Crimean War. At the level of the individual middle-class family, in which the man's provision for his women and children was axiomatic, the possibility of financial ruin was a continual ideological and material threat. The collapse of the finance house of Overend and Gurney in 1866 came to symbolise the fragility of the middle-class way of life and of entrepreneurial capitalism even at its most triumphant. Significantly for this study, one of those it bankrupted was Samuel Beeton (Hyde 1951: 134). The heroic figure of the self-made man was always under threat.

In Beeton's case another dynamic was at work to disrupt the stereotype. Between 1857 and early 1865, when the publishing house was at its most successful, 'Beeton' was not a self-made man at all but a married couple. Isabella Beeton worked more or less continually, from the time of her marriage until her death from puerperal fever at the age of 28, as journalist and then joint editor of the *EDM*, co-ordinator of work on Beeton's new women's magazines, and author of the book by which she is still known (Freeman 1977; Hyde 1951). In the year after her death bankruptcy forced Samuel to sell his titles to Ward, Locke & Tyler and engage himself to work for them (Freeman 1977: 248–51). But by then 'Beeton' had thoroughly transformed the middle-class woman's magazine, begun to re-work the conventions of the expensive ladies' illustrated paper and pioneered the magazine for young women.

The 'domestic woman' of the magazine was both as central and as potentially unstable a figure as her counterpart, the self-made man. In 1851, in an article in the *Westminster Review*, Harriet Taylor set out her argument that the current 'position [of men and women was] equally corrupting to both', although for women to argue for political rights 'requir[ed] unusual moral courage as well as disinterestedness' (*WR* July 1851, repr. Murray 1982: 32–5). It was not until 1869 that John Stuart Mill published his full development of this argument in *The Subjection of Women*, but throughout the 1850s and 1860s there were 'strong-minded women' and disinterested men prepared to voice the case for the rights of women as a group – of access to education, paid labour and the vote, divorce and their own property if married. Middle-class women who failed to marry and had to work (often as governesses) were another endemic problem for the ideology of the domestic, even before they were named as such by W.R. Greg in his 1862 article on 'Redundant Women' (Greg 1862).

The work of gender definition and particularly the re-creation of the domestic woman in the *EDM* must be understood as part of these 'uneven developments', in Poovey's phrase (1989: esp. 1–23). Beeton assumed that women were a group with common interests and located these in the domestic realm. However, 'Beeton' was a working partnership as well as an apparently companionate marriage, and even after Isabella's death Samuel's editorials in the *EDM* spelt out his commitment to women's rights in the public sphere with endorsement of John Stuart Mill's position (*EDM* N.S. 2, III 1867: 332–3). The extraordinary diversity of genres and voices which characterised the *EDM* allowed very different models of femininity to coexist on its pages, which may also have contributed to its success.

That success must be understood too in the context of the growth of the periodical press. Here there was a complex pattern of growth and sudden – if local – reversal. Anyone tracing the history of particular periodicals is struck by how many were short-lived and how others passed from one publisher to another, making the bibliographer's task a nightmare. Whatever the individual difficulties, however, the general trend during the 1850s was one of continued expansion both in numbers of titles and in readership. Periodical publishing was given a great impetus from the lifting of the taxes on knowledge between 1853 and 1861 (Altick 1957; Lee 1976: 42–9). The increased capital investment, improved technology and better communications which characterised mid-Victorian prosperity were also evident in periodical publishing, with the arrival of the Hoe printing press from America and the making of paper from Esparto grass (Lee 1976: 54–9).

The growth of the railways during the 1840s had not only improved periodical distribution, it also produced new sales outlets. Station book stalls, run from 1848 by W.H. Smith with the motto 'All who ride may read', sent sales of books and periodicals soaring to 'unprecedented levels' (Altick 1957: 302; Davies 1983: 46). Even more importantly, rail travel created a new reading public and new scenes of reading. Beeton along with other publishers rushed to produce

'Literature for the Rail', including part-issues and periodicals, and the *EDM*, while not designated 'railway reading', was part of that general process of expansion (Hyde 1951: 54).

CLASS, NATION AND GENDER: THE MAKING OF 'THE DOMESTIC ENGLISH WOMAN'

The title, price and monthly publication of the *EDM* designated a specific readership which it also sought self-consciously to create. Beeton constructed his readers primarily in terms of a universal womanhood centred on home-making. Two decades after its launch *EDM* was still articulating the belief that:

> All households, English and foreign, may be classed under one of the following heads:- 1st. Orderly and clean; 2nd. Clean but not orderly; 3rd. Dirty. We have found the first among the poorest, the third among the richest.
>
> (*EDM* N.S. XVI 1874: 16)

However, as its title made clear, the domestic ideal was linked both to class – that is to 'womanhood' rather than 'ladyship' – and to national identity.

The class connotations need to be read carefully in relation to the price of the magazine. *EDM* was launched at a moment of flux in the development of magazines for women. Mergers had reduced the early ladies' journal titles to just two, the *New Monthly Belle Assemblée* and the *Ladies' Cabinet*, but these in fact had identical contents. Publishers besides Beeton realised that there was an opening for a new kind of magazine, and in 1849 Bradbury and Evans launched the *Ladies' Companion at Home and Abroad* as a threepenny weekly. It was beautifully produced in a large size (7½ × 10½ inches), with signed work from such well known authors as Geraldine Jewsbury, Mary Howitt and Miss Mitford, and a regular recipe column from Eliza Acton. Unfortunately – or fortunately for Beeton – this format was not suitable for the new market and in 1852 it too became a shilling monthly, identical in content to the two existing titles.

Beeton took certain ideas from this magazine – notably the recipe column – but went boldly down-market to find his readership. Two pence for a monthly was unusually cheap and, though less attractive than the *Ladies' Companion* and smaller (5 × 7 inches), the *EDM*'s 32 pages of double-column close type and several illustrations offered good value. The immensely successful *Family Friend* had started as a twopenny monthly in 1849 but it subsequently went weekly (Freeman 1977: 76–7). Dickens had launched his twopenny weekly *Household Words* in 1850, hoping to appeal to 'thousands of all ages and conditions', though it cost double the price of other weekly fiction papers (*HHW* I 1850: 1). The *EDM*'s readers were 'women' rather than 'ladies' but they were middle not working class. Although at the time the most successful women's periodical ever launched, claiming 60,000 readers by 1860, the *EDM* did not succeed in attracting a mass readership any more than *Household Words* had done (*EDM* N.S. I 1860: ii).[1]

An article on 'Marriages Frugal and Otherwise', for example, dealt with budgets from £60–£70 to £500 or £1,000 – from the respectable lower middle class to the very wealthy indeed. It answered 'yes' to the question 'Can we live on £300 a year?' adding: 'Crushing poverty is one thing and no fool will voluntarily risk it. The necessity for exertion is another and few really wise people would wish to be without it' (*EDM* VII 1857–8: 362). The actual readership probably included domestic servants, like one who, though 'only a general servant working out at place for my living since eleven years old' wrote to the magazine 'in a good hand' in 1866 (*EDM* N.S. 2, I 1865–6: 256). Its target, however, was the woman who employed servants. One of the most controversial episodes in its history was a correspondence on disciplining female servants which made one reader's house-maid describe it as 'the sort of books her ladyship reads' ('Supplemental Conversazione', *EDM* N.S. 2, April 1870: 3).

The *EDM* made explicit the relationship of middle-class domestic femininity to national identity. Beeton explained his title by writing rather stiffly: 'If there is one thing of which an Englishman has just reasons to be proud, it is the moral and domestic character of his countrywomen' (*EDM* I 1852: 1). The trope in which 'Englishness' was linked to morality and domesticity through women of the middle class was utterly familiar, indeed banal, by 1852, not least because of the magazines I have already discussed.

The 'Englishness' in which Beeton situated this journal was also metropolitan, a function not just of personal history but of a general trend. The lifting of the Taxes on Knowledge between 1853 and 1861 led to a huge expansion of the newspaper press in regional centres like Manchester, Birmingham and Leeds (Lee 1976: 73 and passim). The magazine press, by contrast, was dominated by London even in the mid-Victorian period. Commercial magazines for women were all published here, as were most of the later campaigning women's journals.

The 'rediscovery of London as a theme' for magazine journalists and novelists did not fully take off until the 1890s, but by the early 1860s the general magazine press already favoured metropolitan titles like *Belgravia, St James's, St Paul's* and *Temple Bar* (Swinnerton 1969: 43). The *EDM* also assumed a London base and a femininity which was that of the metropolis. Despite Britain's expanding empire, the magazine showed little internal evidence of the world-wide readership it apparently possessed. Not until the 1870s did it acknowledge that 'subscribers residing in India, in Canada and in other of our Possession and Colonies' might have difficulty in getting the items of dress which the magazine deemed essential. Its solution was to arrange for a shopping service to be provided, ironically through Madame Goubaud, the French partner of the Beetons' fashion department (*EDM* XVI 1874: 224).

These powerful identifications of domestic femininity with class and nation were developed across the range of genres already familiar from the ladies' magazines: serialised fiction, potted biographies, occasional poems, book reviews, fashion news and articles on 'subjects tending to elevate the female character' (*EDM* I 1852: 1). Beeton's use of these genres was not always safe or conventional, however. In the first series he included Hawthorne's controversial novel of adultery, *The Scarlet Letter*, among more typical serialised romances. Nor was the *EDM* bound by the conventions of a single publishing tradition. One Beeton biographer thinks the magazine looked to the Beauty Books and fashion journals, another that it was the *Family Friend* which provided its immediate impetus (Freeman 1977: 75–7; Spain 1956: 15). In fact it incorporated elements of several traditions: the fashion from Books of Beauty and journals like *Le Beau Monde*; the lively correspondence column and serial fiction from the *Family Friend* and the penny journals; the practical advice from the *Family Economist*; the recipes from Eliza Acton's column in the *Ladies' Companion*.

From these Beeton forged a new feminine genre. Crucial to it were the reinterpretation of the ideal of domestic management and the development of a lively dialogue between readers and 'The Editor' through essay competitions and correspondence columns.

THE DOMESTIC WOMAN AS MORAL AGENT AND PRIZE ESSAYIST

The magazine's re-working of the domestic deployed the discourse of moral management which was now utterly familiar and as likely to be employed by readers as by the editor. The characteristic rhetorical strategies here were aphorism and paradox or oxymoron. Woman is our 'weaker, better half', as Beeton put it in a throwaway line to a correspondent (*EDM* III 1854–5: 96). According to one prize essayist: 'The extent to which the intellectual power of Woman is associated with and dwells in the affections, constitutes their characteristic weakness and their characteristic strength' (ibid.: 76).

The magazine, like the culture, was pervaded with the paradox that women were the moral superiors but the physical and intellectual inferiors of men. The problems of this argument were eloquently exposed in one essay competition on 'Women's Rights'. According to the editor the only essay which argued that women should have access to the professions was 'too discursive in its treatment to be printed' (*EDM* I 1852: 74). This was somewhat disingenuous since the prize-winning essay by Annie C. – the longest – was printed in full. All too predictably, this argued that:

> The immense influence possessed by women in society can never be so beneficently manifested as when suffered to flow in natural channels. These natural channels are emphatically the cares, duties and responsibilities of household life.
>
> (ibid.)

Annie C. pursued her argument into some unexpected places, however, insisting that women should have easier access to divorce and stronger rights of custody over their children than man-made laws allowed. But she attacked female would-be reformers, especially in America, who 'insist on dragging [woman] from the peaceful shade of home – from the sphere assigned to her by All-wise God – and placing her in an un-natural position out in the glaring sunlight' (ibid.: 77). The violence of this language in relation to the demand for rights is a measure of their threat, and perhaps also of the contradictory nature of the magazine's ideological project. The essay competition itself had been trumpeted by 'The Editor' in a letter to his 'Fair Young Friends' as a means of encouraging their competitive spirit and powers of argument, since:

> One and not the least important purpose of the EDM is to raise the intellectual character of our young countrywomen by inducing them to venture into print, our magazine supplying a fit vehicle for giving publicity to their speculations.

> (*EDM* I 1852: 227–8)

Beeton's essay topics ranged from the boringly safe 'The Duke of Wellington's Funeral' to the risky 'Do Married Rakes Make the Best Husbands?' (ibid.: 228, 391). This was an astonishing choice at a time when the management of female sexual ignorance was central to the discourse of the domestic. No more surprising, however, than the project of the essay competition itself with its implied encouragement of intellectual competition and women's aspirations to the public sphere.

The ambiguous status of women's writing for publication was also introduced through the biographies of women writers which featured in the magazine's 'Notable Women' series. Here, however, it was easier to accommodate within the domestic framework because the conventions – and often the characters – of the exemplary biography were inherited from the ladies' magazines: Miss Mitford, Mrs Hemans, L.E.L. (Laetitia Elizabeth Landon), Lady Mary Montague, Madame de Stael and, inevitably, Hannah More (*EDM* I 1852: 1, 33, 92, 129, 193, 353). The essay competition was far more disturbing as it directly urged readers to public expressions of opinion, even if what they had to say was often utterly conventional.

As editor, Beeton printed occasional pieces advocating divorce reform and married women's property rights which were more radical than anything produced in prize essays (*EDM* VI 1857–8: 201–6; V 1856–7: 234). These opinions were always developed within the argument that 'Home' was 'the appointed scene of women's labour'. The lines of battle might be re-drawn at the margins – now taking in divorce reform, for example, now excluding it – but domestic femininity was the more urgently asserted the more manifestly unstable it became. Regular articles on 'Female Education' or 'Woman's Work' made this dynamic painfully clear. 'Married women with families need not go beyond their own home to employ themselves', yet 'all have not homes of their own, some never will have'. Women must be educated in more than accomplishments, but 'of infinitely greater consequence than all the rest' must be 'the cultivation of the heart' (*EDM* I 1852–3: 2–3; VI 1857–8: 348–9).

The heart was constantly evoked as 'woman's most important organ' (*EDM* III 1854–5: 74). In the difficulties of defining 'woman', nature was the court of final appeal and the heart was signifier both of the body and the susceptibility to emotions by which women were defined. This metaphor allowed a blurring of boundaries between the physiological, psychological and social; indeed it was so powerful that it acquired the status of scientific knowledge. It was assumed that 'There is a sex of mind and brain as well as person' and this biological/physiological difference made woman at once morally superior to man and unfit for the vote, the medical profession, the pulpit or the bar.

THE DOMESTIC WOMAN
AS COMPETENT MANAGER

Complex though it was, this moral discourse on women's role was not the only way in which the domestic was constructed as 'the appointed scene of women's labour'. Unlike the earlier ladies' magazines and the popular conduct books by Sarah Ellis, the *EDM* included practical advice on household management: recipes, gardening notes, advice on sick-nursing, child-care and even the care of domestic pets.

The rhetorical tendency here was away from moral generalities towards materiality and detail. Isabella's recipes, for example, were marked by a combination of precision and standardisation, with a systematic presentation of ingredients and method which has been standard ever since.[2] Instead of the heart, the crucial organs here were the hands and the brain; instead of moral self-examination, the acquisition of practical skills and systematic knowledge. In its first article on 'Female Education', the magazine stressed the importance of the heart but went on to suggest similarities between domestic knowledge and science. In cooking, a 'tincture of chemical knowledge' was useful, as was the capacity to understand basic principles and apply them logically (*EDM* I 1852: 2–3). A sense of scientific application was central to the practical aspects of 'Household Management'.

This differed fundamentally from the discourse of femininity offered in earlier magazines and in some sections of the *EDM* itself. First, the skills necessary to prevent moth, cook carrots or clean stains from a floor were not 'natural' but learnt; even 'the love of order, cleanness and neatness' necessary for domestic work had (in a telling phrase) to be 'grafted by habit' upon female nature (*EDM* I 1852: 3). When Beeton, in his opening number, offered to help in the task of making 'home happy', he was defining his magazine as a manual of instruction in the domesticity thus defined.

Second, the lists of 'Things worth Knowing' in the early volumes of *EDM* not only implied a body of domestic knowledge to be learnt, but assumed print as an appropriate medium for its instruction. This displaced a tradition of direct instruction by mothers and older women, though of course 'Mrs Beeton' was and is still constructed as such a figure. The thrust of this both placed work at the centre of femininity and claimed a new status for that work in a modernising and professionalising culture. In a reversal of the usual aphorism, women had to 'do', not 'be'.

The contrast with earlier domestic magazines or the works of Mrs Ellis is nowhere more clearly demonstrated than in the *EDM*'s treatment of sewing and embroidery. Work with the needle had become the defining work of femininity. As a symbol of constrained or suffering femininity in mid-Victorian art, its complexities were too great to be dealt with here. Hood's dying seamstress in 'The Song of the Shirt' and Elizabeth Barrett's young woman poet, training for an English femininity by embroidering slippers, have little obviously in common (Hood 1843; Barrett Browning 1857).[3] Nevertheless, the needle was central to their widely different fictional constructions of womanhood.

From the late eighteenth century magazines for women had carried patterns for embroidery and these continued to be a staple. 'Work' in ladies' magazines always meant fancy, non-functional needlework, a tradition continued in the mid-century by such rivals to the *EDM* as the *Ladies' Companion*. Isabella, like any strong-minded heroine, was unenthusiastic about Berlin wool work, which was the central element to mid-century drawing room needle craft, and she refused to carry Bible story patterns, which she described as old fashioned (Hyde 1951: 85). However, the *EDM* had to include Berlin work patterns and these were a special feature of some of the supplements in the new series.

The major departure in the *EDM*, however, was the provision of patterns for dress-making and a 'Practical Dress Instructor' from which readers could make up their own paper patterns following a step-by-step method. English magazines, unlike the French, had not previously offered patterns for their readers to make up their own dresses. Descriptions and fashion-plates had simply provided a visual model from which to work. It is difficult to exaggerate the importance of this innovation on future publications for women and on the dissemination of 'fashion'. The sewing with which the magazine dealt became explicitly functional; it related to women's work in clothing herself and her family rather than to her drawing-room accomplishments.

This redefinition of the work of domesticity, together with the stress on knowledge and the magazine as educator, gave the woman at home a new status. Hers became a skilled task in a modern world which increasingly stressed literacy and print-based knowledge as necessary for all but the lowest status jobs (Vincent 1989: 95ff). By professionalising the idea of domestic management, 'Beeton' made space within the feminine for the masculine qualities of 'strong-mindedness' and organisational competence which were otherwise repressed. Isabella's book opened with an image of the woman not as an 'influence' but as the head of a complex organisation.

> As with the commander of an army, or the leader of any enterprise, so it is with the mistress of a house. Her spirit will be seen through the whole establishment.
>
> (Beeton 1861: 1)

An aggressive competence was thus inscribed and legitimated within the domestic role. It was this, argues Mary Poovey, which Florence Nightingale drew on when she sought to redefine nursing as a domestic feminine rather than a professional masculine task (Poovey 1989: 170). It was a construction which other 'strong-minded women' were also able to mobilise to create appropriate paid work for women through the development of 'caring' professions later in the century.

It was as domestic managers in this sense that Beeton first appealed to women readers of the *EDM*. Although this model was less coherently pursued in the magazine than in the book, it remained central to both. The association of masculinity with profession, or vocation, was not at issue. Rather, the magazine reactivated the meaning of domestic management as skilled labour and so re-made the domestic as a site of work and of 'woman' as the leader of an enterprise.

Of course, woman was still constructed by the magazine as moral agent as well as practical manager. The domestic continued, and continues, to exist as the domain of both these forms of femininity. In the *EDM* the practicalities of household management were always in danger of being collapsed back into an idea of woman's work as emotional support and loving care. The domestic manager and the caring professional remained only precariously distinguished from that other 1850s construction, 'the Angel in the House'.

THE DOMESTIC WOMAN AS LADY

The redefinition of woman's work was set against another older definition for which I have made the lady in the drawing room the sign. Embroidery patterns were still important. A substantial proportion of every number was given over to elements which offered neither practical knowledge nor direct moral instruction. The 40 text pages in a typical number included 16 of fiction and poetry, 2 of fashion and 1 of music (*EDM* III 1855: 1–39). A definition of the lady in terms of leisure and accomplishments persisted, not as an alternative construction of the feminine so much as an element in the new configuration which the magazine shaped and was shaped by.

The status of household management as work remained uncertain, not only because of the persistence of the definition of domestic work as 'what comes naturally to women', but also because for middle-class men the home was defined as the place of leisure. The magazine constructed 'home' for the woman as a contradictory site of work *and* leisure by offering entertainment for the lady reader alongside its domestic instruction and moralising.

In this the *EDM* prefigured the development of women's magazines as a publishing genre which is simultaneously manual of practical instruction, moral guide and source of pleasure. The mixed nature of the magazine makes it able to accommodate contradictions, but the later history of the *EDM* proved just how difficult it could be to control the meanings of the 'domestic English woman' and of female sexuality. The element which proved most difficult to accommodate within the idea of the domestic was fashion, the signifier of femininity as an erotic surface rather than active hands or loving heart. But it was in the letters pages that female desire became most evident, in the person of the unruly daughter, and it was here, too, that readers participated in the struggle over what it meant to be themselves, domestic English women.

CUPID'S LETTER BAG
AND THE CONVERSAZIONE

The correspondence columns in the *EDM* drew on both the tradition of 'Answers' in the penny journals of the 1840s and the earlier tradition of the Confidante in the ladies' magazines. This double inheritance was at first reflected in two separate columns: the more general 'Englishwoman's Conversazione' and 'Cupid's Letter Bag', which invited intimate revelations on love and romance. These were soon combined under the 'Conversazione' title but Beeton continued to encourage letters about love, romance and sexual relationships as well as enquiries on matters general and domestic.

The case of Albert, for example, which ran for several months was specifically concerned with the nature of the desirable wife (see epigraph, p. 59). Nettie's 'terrible little secret' – that she was in fact utterly incompetent as a domestic manager but *most* amiable, loving and affectionate – suggests the limitations of the domestic as a determinant of desire (*EDM* III 1855: 96). Even more significant is the 'confessional' nature of her letter. The correspondence columns allowed the most hidden parts of the self to be revealed, even the state of one's drawers.

Such revelations and their *double entendres* were the product of Beeton's editorial persona and management of the column. It was standard practice in magazines of the period to print only replies to letters from readers. Beeton followed this model in those parts of the journal concerned with practical knowledge but he developed the 'Conversazione' column by including short verbatim extracts from readers' letters embedded in his own detailed summaries. The scenario was not so much a dialogue of equals, however, as the older, wiser editor dispensing advice to a young, and often silly, female correspondent.

This correspondent was produced – if not as a Miss Madcap – then as the heroine of a romance, perplexed by the difficulties of finding a way to marriage and full adult sexuality. Laura wanted to go to balls against her new husband's wishes but was warned 'Laura, beware, Cupid cannot countenance such coquetry. Make your choice, be steadfast in your love' (*EDM* I 1852: 94). Ada was told that 'a fine spirited girl' as she was should know what to do with the 'gentleman who for ten or fifteen years has been engaged in a series of love affairs' but who now tells her that 'he loves her devotedly and that her love is indispensable for his happiness – *and nothing more*' (*EDM* III 1854–5: 96).

Like 'the Matron' or the 'Old Woman' in the early ladies' magazines, 'the Editor' was constructed by contrast with the readers as old and wise in the ways of the world. Even when Isabella was joint editor, however, the editor's persona was clearly masculine in status, title (frequently invoked) and tone. One element of

Beeton's persona was the schoolmasterly. He revived the tradition of editorial complaint about readers' offerings with remarks like 'Were we not old and steady the fair Blanche's calligraphy would certainly induce us to emigrate' (*EDM* I 1852: 95). Such comments struck the same note as the judging of prize essays, in which a specifically young and female group were criticised by the male editor. However, his tone was more often jocular and avuncular than magisterial and serious. This became more pronounced in later years but was evident from the first 'Cupid's Letter Bag'.

It was one of the contradictions inscribed in the magazine and its definition of the female self that it simultaneously advocated domesticity and encouraged female readers to enter the public arena in print. Isabella Beeton herself, however, the model of a professional female writer, was almost invisible in the magazine. In her volume edition of *Beeton's Book of Household Management* she paid tribute to the contribution of *EDM* correspondents who had sent her copies of their recipes (Beeton 1861: Preface, iii). Yet the sharing of knowledge between equals which this implied was almost as invisible as Isabella herself in the magazine. There the dominant model was of a senior masculine figure teasing and instructing the readers, in whom youth and sexual inexperience were so identified with femininity that they became its metonyms.

The correspondence columns thus marginalised the figure of the adult woman whose competence as writer or household manager was rooted in a mature sexuality. Instead it reproduced female sexuality in the figure of the young person in need of protection and control. What was new was that within the masculine editorial discourse there was a space in which the readers were invited to make their public confession of desire. It was this which precipitated the *EDM* into scandal when it was re-launched in the 1860s.

6

THE FEMALE BODY
AND THE DOMESTIC WOMAN,
1860–80

Be natural but firm.
(Advice to reader, *Young Englishwoman* IV 1873: 414)

Dear Mrs. Englishwoman, I beg – I pray – that you will not close your
delightful Conversazione to the Tight-lacing question; it is an absorbing one:
hundreds, thousands of your young lady readers are deeply interested in this
matter.
(*Englishwoman's Domestic Magazine* N.S. 2 IV 1868: 109)

In 1860, buoyed up by their success, and determined to seize commercial advantage from the lifting of tax on paper, 'Beeton' (i.e. Isabella and Sam) embarked on an ambitious expansion of their magazine empire.[1] This began with a relaunch of the *Englishwoman's Domestic Magazine* in a new and larger format, followed by two new ladies' weeklies: the *Queen* in 1861 and the *Young Englishwoman* in 1864.

The New Series *EDM* had more space for fiction and better quality illustrations, especially for fashion and needlework. The fashion coverage was extended first by Isabella and, after her death in 1865, by her friend Matilda Browne, who created a new and confident feminine editorial persona. The re-making of the magazine meant the re-making of 'the Englishwoman' it addressed, a process fraught with anxiety, as the regularly expanded 'Conversazione' attested.

Freeman, in her useful double biography, argues that the new *EDM* was the result of Isabella's interest in creating a fashion journal, of which an increasing number were coming onto the market (Freeman 1977: 164). But the *EDM* was caught up in several different economies and discourses. Fashion and the growth of the press were crucial, but so was the new gender politics of the 1860s. 'Women' were increasingly defining themselves as a group and demanding civil, economic and political rights, demands which the *EDM* often supported (Levine 1987: 80; *EDM* N.S. 2, III 1867: 279, 332–3; VII 1869: 279; but see N.S. I 1865: 256). Its fiction, however, was inspired by female novelists such as Mary Braddon and Mrs Henry Wood, who defined female desire in terms of 'sensation' rather than rights (Braddon 1862). These different discourses of desire and female sexuality combined with still powerful definitions of femininity as 'housewifely', 'maternal' and 'moral' to form the project of the new *EDM*.

Despite the heterogeneous nature of the magazine as a genre and Beeton's editorial skills, there were moments when these competing discourses could not be kept in equilibrium. In 1865 a series of letters in the 'Englishwoman's Conversazione' erupted into a national controversy over the management and control of the female body. The extended correspondence on tight-lacing and whipping of young girls made the *EDM* notorious and still affects access to it today. Some of the more explicit letters have been razored out of the bound volumes I consulted in Birmingham Public Library and other volumes are still classified for restricted reading in the British Library. Later historians have discussed this correspondence out of its publishing context.[2] In this chapter I return it to the magazine, while reading it as symptomatic of the wider difficulty of constructing a coherent strategy of gender from the diversity of femininities circulating in 1860s middle-class culture.

THE COMMERCIAL CONTEXT

The crucial decision Beeton made with the new series was to confirm that middle-class character: to go up-market. They rejected the option of competing with the penny weeklies, who were making even more specific appeals to women with fashion, needlework patterns and music (Altick 1957: 361; Ellegard 1957: 37; Hitchman 1880–1: 393).[3] Instead they kept *EDM* as a monthly and raised its price to sixpence, with occasional special sixpenny supplements which took the price of the combined volume to a shilling.

In 1860 the shilling monthly magazine was just emerging as central to middle-class reading. Launched in 1859 and 1860 respectively, *Macmillan's Magazine* and the *Cornhill* established this trend by offering good quality fiction and serious articles as well as – in the latter case – high quality illustration. Within the decade ten other quality monthlies were launched, almost all costing a shilling.[4] In common with the penny weeklies these new periodicals addressed 'the family' but their dependence on serial fiction assumed the importance of women in that readership.[5]

Beeton must also have been aware of a number of publications specifically for women which had been launched since they started the *EDM*. These included improving and proto-feminist journals like the *English Woman's Journal* (1858–64) and the *Englishwoman's Review* (1857–9) (which I discuss in Ch. 12). The mothers' magazines continued to be important and were joined by other religious publications aimed at women.[6] Although the alternative femininities of these political and religious magazines affected the New Series *EDM* ideologically, they posed little economic threat because their projects were so different.

Others, however, offered direct competition. Some of these were short-lived, like the *Advice to Young Wives* which lasted barely a year (1859–60) but the *Ladies' Treasury*, launched in 1858 with the subtitle 'An Illustrated Magazine of

Entertaining Literary Education, Fine Art, Domestic Economy, Needlework and Fashion', was a great success and lasted until 1895. Its declared aim 'to illustrate each dear domestic virtue' was very close to *EDM*'s and at ninepence it was, and continued to be, a formidable rival – especially with its supplement, the *Treasury of Literature* (Cross 1985: 191; White 1970: 47).

In this new situation, Beeton's re-making of the *EDM* can be understood as an attempt to maintain their readership and extend it upwards in class terms. The New Series format was only slightly larger than the first (8 × 5 inches against 7 × 4½ inches) but it was thicker (48 pages against 32) and more attractive, with better quality paper and more illustrations including pull-out colour embroidery patterns and coloured engravings of the Paris 'modes'. While the visual and fashion elements were improved, the domestic and practical information was down-graded, with the exception of the needlework patterns. Though the magazine maintained its double function, to 'add in every possible way . . . to the amusement and instruction' of its female readers, this shift away from practical domesticity and towards visual pleasure was crucial.

FICTION IN THE MAGAZINE

The fiction in the magazines ostensibly addressed the readers' pleasure but, partly for that reason, editors had to represent it as 'healthy', improving and protective of female sexual ignorance (*EDM* N.S. 2, XVI 1874: 272). The publication of *The Scarlet Letter* in the first *EDM*, with its scandalous treatment of adultery and the illegitimate child, had been a notable exception.[7] In the New Series notes on recent books and writers continued to deal with a wide range of serious fiction, and there were biographical/critical articles on novelists including Charlotte Bronte, George Eliot and Elizabeth Gaskell (*EDM* N.S. 2, II 1865: 90–5, 102–6, 165, etc.). However, the fiction actually printed in the magazine was much less varied. Although the short stories dealt with a range of subjects, the serial novels – often three or four running side by side – focused unrelentingly on a youthful and beautiful heroine, her quest for a happy marriage, and her encounter with trials and disappointments.

These serials were more inclined to sensationalism than sentimentality, but in either mode they instructed the reader on the pleasures and dangers of becoming a female self. Motifs such as the secret marriage and the aristocratic lover recurred in this fiction as it did across the range of periodicals from penny papers to serious monthlies.[8] Running through the first three volumes of the new series, *The Family Secret* told a typical tale of a beautiful and innocent young girl condemned to love a man her social superior (*EDM* N.S. I 1861: 49, 97, 145, 193, 241; II: 1, 49, 97, 145, 193, 241, 289; III: 1, 73, 121, 184). A secret marriage takes place, but before the heroine can be recognised as the true wife and mother of the heir she endures months of serialised suffering caused by the careless contempt of her lover's family and the machinations of her beautiful but wicked rival.

The 'family secret' in this case is hereditary insanity, a favourite discourse of both medicine and sensation fiction in the 1860s (Showalter 1982: 166–7; 1991). The mad person in the attic, however, turns out to be not a hysterical woman but an eccentric aristocratic man. The heroine, tricked by her rival into entering an asylum and deprived of her husband and her baby son, also loses her reason. At the denouement she is restored to herself – a self defined as maternal, wifely and utterly passive. In contrasts, the energetically scheming Lady Gwendoline is condemned to fashionable lovelessness.

This narrative prefigures such sensation novels as Mary Braddon's *Lady Audley's Secret* or Mrs Henry Wood's *East Lynne* in which the woman who actively pursues her desires generates the narrative interest but must finally be punished. For the heroine, on the other hand typically, 'the curtain closes on the young mother hanging over the cradle of her child' (Helsinger *et al.* 1983 I: 128). Feminist literary critics since Elaine Showalter's (1982: 153ff) discussion of the genre in *A Literature of their Own* have been aware of the tension between the potentially subversive femininity of these narratives and the orthodoxy of their denouement (Flint 1993: 274–93; Helsinger *et al.* 1983 III: 111ff; Pykett 1992). Sensation novels, as Showalter suggests, were all about 'family secrets' (Showalter 1982: 158). They routinely dealt with deviance and violence: madness was the theme of this serial in *EDM*, bigamy and infanticide the next. These were represented simultaneously as 'intolerable . . . in domestic life' and as the key to understanding how 'the family' worked (Helsinger *et al.* 1983 III: 128).[9]

These novels were immensely popular because they allowed the anxieties of femininity to be explored in safety. In the *EDM* such serials both affirmed women's traditional roles as wives and mothers and recognised the difficulties which women had to endure as sexual beings. The ordeals through which the heroine passed – whether they involved bigamy or being snubbed at a ball – the uncertainties of her fate, the relief when she did win through, all afforded pleasures relevant to the problem of being a woman.

More disturbing were those stories in which the young and beautiful heroine failed to marry the man she loved and was punished apparently for her femaleness alone. In *Gilmour's Ward* Miss Peri is an astonishingly voluptuous beauty. Her 'black silk dress' fitted so tightly that it

> revealed the full grace and proportion of her gloriously, luxuriously developed figure. Her waist looked a mere span . . . and from it sprang a magnificent bust and pair of well-rounded shoulders . . . . She was a rich, deep-toned, clear, brilliant brunette, this lady . . . and her age appeared to be seventeen.
>
> (*EDM* N.S. 2, I 1865: 6)[10]

Unfortunately Miss Peri is condemned to die (months later in the serial) of unconsummated love.

Anne Humphreys has suggested that this and similar stories in the magazine reveal an anxiety among middle-class women about their absolute reliance on men for their livelihoods, and indeed for their lives. Though Cinderella performs her part, the Prince is unreliable.[11] Since failure to marry was a failure on the part of the woman, who was left 'redundant', such anxiety ran deep. The 'natural' progress of Miss Peri to household manager and mother hanging over the cradle was not clear and straightforward but liable to interruption and even death.

There was, also, an implicit male anxiety about female sexuality evident in this narrative. The middle-class woman was dependent on a man not only to define her social role but to bring her to adult sexuality; the story of the heterosexual romance delivered her identity as a woman. Miss Peri represented the young woman whose desire must be controlled. Her luxuriously developed figure was the signifier of a terrifying female sexuality which not even the narrative closure of her death could adequately contain.

One reason for this was Miss Peri's existence beyond the serial fiction. With her well-developed bust and waist 'a mere span' she was also the embodiment of the desirable woman in the magazine's fashion-plate and fashion notes. Hers was the fantasy figure of the corset-makers and tight-lacers. The question of whether she represented a male fantasy of female sexuality or a female desire whose passivity was ultimately destructive dominated the 'Conversazione' as well as the fiction.

FASHION AND NEEDLEWORK IN THE NEW *EDM*

More significant even than the fiction was the centrality of fashion and appearance in the New Series. Material on practical knowledge and domestic management never disappeared but it was cut back and occasionally even confined to the answers to correspondents. The existing column on fashion was correspondingly up-graded and Isabella provided regular first-hand accounts of the Paris modes.

Beeton encouraged the view that it was the fashion coverage and needlework patterns which distinguished the new journal:

> Not alone from our countrywomen in England but from the continent of Europe, from America, India and distant Australia do we receive from month to month the most satisfactory assurances that this magazine fulfils the purpose for which it was intended . . . to inform our sisters what is the style and manner of dress in vogue at time of publication, what the fashionable and useful needlework and to add in every possible way, by imaginative and serious literature and well executed engravings, to the amusement and instruction of our readers.
>
> (Preface, *EDM* N.S. III 1861)

In addition, a shilling version was regularly produced with a 'Supplement' which included illustrations of fashion, patterns for dresses and needlework designs and other engravings, all of which were advertised in detail:

NOTICE, The SHILLING EDITION comprises, besides the content of the Magazine, an 8-page Supplement containing illustrations of the CHEMISE RUSSE, New Stitches in Point Russe, Six engravings of the

Newest and most Fashionable Mode of Making Dresses, Hanging Sleeve, Muslin Fichu, Young Lady's Coiffure, Work-Basket Cover, Braiding Patterns, Parasol Cover in Venetian Embroidery, Knitted Square for Counterpanes, Braided Slipper, etc. with full d[i]rections for working and making the same. Also a Fashion Plate of large size and a Photograph of the late Prince Consort.

(*EDM* N.S. III 1861: 144)

Beeton had reason to boast, especially as they had effected a publishing coup in arranging for every number of the magazine to include a coloured steel plate by the French engraver, Jules David, showing the latest Paris fashions (Figure 6.1).[12] David was the artist for the expensive Paris-based magazine, *Le Moniteur de la Mode*, with whom *EDM* established a link (Freeman 1977: 164–5). The publishers, Goubaud – another husband and wife team – provided fashion information, superb plates and – crucially – actual paper patterns for the fashions illustrated. Beeton provided English outlets and advertising for the magazine and for Madame Goubaud's wares and services. In business terms this venture in international publishing was significant and successful (see *EDM* N.S. IX 1864: 377–8; Supplement, X 1865: 58).

The move towards fashion and needlework patterns seemed to hark back to a model of magazine and lady reader like that of *La Belle Assemblée*. The new style *EDM* however, did not simply reproduce the earlier magazines; it re-worked their concept of middle-class domestic femininity for the mid-Victorian era.

This was evident in two particular ways. First of all the meaning of Paris as the fashion capital of the world was itself being re-made. The court of the Second Empire, established in 1852 under Napoleon III and the Empress Eugénie, was marked by its brilliance and extravagance of display. The English 'man-milliner' Worth, who had set up his house with Bobergh in 1858, used his position as court dress designer to create the first modern fashion house (de Marly 1980: 32). Worth created fashion as an art and an industry, in which the manufacture of cloth, the production of garments and accessories and the dissemination of information about the 'modes' were inseparable (ibid.: 39–41 and passim; Wilson and Taylor 1989: 22). His styles dominated not just European courts but also American Society, creating an international market for Parisian fashion.

Although Worth himself did not need to use the press, periodicals were central to these developments. Fashion as a journalistic discourse produced as much as it was produced by fashion as an industry. Beeton, with their regular trips to Paris, their link with *Le Moniteur de la Mode* and their empire-wide readership, were crucially involved in establishing this interrelationship.

In doing so, they perpetuated that ironic double-bind in which fashion journalism was caught as it developed: it made available to as wide a readership as possible what was by definition exclusive and elite. The whole thrust of the fashion in the *EDM* was to render 'dressing in accordance with the latest fashions . . . easy and not too expensive' (*EDM* N.S. IX 1864: 378). It suggested economical ways of reproducing

Figure 6.1 Fashion-plate from N.S. *Englishwoman's Domestic Magazine* (III 1861)

expensive items and welcomed the new sewing machines, on which it ran a series in the 1860s (*EDM* N.S. III 1863: 326, 354, 402, 483, etc.). Though relatively expensive, the paper patterns it sold offered a wide circle of women access to 'the original articles furnished by the first Parisian houses' (*EDM* N.S. IX 1864: 377).[13] Nevertheless, it insisted to the end that a woman should dress appropriately to her situation and income (*EDM* N.S. 2, XVI 1874: 102). Thus while it paid lip service to the idea of dress as a marker of status and class, *EDM* helped to create a mass fashion industry in which all such codes would eventually break down.

The second crucial difference between the fashion in the new *EDM* and that in the earlier ladies' papers was the context of practical domesticity which the first series magazine had so successfully articulated. A feminine ideal which centred on appearance and dress threatened to rewrite not only class distinction but a definition of femininity in terms of the domestic and the moral. In an account of the Ideal Woman the magazine produced both a 'pleasing' appearance *and* dedication to the home as duties of prime importance (ibid.). This tension was compounded by the problem that the fashion-plate represented a woman not only primarily beautiful, rather than useful or good, but one constructed as an object to be looked at rather than an actor or a self.

Beeton deployed a simple but brilliantly effective strategy to negotiate between these feminine ideals. Alongside the fashion-plates Isabella provided detailed descriptions of the modes not only in terms of their visual effect but so that the reader understood how to re-create them for herself, as her use of italic signalled:

> Nearly all dress sleeves this season are made with a seam at the elbow and a turned-back cuff, projecting an inch or two beyond the seam of the sleeve at the bottom . . . . The prettiest and most suitable way of making these dresses is with a plain or *slightly* full body . . . and a pleating of silk ribbon one and a half to two inches wide *placed quite at the bottom of the skirt, below the braid.*
> (*EDM* N.S. V 1863: 141–2)

Most important of all, Beeton linked the fashion-plate with the 'Practical Dress-maker' of the first series by offering not just advice on pattern cutting but actual paper patterns for the 'modes' shown in the plate. These were prepared and tacked together ready for pinning and cutting out, either by the woman herself or by the dress-maker she employed.

The paper pattern was a brilliant device for bridging the gap, or rather the gape, between the reader as 'household manager' on one hand and as fashionable lady on the other. It promised the woman as 'practical dress-maker' a means, through her domestic skills, of realising herself as the woman of the fashion-plate. The 'same' woman could not only accomplish two different feminine identities in her dress, but could move from one kind of femininity to another. Moreover, the woman as skilled manager – as actor and subject – could turn *herself* into the woman as desired object. This did not so much solve the contradiction as offer practical strategies for encompassing it, literally 'paper(pattern)ing' over the cracks. The continued use of this device in women's magazines of the 1990s suggests both the persistence of these contradictory meanings of femininity and the success of this strategy.

The discourse of fashion, both visual and verbal, had a further function in the new *EDM*. It defined a femininity which the woman reader did not yet possess, and which was therefore to be desired. The desire of the reader for the person she was not yet (but might be) was itself complicated by the fact that fashionable woman was presumed to be the object of *male* desire. Women's fashion was designed to 'attract and please' (*EDM* N.S. IX 1864: 377). But the question of whether the desire addressed by the fashion-plate was female narcissism or male heterosexuality was one of those issues which returned in the corset correspondence.

It was clothes, rather than the body, which were the ostensible subject of 'fashion'. Nevertheless, the clothes assumed the body which they concealed, just as desire was defined by absence. Unlike the discourses which had defined woman as emotional ('all heart') or domestic ('hands and brain') fashion produced the female body as the subject/object of desire. Desire and the eroticised body were thus simultaneously represented and concealed in the magazine's discourse of fashion.

The relation of the body and clothes, of femininity and fashion, interacted with a larger set of negotiations about the meaning of the natural and the artful or the cultivated. Here again there was a distinct shift between the two series. In the first series the problem of defining 'natural' femininity had pervaded the discourse of domesticity; in the New Series, while the word 'natural' persisted as a term of ultimate praise, the ideal of woman as the product of art (her own or her dressmaker's) was both more evident and more troubling. The title motif which appeared on the first page of each New Series issue can be read as a visual sign of this. Flowers – symbolic of natural femininity – are arranged in a highly unnatural fashion which obscures rather than frames the title *The Englishwoman's Domestic Magazine* (Figure 6.2).

Enormous strains were imposed by a definition of femininity as at once artful and natural, self-made and given, desired object and desiring self. These were deflected into the magazine's advice and correspondence columns: Myra's 'Spinnings' and the long established 'Conversazione', which continued to be dominated by the persona of 'The Editor'.

'THE SILKWORM'S SPINNINGS'

After Isabella's death her friend, Mrs Browne, took on her role in the Beeton journals as well as assuming the care of the two Beeton children (Hyde 1951: 136; Freeman 1977: 243–60). 'Myra', or 'The Silkworm' as she called herself, wrote both fashion and advice columns for the Beeton empire until her departure in 1875.[14] Her importance for my account is two-fold. In her 'Spinnings' column for the *EDM* she developed a persona which was manifestly feminine and quite distinct from that of the editor. And when she left she established a group of

Figure 6.2 Title page of N.S. *Englishwoman's Domestic Magazine* (III 1861)

women's magazines bearing her name which, along with the titles launched by Christopher Weldon (who had also worked with Beeton), took women's magazine publishing into a new era (White 1970: 55–6).

Although Matilda Browne undoubtedly loosened the style of the fashion sections, 'Spinnings' was her most important contribution to the *EDM*. A chatty column, it foreshadowed the *causerie* which became a feature of magazines in the last decades of the century, with the important difference that these mainly depended on the creation of a very masculine matey-ness like that of a gentleman's club. 'Spinnings', as its title suggested, was feminine in tone and subject matter, and the threads of womanly chat it produced were both explicitly lightweight and implicitly valuable.

Rather than concealing her gender as a writer, Matilda Browne made it central to her persona. She represented herself as a woman sharing readers' fragmented concerns with practical domesticity, fashion and beauty, or the moral and emotional support of others. She moved without embarrassment between these different worlds. In January 1874, for example, she produced a 'recipe for a Happy New Year': 'Take of unselfish love three parts; of cheerful industry, one part; mix and use daily'. This was immediately followed by a promise to keep readers informed of 'novelties I have seen', beginning with a method of casting light on the mirror so as better to perform the delicate business of constructing a chignon (*EDM* N.S. 2, XVI 1874: 34–5).

This apparently inconsequential 'flitting' from subject to subject made Myra an unlikely authority figure or mentor. Instead, her role in the magazine was as the reader's alter ego or friend. One reader consulted her about boys' clothing because 'you have little boys of your own', and added 'I look for your spinnings with a sort of affectionate interest, and feel as if we were friends' (*EDM* N.S. 2, XVI 1874: 222).

This persona depended not just on the tone of her writing. The Silkworm's 'Spinnings' took her from shop to shop, from 'novelty' to 'novelty'; indeed, shopping was her business and the model of femininity she produced from the immense diversity of female concerns centred on shopping. Silkworm identified what was fashionable and novel and told readers where to buy it. She gave addresses of shops, put readers in touch with those who would provide services and generally pioneered what in modern magazines is called the 'advertorial', in which the woman reader and woman consumer become one and the same.

There had been elements of this in the 'Conversazione', and the magazine's relationship with Madame Goubaud meant that its fashion advice sometimes read like an extended commercial for her shop. The magazine had also offered a service for readers in India and other parts of the empire and even acted as a glorified 'Bring and Buy' sale through the 'Englishwoman's Exchange' column. For years it had carried up to 20 pages of advertisements just inside the covers.[15] In the New Series of 1860 these reflected the diversity of available constructions of femininity: advertisements for Beeton's other publications, for sewing machines and cooking ranges, for hair colour, abdominal belts and various medicines including Widow Welch's Pills for Female Complaints. 'Spinnings', however, brought advertising into the body of the text as part of a crystallisation of these different constructions into an image of the woman as shopper, embodied in the person of the 'Editress'.

In constructing a feminine identity around shopping and in creating a sympathetic public persona for herself specifically as a woman writer, 'Myra' re-worked existing traditions of women's place. These were taken up by her and others in the next stage of women's magazines, which I discuss in the following chapters. In the *EDM*, however, her position was relatively marginal. It was the editor and his letters column which defined the magazine.

THE 'ENGLISHWOMAN'S CONVERSAZIONE' AND THE CORSET CONTROVERSY

The 'Englishwoman's Conversazione', established in the first series *EDM*, flourished in the second. Indeed, it was so popular that when Ward, Locke & Tyler launched yet another new version in 1866 they expanded the column from one to three or four pages. A later reader even suggested the magazine should go weekly on the strength of the 'Conversazione' (*EDM* N.S. 2, XVI 1874: 54). Beeton had always been prepared to reproduce some verbatim extracts from letters as well as the summaries and answers which were the standard format for such features. Now he gave as much as a page to an individual letter and allowed conflicting views to develop at length, with a running commentary in which the editor summarised and commented on his correspondence.

Beeton's editorial persona, as in the earlier series, was teasing, authoritative and implicitly masculine:

> A few correspondents – a few? well, never mind the number – are curious about their hand-writing. None very good except Esther; none very bad, except – well, we name no names . . . . A correspondent wants to know what a flirt is. Virgin innocence! You know very well what a flirt is. Did you not – not intentionally, of course, make [alpha], [beta], Gamma and Delta all fall in love with you, including the young man with the ginger-coloured mustache and the lisp! Was it this benighted and betrayed one who says
>
> > Woman's love is like Scotch snuff
> > You get one pinch and that's enough.
> >   (*EDM* N.S. IX 1864: 228)

Readers who wrote in with romantic problems might find themselves answered in a similar vein:

> Georgina is evidently fickle and writes a worse hand than Aurora. She is to be married to a man she 'hates' and is deeply in love with another. Could she not contrive to throw the first man down a well? taking good care, of course, that he did not get up again. Perhaps, however, on second thoughts, it were well to leave well alone.
>
> >   (*EDM* N.S. VIII 1863: 48)

This reference to the notorious novel of bigamy, Braddon's *Lady Audley's Secret*, might have been offered as a jocular warning against reading life in terms of melodrama, but it was certainly far removed in tone from the Mrs Greys of the early century.

Beeton could be serious, however, and his newly expanded column enabled him to express his republicanism and put his case on women's demands for the vote and for education. In 1867 he wrote at some length in support of Mill's arguments for women's suffrage and in the same issue joined in criticism of the Queen, who was still in retirement after Alfred's death (*EDM* N.S. 2, III 1867: 333, 389). Given the tone of his writing and the position he adopted on a number of sensitive issues, it would not be surprising if readers took seriously Beeton's invitation to 'discuss any subject they please[d]' (*EDM* N.S. 2, XVI 1874: 55).

The range of topics covered was extraordinary. In two numbers of 1867 series they included a discussion of Mormon women, 'hints to young mothers', instructions on bottling gooseberries, recipes, sewing hints, a contribution to an ongoing debate on the wearing of chignons, fashion enquiries with answers directing readers to Madame Goubaud's establishment and a discussion on schools (*EDM* N.S. 2, III 1867: 164–8 and 223–4). The domestic, maternal, fashionable and political coexisted on the page.

These numbers also included the two letters which sparked the nòtorious 'corset correspondence' (Steele 1985: 177). A mother wrote that she had returned from abroad to find her daughter being subjected to a 'system of torture', designed by the Headmistress of her boarding school to reduce the waists of her charges to 'absurdly small dimensions' through tight-lacing. Her daughter's 'wasp-waist' could now be clasped with two hands. Her muscles were so weakened that she had to continue to wear a corset, though it now caused minimal discomfort so 'wonderful is the power of Nature to accommodate herself to the circumstances' (*EDM* N.S. 2, III 1867: 165). 'Staylace' responded in the next number that 'from the tone of her letter, [I am inclined] to consider her an advocate of the system she appears to condemn'. Arguing that a waist which could be clasped with two hands was worth a short period of pain, Staylace concluded:

> To me the sensation of being tight-laced . . . is superb. I . . . never feel prouder or happier than when I survey in myself the fascinating undulations of outline that art in this respect affords to nature.
>
> (*EDM* N.S. 2, III 1867: 223)

This exchange precipitated an avalanche of letters, some of which took up the link between pleasure, tight-lacing and 'torture' implicit in the first letter and developed it in more or less explicitly sado-masochistic terms (*EDM* N.S. 2, III 1867: 164, 223, 272, 334, 389, 501, 557, 613; IV, 224, 279, etc.). This continued sporadically in the magazine for years. As late as 1874 Beeton printed several such letters, including a detailed account of a 'spinal instrument' and collars for young women to wear (*EDM* N.S. 2, XVI 1874: 55). The sadistic tone became even more pronounced in a parallel correspondence – begun in 1868 – about the use of whipping to control female servants and girls ('Supplement Conversazione' *EDM* 1870: 1–9). The beating of a young woman servant was one of the staple tropes of Victorian pornographic literature, another genre which, like the letters page, deployed the confessional first-person narrative.[16] This correspondence not surprisingly, therefore, made the *EDM* notorious and brought protests from some 'regular subscribers'; one complained that she had taken the *EDM* for years but was thinking of stopping because

> I have been so ashamed of [the letters] that lending the journal to any of my friends is out of the question . . . I put the book out of reach of any casual observers and where especially no gentleman can read it.
>
> (ibid.: 7)

The notoriety seems to have done circulation no harm (Freeman 1977: 278). Ward, Locke & Tyler, the publishers, were certainly quick to cash in on the controversy with the publication of volumes called *The Corset and the Crinoline* (London n.d., by W.B.L. [1868]), re-published as *The Freaks of Fashion* and

Figure Training; Art the Handmaid of Nature (London, n.d., [1871] by E.D.M.) (*EDM* N.S. 2, III 1867: 224; Steele 1985: 250). They allowed Beeton to produce a special Supplement on the whipping correspondence in 1870, perhaps the most contentious of all these publications. This carried advertisements for such texts as *A History of the Rod* and *Flagellation and the Flagellants* by the Rev. W. Cooper BA (*EDM* 1870 Supplement: 8).

How to make sense of this controversy troubled contemporaries and has divided later critics (see note 2). The argument that the magazine was taken over by a small group of fetishists does not explain its continuing to maintain regular sales over these years; nor why outbreaks of the tight-lacing debate were endemic to women's magazines in the second half of the century and were expressed in a variety of voices. Contemporary accusations that the whole correspondence had been made up by Beeton and were 'a quiz' were indignantly and, I think rightly, refuted (*EDM* 1870 Supplement, June: 3; *EDM* N.S. 2, VI 1869: 164–5). His response to earlier letters had been brisk. 'Serephina', boasting a 15¾ inch waist, was told this was 'absurd' and advised, 'If [she] wishes to enjoy good health and preserve the beauty of her complexion, let her avoid tight-lacing' (*EDM* N.S. III 1861: 144). An even more astringent answer was given to 'La Duchesse' who wanted 'a recipe to make her thin': 'Go out as a Governess on a low salary in a *parvenu* family of self-willed daughters with an indulgent and 'naggy' mama' (*EDM* N.S. IX 1864: 96).

Beeton's editorial personality no doubt helped the 'Conversazione' become a space for this debate, and he was prepared to revive it on several occasions despite having declared the subject closed (*EDM* N.S. 2, VI 1869: 52–3; Steele 1985: 250). However, instead of reading this correspondence as the product of dedicated deviants or a calculating editor or publisher, we need to ask what it meant in terms of the definitions of femininity which the magazine constructed and was constructed by. Although the corset had been worn by Regency beaux early in the century and some men continued to wear a modified form, by the 1860s and 1870s it was identified specifically with feminine dress and the fashionable female body (*EDM* N.S. 2, III 1867: 110, 168). The corset controversy therefore involved the multiple and contradictory meanings of that female body itself (Figure 6.3).

THE BODY IN THE TEXT

Fashion produced sexual difference in a number of ways during this period. The use of aniline dyes developed in the 1850s and 1860s made women's clothing even brighter against the dark male costume (Wilson 1985: 214). However, difference was crucially encoded in body shape. Throughout this period the fashionable and desirable female figure was that of Miss Peri, a small waist between a voluptuous bosom and large hips, exaggerated by the crinoline or the later bustle. The corset produced the 'natural' difference of the feminine body to a heightened (or 'unnatural') degree. It was widely argued that tight-lacing actually altered the shape of

Figure 6.3 Corset advertisement from *Queen* (CI 1897) © Manchester City Art Galleries

organs and bones (Roberts 1977; Steele 1985: 167–71). The debate about whether the result was either healthy or beautiful, however, was fraught with contradictions. The natural beauty which marked the female body was opposed to artificial aids – and hence to 'unnaturally' tight lacing – but also to the male body, perceived as strong and healthy – so the weakness produced by tight corsets was itself a potentially beautiful enhancement of female difference.

As instrument of control the corset also carried a set of meanings which concerned not beauty and nature but society and decorum. The corseted body was the social body, controlled and regulated; the uncorseted body was a social disgrace. None of the correspondents to *EDM* advocated abandoning corsets altogether: the argument was specifically over *tight*-lacing or what constituted abuse. Natural femininity *had* to be trained, and the trained figure was a symbol of the social restraint which marked off mature sexuality from girlhood. Middle-class 'romping girls' had to be corseted in order to learn how to be and bear themselves like women, or as one correspondent put it, 'If you want a girl to grow up gentle and womanly in her ways and feelings, lace her tight' (*EDM* N.S. 2, III 1867: 334–5; N.S. 2, X 1871: 127).

Even in pre-Freudian times, however, it was obvious that such language brought another set of meanings into play. Worn next to the skin and mimicking the shape of the womanly figure, the corset became itself eroticised. This meant that respectable femininity became inseparable from the sexuality it sought to repress and much of the correspondence was galvanised by the attempt to separate the two. Since the corset was a potent symbol in the discourses of both sexuality and 'discipline' or 'training', the correspondence enabled writers to explore the relationship of power and sexuality, though they did so with varying degrees of self-consciousness and with different agendas. In the parallel correspondence on the whipping of girls, the arguments about training and discipline were even more forcibly made and the sado-masochistic elements more evident, especially in the Supplement of 1870 in which the correspondence was collected and taken out of the context of other letters.

The motive and sex of these writers were widely debated. Many of the letters, especially on the subject of whipping, gave male names or pseudonyms. 'Truth' (of Leicester) argued that even the female signatures were fake and went on:

> it is not improbable that some of the men who have been studying for their own base purposes the latest fashions in women's dress, may have taken your magazine on account of the valuable information it contains on such subjects and may have rejoiced at carrying on such a correspondence on such a subject in a feigned name and character.
>
> (*EDM* Supplement 1870: 4)

The ambiguity or 'duplicity' which 'Truth' wanted to impute to these letters, was, however, firmly located in the magazine itself and especially in its attitude to fashion. The argument that men could enter undetected into the feminised world of the women's magazine and there pursue 'their own base purposes' implicitly acknowledged that the legitimate reader and the illegitimate voyeur were indistinguishable. 'Valuable information' on women's fashion could become its opposite, the stuff of sexual fantasy. Hence the importance of placing the correspondence out of reach of 'casual observers and especially . . . gentlemen' (ibid.: 7). It was essential but perversely impossible to distinguish a serious parental discussion about training girls from the sexual fantasies of 'base men'.

But this correspondence threatened an even more disturbing 'Truth'. The corset and the whipping debates had in common their concern with the 'control' and 'training' of girls, yet correspondents like Staylace disrupted that discourse of discipline with an alternative discourse of female pleasure and desire. This discourse was extremely unstable. Women's letters in favour of corsets characteristically elided the pain of tight-lacing with the pleasure of displaying their figures to view: 'Why should *we* who have been disciplined at home and school and laced tighter month after month . . . be expected to hide our figures (which we know are admired) . . .?' (*EDM* N.S. 2, IV 1868: 109). Staylace described the pleasure produced by the feel of the corset on her body giving way to that of viewing the delightful undulations of her figure in the glass. For her a sexuality of 'sensation' gives way to a sexuality of the gaze. This move resonates with late twentieth-century arguments that women's desire can only exist culturally in what Irigaray calls the 'dominant scopic economy', that is an economy of pleasure in which woman is relegated to 'passivity', to being a 'beautiful object' (Marks and de Cortivron 1981: 101).[17] Yet it is significant that Staylace occupied simultaneously the position of subject looking and beautiful object. She represented herself to readers, who were defined as women, in terms of their active pleasure in looking both at their reflection in the mirror and at the fashion pages in the magazine (Figure 6.4).

The difficulties of reading this correspondence today extend from the most specific (how do we know that 'Staylace' is not a male pseudonym?) to wide-ranging questions about the relevance of late twentieth-century theorising of

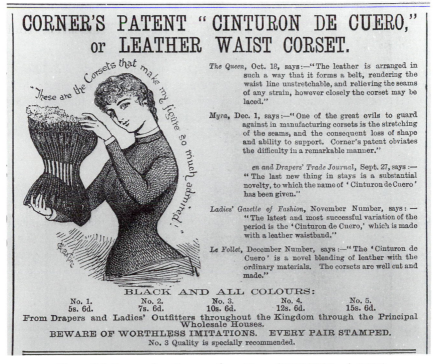

Figure 6.4 Corset advertisement from *Queen* (LXXVII March 1885)
© Manchester City Art Galleries

female desire to earlier periods. Certainly in the struggle to be 'natural but firm', as a correspondent to another Beeton journal put it, the importance of the female body as erotic surface, as beautiful object, returned again and again. In the next chapter, I pursue the question of the visual within the economy of desire in terms of another Beeton journal, the *Queen*. However, contemporary reading of the corset correspondence, like discussion of the sensation novel, turned on an anxiety not only about the control of female sexuality but about maintaining sexual difference itself. Dependent on that primary difference were all the other oppositions which the correspondence showed to be so slippery: art and nature; the sexual and the respectable woman; valuable information and base desires. The 'domestic English woman' was a signifier whose signified was radically unstable.

This correspondence also resists our late twentieth-century descriptions of female desire as necessarily either narcissistic or sado-masochistic, as either hetero- or homosexual, as either active or passive. It constantly disrupts such attempts to bring it to a closure, just as Beeton's efforts to signal the end of the correspondence were constantly swept aside by new letters.

7

RE-MAKING THE LADY: THE *QUEEN*

When we write for women, we write for home. We shall offend very few when we say that women have neither heart nor head for abstract political speculation; while as for our liberties, or our political principles, they may safely be left to men bred in the honest independence of English homes.

(*Queen* I 1861: 1)

In whatsoever proportions the graver rights and duties of life are adjudged and distributed, to Woman beyond all dispute belongs the casting voice in social usages and manners.

(*Ladies' Companion* XXVII 1850: 8)

In 1861 Beeton launched a new journal for women, the *Queen*. Though Isabella's death forced Samuel to sell the title 'on very easy terms' within a year, this was to be the most successful of all the Beeton periodicals, surviving into the 1990s (Watkins 1985: 187). It pioneered and remained a significant example of a new kind of journal for women. Contemporaries called them 'class' papers; I describe them as 'ladies' illustrated newspapers' because they brought the concept of the lady, the techniques of illustration and the category of news into dynamic relationship with each other. They carried the woman's journal form forward through the 1860s to the end of the century and beyond and are the subject of this chapter.

The *Queen* was dedicated to a female sovereign and claimed to be 'for women', 'about women' and 'EDITED by a LADY'. It constructed a readership of 'ladies' rather than 'domestic women' (*Q.* II 1862: 96). Like its later imitators and rivals, it assumed an annual income well above the £300 which marked the respectable middle class. In 1885, when senior male workers in insurance, banking or the civil service earned less than £200 a year, the *Queen* advised its readers:

You may live very comfortably on £800 a year but, if your family be at all large, it will require careful management and allow but a narrow margin for [the pleasures] which make life worth living.

(*Q.* LXXIX 1865: 102; cf. *EDM* N.S. 2 IV 1868: 22; Read 1979: 26)

'When we write for women, we write for home' the *Queen* asserted in its opening number, but neither term meant here what it did in the *Englishwoman's Domestic Magazine*. This 'home' was neither the product of woman's moral management nor of her practical skills but a domestic theatre in which her femininity – defined in terms of beauty, dress and deportment – was displayed. These papers confined practical housework to their 'Answers to Correspondents' and occasional articles on 'Cuisine' for entertaining. They paid scant attention to the minutiae of family relationships in either fiction or correspondence columns. *Queen* carried little fiction of any kind and eschewed the usual stories of love won through suffering. It specifically rejected letters on 'merely personal and private matters', including romantic problems of the 'Conversazione' variety (see 'Rules for Correspondents', passim). Instead it developed a policy of 'Answers' for each of the paper's different Departments – providing information on etiquette, appearance and dress, and from the 1880s music and travel. None of these printed readers' letters.

The *Queen* redefined the space of the woman's journal by calling itself a newspaper rather than a magazine and adopting the characteristic broadsheet format. But the project of creating a feminine 'news' was fraught with difficulty. 'News' was traditionally political and public, and therefore masculine; women had 'neither heart nor head for political speculation' (*Q.* I 1861: 1). Resolving this problem proved difficult and I discuss it in more detail below. In searching for a suitable format, however, the *Queen* took for its model not *The Times* or the *Daily Telegraph* but the *Illustrated London News*, which had pioneered picture-based stories and developed a news journalism centred on the visual.

The development of improved technologies for picture reproduction in the 1870s made visual pleasure increasingly important in all kinds of journalism (Shorter 1899). In the ladies' papers, illustration was specifically linked to representations of the clothed female figure. 'Fashion' was not only a crucial signifier of femininity, it also met the demand for 'news' since its concern by definition was the new. However, the meaning of illustration in these papers was complex. Among its determinants were the need to find a feminine news, the emerging fashion industry, the publishing tradition of the illustrated periodical and associated advances in print technology, and the inherited ideal of female beauty which persisted in high art. All these elements combined to create a femininity of surface rather than depth, of appearance rather than moral management.

Historically this may be understood as casting back to an earlier aristocratic model of the female self. Certainly the 'lady' of the late nineteenth century was a signifier of the continuing vitality of the aristocracy in British economic and social life, but she was also a radical reinvention of aristocratic femininity in the context of a popularising press. This was most dramatically evident at the end of the century in relation to the Queen herself, but similar processes were a work on lesser ladies (Cannadine 1983).

Just as fashion journalism depended on simultaneously identifying what was exclusive and making it widely available, so these ladies' papers produced a femininity which was both class- and status-specific *and* available to the aspirational reader, whoever she was. Although it explicitly constructed an upper middle-class reader with an above average income, *Queen* was almost certainly read by those for whom such a style of life was an aspiration or even a fantasy – just as contemporary magazines like *Vogue* or *Elle* are read and even bought by those who could never afford the clothes they picture.

The ladies' newspaper above all produced femininity as a text available for reading. The masculine reader might engage with this femininity only as an object of his gaze. The feminine reader, however, not only read but used her reading to reproduce herself as another feminine text, available in turn to other knowledgeable readers.

THE DEFINITION OF 'FEMININE NEWS'

The *Queen* was not the first ladies' newspaper. This was the appropriately named *Lady's Newspaper* (incorporating the *Pictorial Times*), which had been launched in January 1847 and was to merge with the *Queen* in 1863. A large (quarto size) sixpenny illustrated weekly, it offered 14 pages crammed with

> Fashion, the Work-table, Festive Meetings, Striking Events, the Court and Fashionable Assemblies and a consecutive novel of interest . . . all the great interests of society [including] Emigration and the Amelioration of the poor . . . the best in Art, Science and Literature . . .
>
> (*LN* IX 1851: 1)

It was an eclectic mix. Some elements, like the illustrated fashions, the needlework and the articles on 'Illustrious Women of our Time', recalled the *Lady's Magazine*, which was dying just as the *Lady's Newspaper* was being born (*LN* XI 1852: 99, 112, 155). Others, like the 'Frightful Murders', 'The Robbery of a Lady' and the 'Calamitous Occurrence and Loss of Life' more closely resembled the cheap sensational newspapers (*LN* IX 1851: 90–1). This diversity also characterised its views on such matters as women's dress, where it both advocated the wearing of bloomers and gave precise details of dresses 'made by tasteful milliners for ladies of distinguished taste' (*LN* X 1851: 238; XI 1852: 17). At least it was not a dull paper. It survived despite – or perhaps because of – its contradictions, though there is evidence it was in financial difficulty by 1863 when it was rescued by merger with the *Queen* (March-Phillips 1894: 661).

The early days of the *Queen* were similarly marked by an energetic, even frenetic, eclecticism. Its first numbers were crammed with illustrations of dreadful accidents, accounts of royal and court functions, gossip, snippets of news and satiric sketches both visual and verbal. Two re-launches quickly followed. The first, in April 1862, gave it a new proprietor, a more serious tone, fewer railway accidents and a bid for the 'class' market (Watkins 1985: 187).[1] It was only in 1863, however, when the two papers merged to become the *Queen; the Lady's Newspaper*, that Cox, who had bought the title, settled on the formula which laid the basis for its success.

During the 1860s and 1870s the *Queen* had few imitators and those were short-lived, perhaps because – as one of them explained – it was still difficult for ladies' papers to be accepted as 'real' newspapers (*Ladies* I 1872: 110). In the 1880s and 1890s, however, other weekly ladies' papers began to appear with similar format and at the same price: the *Lady's Pictorial* (1881–1921), the *Gentlewoman* (1890–1926) and *The Lady* (1885– ; though it later dropped its price to three-pence).

As this brief history shows, a formula which successfully combined the female reader and the masculine category of 'news' was not easy to develop. The *Queen* in an early number declared:

> The problem which we have set ourselves is how to provide a weekly record and Journal which ladies can read and profit by; one in which their under-standing and judgement will not be insulted by a collection of mere triviali-ties but which will be to them a help in their daily lives.
>
> (*Q.* II 1862: 96)

Achieving this involved first of all finding a suitable editorial tone and persona. In its re-launched version the paper was consistently serious and, unlike the ladies' magazines, kept its promise to treat its readers as grown-ups, not 'like children or dolls' (ibid.). It also rejected the specifically masculine voice adopted by Beeton as editor of *EDM*. Instead it sought to create an editorial persona which was ungen-dered: masculine, insofar as its tone was detached and magisterial, but feminine because – as readers were reminded from time to time – the 'editress' was indeed a lady. The name and character of Helen Lowe were, however, unimportant. Readers were advised:

> Our editress told you the other day that a good deal of the Queen is written by men; quite true and these men will remember that they address women whose sense and accomplishments are quite equal to their own . . . the Queen . . . will sometimes address you as if a Lady speaks (as she will speak) and sometimes as if a gentleman spoke, but never as if an idiot spoke.
>
> (*Q.* II 1862: 147)

In this familiar manoeuvre the paper was established as a feminised space but the grammatical clumsiness suggests the difficulty of that manoeuvre in a newspaper.

The fundamental problem of defining women's news was that the category 'news' must involve politics but: 'As our readers are well aware, politics are, by the very nature of the constitution of our journal excluded from its columns' (*Q.* LVIII 1875: 105). Appealing to women's moral 'influence' on their men was the usual way of resolving this dilemma:

> Now and then, of course, sounds from the area of political conflict penetrate even into our quietude . . . . Now and then, also, matters which bear upon the welfare of large classes of the community . . . it is the privilege of women to sympathise in and help forward all efforts which are to benefit human beings in anyway.
>
> (ibid.)

The first number of the combined *Queen; the Lady's Newspaper* ran an editorial on the Ladies' Galleries in Parliament. Just as the ladies in the Galleries looked down on the political scene from a position both removed and elevated, so their role was to listen and to remind their men that 'labourers were also human beings' (*Q.* I 1861: 114; see also *Q.* LVIII 1875: 105).

As the editor explained:

> It is the fashion for those who make the laws – that is men – to say that ladies having nothing to do with what takes place in Parliament. Nothing could be more unjust, more illogical or untrue than this. It is true that women do not sit in Parliament, and no true woman who respects her sex and knows its rights and duties, hopes they ever will; but that is no reason why they should not take an interest in proceedings which so vitally affect their interests and those of all who are near and dear to them.
>
> (*Q.* II 1862: 97)

The separation of the masculine sphere of law from the feminine one of humanity and love was – in a now familiar contradiction – regarded as both necessary and damaging, hence the need to humanise, or feminise, the public world. The circularity was inescapable – except in self-proclaimed fictions like Elizabeth Gaskell's *North and South* (1855). This doctrine of women's humanising influence enabled the paper to include political comment – even on matters as far removed from the drawing room as Plimsoll's Naval reforms (ibid.).

The *Queen* went further, however. It argued that it must give space to matters affecting *women* as a group because the readers' commitment to humanity in general depended on a particular concern for 'the well-being of women' (ibid.). The lady was bound to other women by a commonality of gender which in certain cases could transcend distinctions of class. The promise of 'news' for ladies therefore included a commitment to inform readers about those aspects of the public world which were of interest to them and which other papers neglected. The 'Gazette des Dames' began cautiously, prioritising court news, but gradually its coverage became wider. Under the new catch-all title 'What Women Are Doing' it was soon offering reports on education, literature, public campaigns and debates about political and social rights as well as Society news.

From the 1860s its editorials dealt seriously with women's position, not only in politics, but in higher education and employment. Through the 1880s and 1890s and into the early twentieth century, *Queen* and the other ladies' papers provided cautious but not unsympathetic comment on the demands for wider access to political and social rights, including accounts of campaigning groups and meetings and examples of women's political activities. The readers were assumed to want political information which would be of direct interest to them as women, not just as the spouses or daughters of important men.

What it meant to be a 'Political Lady', however, remained contested, particularly around the issue of the vote. The *Ladies* (1872), an early rival of the *Queen*, was outspoken in its belief that domesticity was compatible with political rights, arguing that 'women who care for the franchise are often better housekeepers than those [who do not]' (*Ladies* I 1872: 46, 22). It may be, as Cynthia White argues, that the *Ladies* failed because it was too advanced but the *Queen* also reported meetings of the National Society for Women's Suffrage and had given a generous review to John Stuart Mill's ideas on women's rights (*Q.* XLVI 1869: 46, 47, 50ff, 141–2, 145). Throughout the century it continued to report the suffrage debate relatively objectively as well as reminding readers that women were active on School and Poor Law Boards (e.g. *Q.* LXXVIII 1885: 412; LXXXIX 1891: 274).

None of these ladies' papers openly advocated women's suffrage, however. The *Queen*'s attitude to the *Englishwoman's Review* – a journal dedicated to women's rights – was typical. It simultaneously recommended the *Review* to its readers and distanced itself from the *Review*'s position, arguing that 'we want equality not identity' (*Q.* LVIII 1875: 121). These reports sat oddly with the papers' constant rejection of 'strong-mindedness' and occasionally satiric representation of the 'woman's rightist', like the *Gentlewoman*'s 'Gentlewoman of the Future' series, which featured such unlikely figures as the female MA, MD and QC (*G.* I 1890: 151, 187, 223). These contradictions make reading the 'What Women Are Doing' columns problematic. Are such representations comic or celebratory (Figure 7.1)?

The constant presence of such ambivalent or deviant femininities in the ladies' papers provided readers with at least the potential for producing their own definitions of the 'political lady'. In 1892 the *Gentlewoman* polled its readers directly on the issue of women's suffrage. Of a total readership claimed as 47,000, 9,459 readers voted: 8,301 in favour and 1,118 against (*G.* IV 1892: 92). This result suggests that by acknowledging the existence of women's rights the papers had provided a space in which readers could in Foucauldian terms 'reverse' the discourse and begin to contest the meaning of the ladies' public role. Typically, the *Gentlewoman* continued to print accounts of suffrage meetings side by side with satiric representations of female voters (*G.* V 1892: 41).

'NEWS' AS NOVELTY

Public politics never formed more than a small element of the diet of 'news' in these journals. There was, however, another kind of public space which the lady did inhabit. Against the masculine world of politics the social world of entertaining, leisure and cultural events was completely feminised. The *Queen* therefore invented a whole range of 'news' categories which turned on the fashionable social life of the aristocracy and London Society. In 1885 these were:

> Balls, Bazaars, Boudoir, Charity, Cuisine, Drama, Dress, Entertainments, Etiquette, Fashionable Marriages, Garden, Gazette des Dames, Housewife, Illustrations, Leaders, Library, Miscellaneous, Music, Naturalist, Pastimes, Portraits, Private Theatricals, Studios, Tourists, Work-Table.
>
> (*Q.* LXXVIII 1885)

This list demarcated the space – bounded on one side by class and on the other by

Figure 7.1 'What Women Are Doing' from *Queen* (LXXVII 28 March 1885: 314)

gender – in which the multiple meanings of 'the lady' could be mapped out. These were inseparable from the meanings of her 'home'.

'Home', like femininity itself, was both always already there and constantly having to be created. In the tradition of the ladies' magazines, these papers offered to help the reader produce her 'home' through the management of her own and her household consumption. Instead of vague generalisation, however, the imperative to maintain oneself between 'extravagance and meanness' was spelt out by the *Queen* in specific detail (*Q.* LXXXIV 1888: 38). The practice of directing readers to named shops or suppliers became more and more insistent in the 1880s and 1890s until the *Queen's* extensive dress news became virtually an 'advertorial', like Myra's 'Spinnings'. This detailed advice extended from the fashion and dress sections to include other parts of the paper where specific items for household use were described or illustrated and readers advised where to buy them (e.g. *Q.* LXXXIV 1888: 409, 499, 640–7 and passim). Direction were usually given to the London shops but sometimes the paper advised on shopping in other cities such as Manchester or Leeds (ibid.: 495).

News thus became 'novelties'. The novelty, whether a ribbon or a knick-knack, was a visible sign of the woman's skill as a purchaser and her up-to-date knowledge of the latest fashions, a knowledge the paper provided. The reader could therefore not only regulate her own consumption to produce the right kind of home and self, she could also recognise and read the signs other women produced. This knowledge had constantly to be up-dated, since the 'novelty' was by definition always ceasing to be novel. Novelty and periodical thus worked together to create a recurrent pattern of consumption.

Advertising was even more significant than the advertorial in recreating consumption as feminine knowledge. It had always been a feature of the ladies' papers but it grew in importance both economically and visually until by the mid-1880s it was underpinning their finances and occupying half their pages. The *Queen* pioneered the relationship between the periodical and the advertiser through which the 'advertorial' became recycled as pure advertisement. An endorsement in its columns became the basis of producers' self-advertisement 'as recommended in *Queen*' (White 1970: 67). This blurring of the distinction between editorial copy and advertisement was to have profound effects on women's magazines which I discuss in Chapter 10. It was central to that general shift towards redefining femininity as consumption which the ladies' papers undertook.

EMBROIDERY AND THE HOME BEAUTIFUL

Nowhere in this shift clearer than in the well-established tradition of the 'Work-table' department. In magazines like *EDM* the Berlin wool and other patterns had the double function of providing lady-like occupation and enabling the lady to embellish the house with products of her skill. The *Queen* continued this tradition but gradually extended its advice to take in more general buying for the home.

This transition was institutionalised in the 1890s when the Work-table became a 'What to Work and What to Buy' section (see post-1891 vols).

At the same time this column, and the paper as a whole, began to address the creation not just of single 'works' of embroidery but of whole rooms or even the 'Home Beautiful', for which the paper advised on decoration, materials and furnishing patterns (*Q.* LXVII 1880: 387). This shift was evident also in the more down-market *Myra's Journal* and in later magazines like the *Lady's Realm* – which ran the series called 'The Home Beautiful' – but in the ladies' papers it became central (*LR* II 1897: 105, 231, 353, 470, 586, 699: III 115, etc.).

The reader's 'home' was evidence of her management of consumption both in class and gender terms. Her status lent her purchasing power and her gender allotted her the task of purchasing, but these must be deployed with 'taste'. *Queen* stressed this aspect of 'home' from the start by commissioning a series of articles from Charles Locke Eastlake which were re-worked in his popular book, *Hints on Household Taste in Furniture, Upholstery and Other Details* (Watkins 1985: 191). Taste became the crucial marker of a woman's knowledge and management skills. It was an essentially *visible* quality, evident from a detailed scrutiny of the furnishings, the choice of colour and the ornaments in her home.

This preoccupation entered other sections of the paper, above all in the illustrated interviews with celebrities 'at home'. This genre, a characteristic invention of the new journalism of the 1880s and 1890s, was not of course confined to the woman's press but ladies' papers used it extensively, in part because it was a development of that well-established genre, the 'illustrated life of a notable woman'.

The *Lady's Pictorial* ran a typical series on 'Notable Women Authors of the Day' which was later published by Helen Black in volume form. Each woman was represented in terms of her appearance and that of her room, rather than in terms of her achievement as a writer. Helen Mathers's room showed her refined and artistic taste:

> its soft Axminster carpet of amber colour shaded up to brown gives the keynote to the decorations, which from the heavily embossed gold leather paper on the walls to the orange coloured indian scarves that drape the exquisite white overmantels (now wreathed with long sprays of ivy, grasses and red leaves) would delight the heart of a sun-worshipper as Helen Mathers declares herself to be.
>
> (Black 1906: 69)

This interview borrows from the home decoration pages to provide an exemplary reading of the author's room as a text. It taught the reader how to recognise 'a refined and artistic taste' when she saw it, but also of course constrained her to produce her own home as a text which could be subjected to the scrutiny of others. This knowledge was therefore a source of anxiety as well as power. The papers' advice on decorations, the advertorials and advertisements for furnishings, the articles on well known women 'at home' and the 'Answers to Correspondents', all contributed to this anxiety at the same time as they offered the means (temporarily) to allay it.

The meanings which circulated round the concept of 'home' in the ladies' papers centred on the phrase 'At Home', which signified not that a lady was physically in her house, but that she was prepared to receive guests.[2] 'Home' in this sense was the site of that ritual exchange of courtesies which characterised middle- and upper middle-class social life (Davidoff 1986). Social relationships beyond, as well as within, the family circle were the lady's responsibility and in discharging them her household management, her taste in decoration and furnishings and her own dress and behaviour would all be under scrutiny.

In the *Queen* the femininity of the readership was defined in relation to that elite called 'Society', 'the Upper Ten Thousand' as they were called. This was also the title of *Queen*'s column of Society news. For women, entry to this upper echelon was possible only through presentation at court, that is through reception by the Queen or her representative when she herself was 'at home'. Once presented, a girl was 'out' in Society and became a woman or rather 'a lady'. It was a rite of passage whose form changed hardly at all during Victoria's reign.

THE QUEEN, THE COURT AND ETIQUETTE

Representations of Victoria both visual and verbal in the popular press were crucial to re-working the meaning of the monarchy during her long reign (Homans 1993). Invoked across the range of women's periodicals, the image of the female monarch was particularly important in the lady's newspapers. The *Lady's Newspaper* had carried her head on its title page, surrounded by ribbons carrying the words 'Literature', 'Accomplishments', 'Duties', 'Amusement' and 'News'. Despite his republicanism, Beeton recognised the importance of the idea of the Queen for his project and his paper too was dedicated to her, its masthead featured Windsor Castle and the royal coat of arms appeared above its editorial.

A public but non-political figure who was also a woman seemed the obvious answer to the quest for women's news and it was unfortunate for Beeton that, when he launched *Queen*, Victoria was about to retreat from the world to mourn for Albert. The early pages of the *Queen* were full of illustrated accounts of Her Majesty's visits and activities. In the years of Victoria's withdrawal from public life, this kind of copy became more difficult to obtain, though the *Queen* routinely reported on books she had received and drives she had undertaken (e.g. *Q.* II 1862: 163).

The values vested in the Queen, however, were less dependent on what she *did* than what she *was*. Victoria represented at the highest level that feminine influence which could humanise the political. As womanliness enthroned she was essentially *like* the female reader, above all because she was a wife and mother to her family (Homans 1993). The idea of the Queen as mother, always a resonant one for the women's press, sustained an interest in other members of the Royal

Family during her seclusion and provided a means of recreating her in the media in the period of her return to public life.

The marriage of Victoria's youngest daughter, the Princess Beatrice, in 1885, was important in this process. In common with other women's journals the *Queen* produced a special edition representing the marriage as an essentially family occasion in which the public power of the crown was humanised, or rather feminised, by the Queen (*Q.* LXXVIII 1885: 82–4). Victoria's approval of her daughter's match was described as 'in accordance with all that we know of the true womanly instincts that lie behind the throne' (ibid.: 81). There was an evident contradiction here. The papers which defined this as family occasion also created it as 'news', that is public event. Moreover, the special wedding supplements provided an excuse for even more lavish illustrations than usual. The genre of illustrated news produced the event as public spectacle rather than private feeling.

Royal news was only one end of the spectrum of those more general categories, 'court news' and 'Society news', which were a staple of all the ladies' papers. This included state occasions, functions at great houses and on the key dates in the social calendar of the Upper Ten Thousand. For the young woman of the upper class the annual round of the 'Season' was essentially a marriage mart, and marriage remained her only route into adulthood, both sexual and economic. The ceremony of presentation at court which initiated her into Society was therefore described in great detail in the ladies' journals as were the 'Fashionable Marriages'. These marked the lady's rites of passage.

These events, steps in the process of becoming 'a lady', were produced in the papers in terms of visibility. The girl entered Society by coming 'out', that is becoming available to the gaze. The Society lady was defined in terms of where and how she was seen. Illustration became increasingly important in Society news, especially after the development of the half-tone plate in the 1880s and 1890s, when even Society marriages were represented by small inset pictures of the bride and social events such as the Henley Regatta by full page plates (e.g. *Q.* XCVIII 1895: 104). While early Victorian issues of the *Lady's Museum* had given two-line descriptions of those presented at court, by the 1890s *Queen* was offering full-page sketches of the debutantes in their dresses (*Q.* XCIX 1896: 447, 450–1).

The lady was also produced by rules of conduct. Court procedures were formally codified during the early years of Victoria's reign and certificates of presentations, along with a manual of instruction, began to be issued in 1854 (Davidoff 1986: 24ff). This formalisation of behaviour, along with the regularity of the social Season and precise delimitation of its numbers, allowed Society to appear as somehow stable and fixed. The same process of regulation informed the advice columns of the papers, where instruction in the minutiae of manners promised to prevent 'breaches of etiquette' (*G.* I 1890: 56). The *Gentlewoman* in its opening number announced that readers wanting advice on

points of etiquette or matters concerned with Court and social life may write under a nom de plume enclosing the coupon to be found at the end of the paper to Savoir Faire.

(ibid.: 21)

This advice was needed, however, precisely because the boundaries of acceptable behaviour were unclear;

> Though the Queen has lived in touch with the very humblest of her subjects and has withdrawn in great measure the barriers which formerly so completely isolated the Sovereign from the people, the familiarity which endangers respect can never be tolerated and certain rules can never be set aside at Court or in Society.

(ibid.)

The importance of the etiquette advice offered in all the ladies' papers was that, like the articles on home decoration, it constructed a model of the lady in which every detail was important. This knowledge enabled the reader to recognise a lady from the minutiae of her conduct and to produce herself in similar detail. The anxiety addressed by 'Savoir Faire' in the *Gentlewoman* and the *Queen*'s answers to questions on etiquette was pervasive, not least because it could not be openly acknowledged. Those seeking advice were not only anxious because they were ignorant but anxious to conceal their ignorance, hence the *nom de plume*. The papers produced the anxiety along with the knowledge and insisted upon it week after week.

Since the social sphere was feminised, it was the particular responsibility of the lady to ensure the proper conduct of Society and the maintenance of its hierarchies. Gender difference here seemed to offer not grounds for constructing a shared femininity but codification of the terms in which women were to be distinguished from each other. However, the papers undermined the meaning of these distinctions even as they provided advice on maintaining them. For if it were possible to learn from the papers how to conduct yourself like a lady, then the social barriers were indeed in danger of being breached.

The ironic double-bind was even more evident in the vast amount of advice on dress and fashion which the papers covered. In these articles, visibility and the 'tasteful' regulation of detail were both at work to produce the lady. Not surprisingly fashion 'news' occupied more space in the papers than any other single topic.

DRESS AND ILLUSTRATION

All the ladies' papers made appearance central to their definition of themselves as well as their readers. This message was carried primarily by the wealth of high quality illustration. Just as *La Belle Assemblée* had used the best paper and copperplate, so these papers offered the best of late Victorian/Edwardian print technology, especially in picture reproduction. *Queen* in the mid-1880s ran two full-page illustrations for every three pages of text, deploying a variety of illustrative genres and techniques. The other papers were even more adventurous. In the 1890s they carried pictures on almost every page and even experimented with lay-out, though always within the three-column newspaper format.

Advances in print technology and the development of a 'new journalism' which stressed visual interest had revolutionised the appearance of much of the periodical press by the end of the century and led to quality general magazines like the *English Illustrated* or the *Strand.* Illustration in *Queen*, therefore included not only the usual fashion and needlework but reproductions of recent paintings, portraits, illustrations of 'news' items and general pictures of sentimental cherubs and children in winsome poses.

Insofar as they defined current 'taste', these illustrations related to the material on home decoration, but they had a more important role in adding to the readers' cultural capital. A knowledge of current developments in the arts was essential to the lady's class position. It showed she had both the material wealth and the leisure from paid employment which made such knowledge possible. Much of *Queen* was given over to providing such capital, with accounts of theatre, music and books, reproductions of paintings from the Royal Academy or other contemporary exhibitions, and illustrations of studios and other places where the decorative arts were pursued (see e.g. *Q.* XLV 1869: 141; LXVII 1880: 389, 412–13).

As with the book reviews in the *Lady's Museum* of the 1840s, to read these elements of the paper only as providing class-specific knowledge is to deny the aesthetic and intellectual pleasures which they also offered the reader. One of these may have been the potential of a discourse of high art to interrogate the meanings offered elsewhere in the paper. Primarily, however, the quality and the number of illustrations created a sense of luxury or excess. This was emphasised in the *Gentlewoman* by the use of heavy expensive paper, which coded its own femininity just as the late twentieth-century 'glossy' magazine does. Above all the wealth of illustrations created, even more insistently than in the magazines, a femininity and a feminine reading defined by appearance.[3]

The clothed female body dominated these magazines, both in the fashion-plate and the other illustrations. In a typical number of 1885 – not counting the special offer colour plates or the advertisements – there were four full pages of dress illustrations, each showing a row of female figures with the anatomically impossible body-shape of current fashion (*Q.* LXXVII 1885; see Figures 7.2, 7.3, 7.4). As in the *EDM* the clothes both concealed the body from neck to foot and accentuated its femininity. Almost all the other full-page illustrations showed female figures, including a woman artist, a music lesson, a page on 'What Women Are Doing' and a photograph of the Duchess of Albany bending over the cradle of her child. The only male figure in this issue was the late Duke of Albany, represented by a photograph of a memorial bust as though the visible body had become exclusively identified with femininity.

The visible body, like the magazine was defined by the intersection of femininity and wealth enacted in 'fashion'. The language of the 'fashionable' in *Queen* seemed to look back to the beginning of the century with its aristocratic ladies on

Figure 7.2 Fashion page from *Queen* (LXXVII 28 March 1885: 319)

102

No. 13, AFTERNOON CONCERT DRESS.

Skirt and vest in green casimir, striped with velvet. Tunic and blouse plastron in lichen-green, tufted with chenille. The tunic is gathered at the waist, and draped *en pouf*; the full plastron forms a double bouillonné. The demi-long sleeves terminate with lace. The vest is plaited at the back. Pattern of jacket, 2s, 7d.

Figure 7.3 Fashion page from *Queen* (March 1885) detail

Figure 7.4 Fashion page from *Queen* (LXXVII 28 March 1885)

display at Society events or on Rotten Row. Dress and court news were once again indistinguishable, but now they were linked not only by a model of female visibility but by the new economy of fashion which I discussed in the last chapter. Though the British court was very different indeed from Second Empire Paris, the same processes were at work. Indeed it was papers like *Queen* which made them work. In representing a Paris dress simultaneously as fashion item, Society news and consumer guide, the paper was producing 'fashion' as a discourse and as an international business.

Dress in these papers was no longer a simple signifier of status and femininity, but a complex language in which class, wealth, age, marital position, season and time of day were all significant. As with the minutely regulated behaviour which constituted etiquette, so fashion depended on minute differences of material, cut or decoration which to the modern eye are almost impossible to distinguish. But unlike manners, fashion was represented not as fixed and codified but as constantly changing. The papers created this flux and taught readers how to ride it. They offered the knowledge necessary to read others off from their dress and also to produce oneself as a fashionable lady, with the aid of paper patterns and shopping tips. The discursive and the economic were inextricable.

Like the etiquette column, the fashion pictures were caught in the paradox that the value of what they offered depended on an exclusivity which they both created and undermined. The dress patterns in the *Queen* were not cheap but they were a great deal less expensive than costumes designed and made at the House of Worth.[4] Both the expensive dress and the expensive magazine also had an after-life once their first owner had discarded them; they were passed on to maids, exchanged through such columns as the *Queen*'s own 'Exchange and Mart', and sent to second-hand shops (Wilson and Taylor 1989: 38ff). Beyond the ladies' papers there were cheaper journals, like those associated with 'Myra' and Weldon, extending access to fashion down the social scale. As commercial ventures they were under pressure to extend the idea of 'the lady' to a wider and wider circle of women. By the 1890s even suburban housewives like Mrs Pooter in the *Diary of a Nobody* could aspire to be *á la mode* (Grossmith 1892: 69). In 1887 Oscar Wilde declared that the word 'Lady' in the title of the *Lady's World* carried a 'certain taint of vulgarity' because it suggested another magazine dedicated to 'mere millinery and trimmings'. He would only take over its editorship if the word 'Woman' were used instead (Ellman 1988: 274–8).

The meaning of fashion as the mark of 'the lady' was therefore contested, even within the fashion pages of women's journals. In the *Queen* and its rivals dress became ever more elaborate and visibly expensive as the century progressed. By contrast, 'Myra' in her Journal of that year suggested economical ways of being fashionable and argued that:

> we dress to add to our charm and to make our personality pleasant to our dear men and not merely to parade the wealth of our husbands and the taste of our couturier.
>
> (*Myra* I 1875: 21)

The instability of the meaning of fashion generated an anxiety which was not confined to the ladies' papers. Their construction of a femininity which could be read from its surface threatened once again the whole discourse of the domestic woman and of moral management. This threat was dramatically evident because Worth's extravagant costumes were designed and worn by the Parisian demimonde as well as the court. Instead of providing a sophisticated code for distinguishing between ladies, fashion had collapsed that most fundamental divide. Extravagant dress and the presentation of the self as spectacle had become the signifiers of both the lady and the prostitute.

In 1868 this anxiety erupted in controversy over an article in the *Saturday Review* by the journalist Eliza Lynn Linton. Linton invoked the ideal of the English Domestic Woman, or the 'fair young English girl':

> a creature generous, capable, modest; something franker than a Frenchwoman, more to be trusted than an Italian, as brave as an American but more refined, as domestic as a German and more graceful . . . a girl [of] innate purity and dignity of nature.
>
> (*Sat.* XXV 1868: 339–40)

105

However, under the baleful influence of fashion this paragon of inwardness had now become

> 'The Girl of the Period' . . . a creature who dyes her hair and paints her face, whose sole aim is unbounded luxury and whose dress is the chief object of such thought and intellect as she possesses.
>
> (ibid.)

When 'the English Girl' adopted 'the extravagance of fashion', according to Linton, she put on the appearance and therefore also the qualities of the French demi-monde and put off the 'tender, loving, retiring or domestic' behaviour proper to English womanhood.

Linton's concern was in part to maintain a discourse in which the prostitute was not just outside society but beyond language itself, that 'class of woman whom we must not call by their proper – or improper – name' (ibid.). Instead, she sought to recover a femininity of inner value, 'the English ideal woman, the most beautiful, the most modest and the most essentially womanly in the world'.

Linton's position was not consistent, but this argument rested on an understanding of dress not as a sign of inner quality but an agent which shaped it. Fashion 'vitiated' the taste of 'the Girl of the Period' and therefore also her morals. This reversed the dominant formulation of the ladies' papers which consistently defined fashion and display as the signifiers of the domestic economy, as texts from which the lady's character could be read (e.g. Q. XLV 1869: 51, 116). It was the instability of this formulation which allowed 'the Girl of the Period' to capture the public imagination. She became a 'famous topic at dinner-tables, a journalistic catch phrase, the title of several publications and the source of endless jokes' (Helsinger *et al.* 1983 I: 113; Pykett 1992). This is evidence both of the continuing struggle to maintain sexual difference and a historically specific anxiety about the maintenance of that difference through the (self-)control of women.

'THE GIRL OF THE PERIOD' AND THE SEXUAL CONTROL OF WOMEN

The femininity of spectacle which the ladies' papers created was constantly being returned to the work of moral and domestic management. The visible depended always on careful regulation of the invisible, just as the fit of the lady's dress depended on the corset.

Underpinning the home beautiful was the work of the domestic servant and a woman's regulation of her home was nowhere more evident than in the success with which she managed this other woman. The servant 'problem', as defined in these papers, was multiple; finding, training, keeping and controlling. *The Lady* built its reputation on its small advertisements in which employers and would-be servants sought each other, and – in yet another re-working of upper-class British femininity – the magazine still performs this function in the 1990s.

In the *Queen* the 'problem', like the servant herself, was everywhere assumed but rarely visible. An occasional series on 'Why Don't We Get Good Servants?' argued – as Isabella Beeton's *Household Management* had done – that the control of servants was a matter of moral rather than commercial management: 'fair ladies who are so kind and gentle in all the other relations of life, look not upon hard, toilsome service as a mere money question' (*Q.* III 1862: 98). Readers were urged to remember that servants too had feelings and worked better when they were well treated, but that kindness should be carefully regulated:

> while you warm their attachment and stimulate their fidelity by showing you take an interest in their welfare and happiness, discreetly avoid over-indulgence and familiarity, which always nurtures a disastrous sequence.
>
> (ibid., see also 385; *Q.* XCV 1894: 74, 386)

The management of servants was therefore about the regulation of appropriate models of the self. Providing suitable reading was part of the mistress's task and there were periodicals as well as domestic manuals specifically designed to be bought for servants (James 1982). One writer in *Queen* recommended that servants be given Tennyson, Longfellow and Shakespeare as well as 'novels with a good moral tendency' to counteract the influence of lurid penny fictions and sensation novels (*Q.* LXVII 1880: 19). What the servants made of this reading was not of interest to the *Queen*, though servants undoubtedly read and discussed their mistresses' journals. But when servants began to organise themselves in the 1890s, they produced their own rather different kind of periodical, the *Female Servants Union News* (1892).

Just as the home depended on the invisible work of domestic servants, so the clothes discussed in *Queen* depended on the work of dress-makers, milliners and shop assistants. For these women, needlework was not a matter of accomplishments but of necessary and poorly paid labour. 'Myra' assumed that readers of her journal would combine 'economy and good taste' by making their own dresses and it may be that the readers of *Queen* occasionally did likewise (*Myra* VII 1881: 28). Certainly it carried advertisements for domestic sewing machines and, in the 1880s and 1890s, for the increasingly high quality ready-to-wear clothing, especially mourning wear (Figure 7.5; *Q.* LXXVII 1885: unnumbered ads pages passim, esp. fifth page). All the ladies' papers, however, assumed a reader who relied mainly on her own private dress-maker or on the organised clothing trade.

For workers in these sweated industries – largely women or Jewish immigrant men – the relentless demand to be seen in the latest fashion and the concentration of Society events in the Season meant long hours in appalling conditions either at home or in crowded workshops. The fashionable lady was the product not just of a visible difference from the woman worker but of her direct exploitation. This relationship could not remain entirely hidden, however. In art the needlewoman was a recognised icon of female suffering, and the sweated labour and the long hours of shop-workers began to be documented and publicly discussed during the last years of the century (Nead 1988; Wilson and Taylor 1989: 68–71).

107

Figure 7.5 Advertisements from *Queen* (LXXVII 28 March 1885)

108

Occasionally, then, the responsibility of ladies towards those who made their dresses or served them in shops surfaced in these papers.

For the lady this raised more complex issues of moral management even than the domestic servant. John Ruskin's 1865 lecture on women's education, 'Of Queen's Gardens' (popularised as the second half of *Sesame and Lilies*), was immensely influential in this debate. Ruskin claimed that since the title 'lady' was being universally adopted, ladies must extend their responsibilities for the material and moral welfare of their inferiors to women outside the home as well as those within it (Ruskin 1865). The practice of personal charity became an essential aspect of the lady, especially making clothes for 'the poor', for which the needlework pages of *Queen* sometimes provided patterns (*Q*. LVIII 1875: 165). Beeton's model of household management contributed to the development of new kinds of charity organisation and social work for the lady, which *Queen* charted sympathetically (Vicinus 1985; Walkowitz 1994: 54–6).

Charity 'work' in these papers, however, was more often confined to making needle- or fancy-work objects for sale at the various charity bazaars. These were essentially social events and became a significant category of news in *Queen* from the 1880s. High visibility among one's upper-class peers, therefore, replaced the visit in which 'the poor' and their homes became the objects of the lady's scrutiny.

Very occasionally, *Queen* suggested that the lady reader move beyond the exercise of 'influence' on men to take a direct interest in the conditions of seamstresses and women shop assistants. They had power to improve the working conditions of these women, for example, by taking a 'Pledge' not to shop late in the afternoon or by not demanding that dresses be made overnight (*Q*. XLVI 1869: 15). This was close to Ruskin's ideal of extending the domestic relations of mistress/servant into the market-place. It was never extended into a systematic campaign or boycott.

The lady's concern for such workers was always for their moral welfare at least as much as their material well-being. In fictional and pictorial accounts it was precisely the milliners and poorly paid female seamstresses, who were most likely to be tempted into the life of prostitution (Gaskell 1853; Nead 1988: 103 and passim). Like the lady's maid, they were required to walk unattended through the ambiguous terrain of the city's public spaces (Walkowitz 1994: 41ff, passim). Their visibility in the streets in what were often lady-like clothes blurred that distinction between the respectable and the fallen which Linton was so anxious to maintain. Their bodily texts were open to misreading by male passers-by.

In an attempt to control the sexuality of such women, the government passed a series of Contagious Diseases Acts between 1864 and 1869, the year after Linton's article. Contagious or Venereal Disease was endemic in the armed forces and the Acts gave police powers to institute the medical inspection of prostitutes in garrison towns as a preliminary to a more general extension of their powers over 'the painted ladies' of the street (Walkowitz 1994: 22–3). The double sexual standard encoded in the Acts provoked a campaign in which respectable middle-class women, led by the clergyman's wife Josephine Butler, expressed their solidarity with their working-class sisters and publicly contested the assumption that female sexuality must be controlled because male sexuality could not be.

Outrage was also provoked by the ambiguity which enforcement of the Acts revealed in the texts of dress. Legislators assumed that the police would readily identify prostitutes from their appearance alone. Instead respectable working-class women were apprehended simply for being in the street and even a middle-class woman waiting for a bus was apparently in danger of being mistaken for 'a social problem' (ibid.: 50).

The campaign, the repeal of the Acts and the subsequent development of the social purity movement impinged on the ladies' papers only marginally, but the instability of the meaning of fashion and its association with female sexuality remained central to their working. Unlike Butler, who constructed the fallen woman as victim and repentant sinner, Linton argued that the difference between the virtuous woman and the prostitute must be vigorously maintained. This necessity only arose, however, because at heart these two were much alike. Indeed the problem of the demi-mondaine for Linton was that she had all that the pure young English girl 'most passionately desired' (*Sat.* XXV 1868: 339): '. . . the demi-monde have all that for which her soul is hungering and she never stops to reflect at what a price they have bought their sensuous pleasures' (*Sat.* XXV 1868: 339–40). It was the seductive power of fashion which Linton feared and it was her recognition that fashion addressed desire and women's pleasure which energised the debate she initiated.

Advice on dress, like that on manners or home decoration, concerned the constant labour of creating an appropriate self which was the subject of all women's magazines. But the fashion pages, as I have argued, were also about plea-sure and desire. 'Myra' articulated the assumption, made everywhere in these papers, that fashion produced women for the attention of 'our men'. Fashion for her was male heterosexual desire inscribed on the visible surfaces of the female body.

'Fashion' in these illustrated papers, however, also depended on a seduction of the female reader who was actively seeking her own desire. *Queen* invited its readers simultaneously to identify with and objectify the female images on the page. Illustrations functioned as both instructive text, providing information on how sleeves were worn this year or how to make a chignon, and as a source of plea-sure. This fractured text addressed a reader whose feminine identity was neither passive nor active but constantly in process between the two. In the privacy of her own home or sharing the paper with her female friends the woman reader could appropriate its representations of the female body in different ways, from identifi-cation through erotic desire and back again.[5]

The range of possible readings open to any one reader must depend crucially on the historical context of her reading. We do not yet know enough of that context to guess how far it was possible for readers of *Queen* consciously to appropriate its fashion-plates in terms of same-sex desire. We do know that 'passionate friend-ships' between women were culturally acceptable and even common (Raymond

1986). However, the pleasures of the illustrated papers, like the identity of the lady, were not monolithic and nor was the control of female sexuality absolute in their pages. The pleasures they offered were polymorphous, even if they were not perverse.

'The Girl of the Period' was succeeded in the 1880s and 1890s by other images of insubordinate young womanhood around which the contradictions of femininity were dramatised. 'The Revolting Daughter' and 'the Girton Girl' were related to each other and to the most important of all these figures 'the New Woman'. However, they should not be collapsed together. Each signalled rather different lines of fracture in the image of the lady. It is significant that in the 1890s *Queen* employed Linton to write leading articles on a regular basis. Linton's own position as an independent journalist separated from her husband demonstrated precisely the contradictions which made it so necessary and so difficult to maintain the discourses of restraint and domesticity at the centre of female reading. In the 1880s and 1890s that difficulty became even more acute.

Part III

NEW WOMAN,
NEW JOURNALISM,
THE 1880s AND 1890s

8

THE NEW WOMAN
AND THE NEW JOURNALISM

Who cuts her back hair off quite short
And put on clothes she didn't ought,
And apes a man in word and thought?
                              New Woman.

Who rides a cycle round the town,
In costume making all men frown
And otherwise acts like a clown?
                              New Woman.

Who's sweetest of the sweet, I say,
Because she throws not sex away,
Is always lady-like, yet gay?
                              True Woman.
                (Entry to a competition to define
the New Woman, *Home Chat*, 21 Sept. 1895: 29)

'Nowadays all the married men live like bachelors and all the bachelors like married men.'
'*Fin de siècle*', murmured Sir Henry.
'*Fin du globe*', answered his hostess.
                        (Oscar Wilde, *The Picture of Dorian Grey*,
                              1861, in Maine (ed.) 1948/1961: 137)

The label 'New Woman' was instantly recognisable by 1895 when readers of *Home Chat* entered a competition to define her.[1] Since 'costume' was the crucial marker of sex, rejection of traditional female dress precipitated acute anxiety about all the differences maintained by the sexual norm. No wonder it was often diffused in a joke (Ardis 1990: 11; Showalter 1991; Strachey 1986a). The label 'new', like other 1880s and 1890s terms for deviant women ('redundant', 'odd', 'wild' and 'revolting') was an attempt to pin down and therefore to control women and the meaning of sex/gender relations.

The 1880s and 1890s were also the decades of the 'New Journalism'. To contemporaries it seemed that in the press, as elsewhere in the culture, traditional

115

welcomed and some deplored. The New Journalism, like the New Woman, was taken as both manifestation of and symbol for a more general crisis. Across Europe and North America, the period defined itself as marked by innovation in a range of cultural and social forms from Art Nouveau to the New Unionism but also simultaneously as dying, decadent, *fin de siècle* or even *fin du globe*. This widespread and ambiguous sense of transition was given a particular nuance in Britain by the relative decline of the British economy, the emergence of working-class and socialist political activity and the development of a new kind of monopoly capitalism and a new imperialism which focused on Africa.[2]

The rest of this book explores how the 'new' femininity and the 'new' press defined each other. The last three chapters offer readings of particular magazines as representative or significant sites for this process and take my history into the twentieth century. In the three chapters of this section, however, I lay out in more general and theoretical terms my argument about the interaction of femininity and the development of the magazine in the 1880s and 1890s.

GENDER, SEX AND THE MEANS OF REPRESENTATION

It was not only the instability of femininity in the mid-1890s which caused anxiety; it was also a sense of crisis in late Victorian masculinity and male sexuality. Popular representations of 'Woman', like Ayesha in Rider Haggard's bestselling novel, *She*, were at least as much about masculinity and male bonding as about the mysterious and deadly powers attributed to femininity. The 1880s and 1890s were marked by radical re-workings of the meaning of masculinity through the public schools, the creation of football and cricket as mass cultural events, and the spread of imperial adventure stories as popular reading for boys (Bristow 1991). The Campaign against the Contagious Diseases Acts had opened up the debate about the double sexual standard and the question of the control of male as well as female sexuality, whether that control was internalised or enacted in legislation (Smart 1992; Walkowitz 1994). In the press, coverage of the Ripper murders produced masculinity as an area of contention, while New Woman novelists and the social purity campaigners alike insisted on the centrality of male sexuality to the crisis of gender identity at the end of the century (Jeffreys 1985; Walkowitz 1994).

This crisis was bound up with the emergence in these decades of a male homosexual identity in the public discourses of law, medicine and literature (Dollimore 1991: esp. 21–35; Foucault 1981; Weeks 1981: 96–121). The Labouchère Amendment to the Criminal Law Amendment Act of 1885 'brought all male homosexual activity into the scope of the law' (Weeks 1981: 102). Meanwhile 'Decadent Artists', notably Aubrey Beardsley and the admirers of Pater, developed a coded literary discourse of homo-eroticism. The trial of Oscar Wilde in 1895 not only brought the discourses of law and literature together, it was a dramatic demonstration both of the existence of this deviant male identity and the social necessity for its absolute destruction.

The New Woman and the Decadent Artist were signs of this crisis of gender identity which extended beyond questions about 'true' masculinity or 'true' femininity to a more radical questioning of the relationship of gender and sexuality. The difficulty of identifying the eligible man was a stock motif of fiction (Gaskell 1866). The new problem was defining a man's sexuality when behaviour, dress and deportment – the marks of gender – could not distinguish the heterosexual man, married or unmarried. Wilde's argument that the mask was the truth, life imitated art and not the other way round, rejected all received ways of reading the truth of the self, whether as artist or as sexual being (Maine 1948/1961: 921). Even more than 'the Girl of the Period' debate, which also dealt with the relationship of appearance and the gendered and sexual self, this brought into question the very possibility of a coherent sexual identity.

Ideological struggles around gender, sexuality and the body were obviously not 'new' in this period but they took on an unusual intensity and importance. For a short time, a space opened up in which radically new formations seemed possible. Within that space, however, men and women continued to be differently positioned. There was no positive public discourse, however coded, of female same-sex desire.[3] Since both medicine and Parliament were open only to middle-class men, they enacted the legislative and medical control of sexuality over women, the working class and children as well as 'deviant' men. Gender inequalities complicated the struggles over sexuality and were in turn caught up in the inequalities of class. Ironically, middle-class and feminist-inspired attempts to control male sexuality through legislation on prostitution and the age of consent for girls came to bear most heavily on working-class women in the succeeding years (Bland 1992; Weeks 1981: 87–8).

The difficulties of defining a self and a politics as gendered, sexual and embodied were explored in a range of discourses and practices; in medicine, especially in the new science of 'sexology' and the emerging discipline of psycho-analysis; in the legal regulation of sexuality; in the campaigns around social purity; and in polemical and fictional writing on marriage and sexuality.[4] In most of these it was the deviant woman who became the signifier of gender crisis, notably in a series of novels associated with the idea of 'the New Woman'.

The close link between New Woman and New Fiction opened up the confusions about changing socio-sexual roles to another set of debates about the relationship of the written word to the 'real' world.[5] The argument that the 'New Woman' was simply an invention, a myth which did not correspond to reality, was endemic in discussion of her. As Ann Ardis argues, this was in part a strategy of containment (Ardis 1990: 13). Defining the deviant woman as fictive removed her from the 'real' world of social reform and personal relationships. This involved not only denying her 'real' power but also denying that literature was part of that world. As the much-quoted *Punch* rhyme put it:

There is a New Woman and what do you think
She lives upon nothing but Foolscap and ink!
(*Punch* 26 May 1894: 252)[6]

However, it was not easy to separate the real from the inventions of print so neatly. The next couplet of the rhyme acknowledged the failure of its own strategy:

> Though Foolscap and ink are the whole of her diet
> This nagging New Woman can never be quiet.
>
> (ibid.)

Against the argument that literature was irrelevant, or at best an inaccurate reflection of the real, was the widespread belief in its capacity to enter into and shape the lives of readers. The Besants and Lintons, who deplored the representation of New Women in fiction, did so because they feared the power of such writing to destroy the family as the foundation of society (Ardis 1990: 22–3). Conversely, women writers like Sarah Grand turned to fiction because they believed reading was central both to the formation of individuals who identified themselves as 'New Women' and to the collective meanings of the term. This position is shared by modern critics like Kate Flint for whom: 'New Woman fiction may be said to have created a community of women readers who could refer to these works as proof of their psychological, social and ideological difference from men' (Flint 1993: 305). Lyn Pykett points out that writers like Grand came themselves to represent the New Woman for their readers, a shift made possible because the printed word was perceived as at the centre of the political struggle over gender relations (Pykett 1992: 177).

The debate about the New Woman Fiction was crucial to the larger question of the place of print in the politics of gender formation. Fiction became a metonym for the whole range of linguistic practices at work in the culture of print. This was not only a matter of content but of how print worked to create gendered selves and of how gender entered the forms and institutions of print. Contemporary and recent critics have ensured that this dynamic has been much discussed, but very rarely in that discussion has the periodical been regarded as a text in its own right. Yet the periodical, encompassing as it did a range of positions and almost all the genres in which the debate was conducted, was the crucial site for the debate around the meaning of gender, sexuality and their relationship. In it, articles appeared next to serialised novels. Reviews, news reports, caricatures and sketches, jokes and competitions, short stories, interviews and potted biographies, readers' letters and even advertisements were all deployed to define the femininity which New Women brought into question.

In that process women were actively engaged, not only in defining themselves, but in shaping the press, as it went through its own late Victorian crisis. The forms of journalism which were put into place in these decades not only defined femininity but were defined by it. The new press came to be associated with a range of characteristics which were traditionally 'feminine', especially its tendency towards sensation and the personalising of information.

The new press also defined women as central to its readership, both in general publications and through the development of an extensive sub-genre of specifically targeted journals. It was in these decades that the 'woman's magazine' assumed the important place in publishing which it still has. These new magazines were in large part concerned with asserting 'True Woman' against the various deviant femininities subsumed under the labels 'new' or 'modern'. However, the Truth of femininity proved difficult to pin down in these simple oppositions.

THE NEW PRESS AS DEMOCRATIC

But we have to consider the new voters, the *democracy*, as people are fond of calling them. They have many merits, but among them is not that of being, in general, reasonable persons who think fairly and seriously. We have had opportunities of observing a New Journalism which a clever and energetic man has lately invented. It has much to recommend it; it is full of ability, novelty, variety, sensation, sympathy, generous instincts; its one great fault is that it is featherbrained.

(Matthew Arnold, 'Up to Easter', *Nineteenth Century* May 1887: 638–9)

Matthew Arnold is usually credited with inventing the term 'New Journalism' and making its 'virtues and vices . . . the topic of the town' (Schults 1972: 30). As the New Woman existed only in relation to an implied 'true' woman, so Arnold constructed the New Journalism round a set of implicit oppositions. Persons and journalism which were 'reasonable' 'fair' and 'serious' were set against the unreasonable masses, the new 'democracy' with a press appropriate to it. If contemporary society was poised between 'Culture and Anarchy', as Arnold had argued, then it was clear on which side New Journalism lay. The class element in this analysis was explicit. It is also significant that the phrase 'New Journalism' was coined in an article on Ireland, England's oldest colony, and that the opposition of 'reasonable' against 'featherbrained' implicitly mobilised the vocabulary of gendered identity. Arnold assumed as his norm the English male middle-class reader to whom the New Press represented those 'others' against whom he must define himself.

The meanings of 'New Journalism', like New Woman, were plural and contested. A month before Arnold's article appeared, the *Saturday Review* defined 'New Journalists' as products of improved print technology and increased finance (Brake 1994: 96). However, Arnold's situating it in the context of the 'new democracy' was to inform discussion of the press down to Richard Altick's still definitive study of the *English Common Reader* (Altick 1957: e.g. 376). Whether they shared Arnold's pessimism or not, contemporaries agreed that a new press was coming into being with a readership that extended down the social scale as never before and they assumed these new readers were products of the 1870 Education Act which provided for the first time a comprehensive system of primary education in England.

Newnes, whose magazine *Tit-Bits* pioneered the New Journalism, explained its success in precisely these terms:

The demand for cheap, light literature was at that time steadily and rapidly increasing. The Compulsory Education Act of 1870 had been in force for some ten years. There were no illiterates among the growing generation.

(Friederichs 1911: 51)

George Gissing's novel *New Grub Street* satirised this New publisher through his character Whelpdale, whose idea was a paper:

> [which would] address itself to the quarter-educated . . . the new generation that is being turned out by the Board Schools . . . . People of this kind want something to occupy them in trains and on buses and trams . . . what they want is the lightest and frothiest of chit-chatty information – bits of scandal, bits of description, bits of jokes, bits of statistics, bits of foolery.

(Gissing 1891/1968: 496–7)

But Walter Besant, journalist, novelist and founder of the Society of Authors, welcomed it:

> . . . reading, which has always been the amusement of the cultivated class, has now become the principal amusement of every class, all along the line from the peer to the chimney sweep we are reading. Some of us are said to be reading rubbish. That may be but it is better to be reading rubbish than to be drinking in bars and playing with street rowdies.

(Besant 1899: 79)

All the evidence suggests that literacy did not rise suddenly and uniformly after the 1870 Act but slowly with regional and gender variations throughout the century (Vincent 1989). Nor were the innovations in print as radical and sudden as these contemporary accounts imply. However, as with 'Woman', so with 'Press', the term 'New' usefully indicates the distance from the 1840s and 1850s. Crucially the concept produced the press it described. Newnes and other publishers helped to create the new reading public by affirming its existence through magazines like *Tit-Bits* and papers like the *Pall Mall Gazette* and the halfpenny *Mail* (Altick 1957: 355, 396).

The nature of the readership of the new press was also more complex than contemporaries allowed. The idea that its crucial marks were cheapness and the inclusion of the lowest in society, the metaphoric chimney-sweep, were particularly reductive. Although hundreds of penny and halfpenny publications extended the periodical to new groups, surveys by Charles Booth in London made clear that a third of the population remained throughout this period in poverty so absolute that even a regular penny was beyond their means (Fried 1969). At tuppence a week, *Tit-Bits'* regular readers were almost certainly shop assistants, office workers (including the women 'type-writers') and other members of the expanding lower middle class, the suburbanites whose growth in numbers and in collective spending power made them an obvious market (Flint 1986). Sixpenny 'New Journalistic' publications which claimed a mass readership were clearly not aiming at a working-class market and even penny magazines like *Woman* were largely targeting the middle class.

120

New Journalism was, therefore, both less and more extensive than Besant and Gissing argued. There were still those excluded as readers – particularly working-class women, who even in the early twentieth century had less time, money and leisure than their men to give to reading (Lady Bell 1907: 207, 236–7). They may have been literate. This did not mean they had the material and cultural space in which to become regular periodical readers, let alone purchasers. The new press encompassed more, however, than cheap papers for the working class. It was also and crucially about changes in lower middle and middle-class reading. The greatest demand for periodicals still came from these groups, who had relatively more to spend on non-essentials than in the 1870s and were also more likely to be travelling to and from work as 'commuters', a term newly imported from America. The railway libraries of mid-century had been aimed at those going on long train journeys. The magazines and papers of the 1880s and 1890s were often designed to be read on the short daily journey to and from work by train or tram for which the tit-bit was the ideal form.

Contemporary anxiety that these developments would mean the whole press was reduced to the type of the lowest was also misplaced. Though there were strong pressures towards formula writing and homogeneity these were countered by an equally powerful trend towards increasing diversification and specialisation within an already multi-layered press. Whole sub-genres developed with different readerships, style and subject matter. The sporting papers proliferated into specialist journals on football, cycling and fishing while serious journals like the *Academy* had new rivals in specialist publications, like *Mind* (begun in 1876) or the *English Historical Review* (launched 1886). Against the democratising trend appeared a rash of magazines for the Upper Ten Thousand, including some of the ladies' papers discussed in the last chapter. It was also in this period that the avant-garde 'little magazine' was established as a periodical genre. Proudly anti-democratic, the *Yellow Book* and the *Savoy* depended on the technology and used some of the devices which characterised popular middle-class print. Yellow press and *Yellow Book* were connected as aspects of that diversification of the market, which, more than a thoroughgoing democratisation or standardisation, characterised the New Journalism (Mix 1960; Stokes 1989).

DEMOCRATISATION AND GENDER

The discourse of class was explicit in the debates on popular print. Anxiety about women's reading was equally persistent but more diffused.[7] It erupted in the 1890s in a furious debate precipitated by the novelist George Moore on whether the sexually ignorant young girl must continue to be, as she had been for decades, the implied reader of British fiction. This in turn fed into the debate on sexuality and the New Fiction and also precipitated the collapse in the mid-1890s of the whole Victorian structure of fiction publication and regulation by the libraries (Grierst 1970: 120ff; Moore 1885).

In contrast to the critics, the new print entrepreneurs made the woman reader rather than the chimney-sweep the signifier of their democratic readership. Harmsworth, the future Lord Northcliffe, identified 'woman appeal' as crucial to the New Journalism (Clarke 1950: 84; Pound and Harmsworth 1959: 200, 202). Newnes, in a revealing narrative of origins, described how the idea for *Tit-Bits* came to him as he read 'tit-bits' from the newspaper aloud to his wife over the tea table (Friederichs 1911: 55). Her pleasure inspired him to create a paper designed for her consisting only of such tit-bits. The woman at home as type and symbol of the periodical reader was in itself not new, as I have argued, but in the New Journalism she assumed a new importance.

First of all, the woman reader was identified as an important consumer of the general periodical, even the newspaper. When Harmsworth's *Daily Mail* began in 1896 he specifically identified 'movements in women's worlds – that is changes in dress, toilet matters, cookery and home matters generally' as essential to the new kind of daily paper (Pound and Harmsworth 1959: 175, 200). Of course, these were confined to 'the ladies' page' and elsewhere in these papers ridicule was lavished on any other kind of 'Women's Movement' (March-Phillips 1895: 186).

Second, and significantly for this study, Harmsworth put magazines specifically for women at the forefront of his publishing business and his major rivals, Newnes and Pearson, followed him. It was in this period that magazines for women moved to the place they have ever since occupied at the centre of popular publishing. Between 1880 and 1900 I have been able to identify over 120 new magazines for women. Many were short-lived but some, like the penny domestic magazines *Home Notes* and *Home Chat*, survived until the mid-twentieth century, material evidence of a continuous publishing tradition extending from the New Journalism to the present.

In women's publishing, as in the general press, New Journalism meant diversity not just cheapness. The category 'woman' was itself divided into 'mothers', 'girls', 'fashionables', 'women at home', 'ladies' and so on. What united this diversified readership – with the exception of the radical periodicals which I discuss in Chapter 11 – was a femininity defined implicitly in opposition to the New Woman. Harmsworth's positioning of woman 'at the heart' of popular reading mobilised the crucial metaphor of domestic femininity within the New Journalism. Likewise Newnes's story of the origin of *Tit-Bits* assumed the woman at home whose knowledge and pleasure was controlled by her husband. The definition of this true woman was itself continually fractured and in the making however, a process which shaped the women's commercial press in ways I map out in the following chapters.

TECHNOLOGY, THE PRESS AND THE MARKET

New Journalism was defined importantly but not solely by readership. As the *Saturday Review* had pointed out in 1887, it was improvements in the technology of print production and changes in the financing of the industry which made possible the increased scale of the New Journalism (*Sat.* LXIII 1887: 578–9; Brake 1994: 97). Here again, there was no sudden increase in growth or efficiency but at every level of the production process – print, paper-making and techniques of illustration – mechanisation enabled the mass press to flourish. Crucially important were the technology for using woodpulp, which made available the cheap paper sources necessary for mass production, and the rapid development in the 1880s and 1890s of processes for reproducing photographs, especially the half-tone block (Plant 1974: 190–205; 318–19).[8]

The general economic trend towards large businesses with ready access to capital was evident also in publishing where the periodical press began to be dominated by a few large firms. Newnes, Harmsworth and Pearson were the first of the 'press barons' each of whom owned multiple titles and financed them not through joint-stock companies but by flotation on the stock exchange.[9] Family-run and small private companies continued to exist but the 'Northcliffe revolution' was overtaking them.

These 'new' publishers deployed publicity stunts, prizes and free offers on a scale which publishers like Beeton could only have imagined. Newnes, for example, offered free death insurance for anyone killed in an accident who had a copy of *Tit-Bits* on them (Pound 1966: 24). But the key to the new finance was the systematic development of advertising as a source of revenue. Newnes and Harmsworth, although reluctant at first, quickly realised the importance of integrating advertising into their empires at both an organisational and textual level (Pound and Harmsworth 1959: 259; Friederichs 1911: 84–5). Advertising managers were appointed to the publishing staff and – a crucial move in the development of the modern industry – properly vetted circulation figures were produced in a bid to attract advertisers (Williams 1961: 223–4).

Finally, the New Journalism produced and was produced by new patterns of working. The establishment of the Publishers' Association, the Society of Authors and the Booksellers' Association in the 1880s and the 1890s marked a crucial moment in the long process of professionalisation and specialisation of this industry (Cross 1985: 204ff). At the same time, the literary agent emerged, a new figure in the literary market. These processes were not confined to the periodical press but that press was central to the revolution in print production which Gissing described so bitterly in *New Grub Street*.

THE NEW JOURNALISM AND THE 'FEMINISATION' OF THE PRESS

The tendency towards the 'tit-bit' rather than the extended article was invoked in these debates as evidence that the new readership was 'quarter-educated', incapable of sustained attention. However, the '2-inch' article was only one element in the set of formal and textual qualities which defined the new press and which Arnold had addressed.

Crucially, the new press was visually more exciting. Tit-bitty journalism broke up the columns of the printed page but this was even more dramatically the effect of increasing use of headlines and cross headings (Lee 1976: 121). Above all, the new technology for picture reproduction made it possible to provide good quality illustrations more cheaply than ever before and lavish use of illustration became a hallmark of the new press. When Newnes entered the sixpenny magazine market in 1892 with the *Strand Magazine* he envisaged 'a picture on every page' or at least every double spread, making established sixpenny monthlies which had no illustrations look dowdy by comparison (Cross 1985: 209; Pound 1966: 30; Shorter 1899).

Second, the New Journalism stressed what came to be called 'human interest', an emphasis evident in every aspect (Lee 1976: 121; O'Connor 1889: 423). The new periodical typically represented itself as the readers' friend rather than mentor, cultivating an intimate rather than authoritative tone. The tendency was towards a style which if not always chatty was certainly closer to that of conversation than had been the case in most mid-Victorian journalism (Lee 1976: 130). In its reporting, it emphasised the personal angle. The genre which it was credited with inventing was the interview. This combined elements of those well-established journalistic genres, the reported public speech and the potted biography, but, unlike these, it personalised both parties involved, the public figure being interviewed and the journalist/interviewer (Schults 1972: 61–5). It is not surprising that another genre which became popular at this time was the gossip column, or *causerie*. All these contributed to produce a press which represented itself as the site for the exchange of personal views, gossip or 'chat' rather than, or as well as, impersonal judgement.

As with other aspects called 'new', much of this long pre-dated the 1880s. However, as with the changes to the look of the page, there was a shift in gear, a new concentration of these tendencies in the rapidly growing popular press of the 1880s and 1890s. The sense of this as a radical break from the past was also related to the third characteristic which was attributed to the New Journalism by Arnold and others, namely its 'sensationalism'.

The specific charge of 'sensationalism' was provoked by W.T. Stead, the 'clever and energetic man' Arnold credited with inventing the New Journalism. Stead brought to the *Pall Mall Gazette*, which he joined in 1880, a commitment to campaigning journalism on behalf of those he perceived as disadvantaged (Schults 1972: 20ff). His ideal of a democratic press therefore went beyond simply providing reading for a wide public. His tactics were designed to shock his readers into awareness and to that end he employed all the devices which came to signify the New Journalism: the emotive headline, the cross headings and the interview – whose use he pioneered in British papers.

Stead was in a well-established tradition of British journalism going back to the

Chartist, G.M.W. Reynolds, in which sensationalism was linked to social and political radicalism. Stead's most notorious campaign, the 'Maiden Tribute of Babylon', on the prostitution of young girls in London, scandalised readers because Stead personalised the story in the most dramatic way by describing how he had bought a girl of 13 and taken her to a brothel. 'Sex' had long been a journalistic staple. Stead not only brought it into a 'respectable' middle-class paper. He made it central to journalism as political intervention. The Criminal Law Amendment Act, which its supporters saw as a measure to protect young working-class women against the predatory upper-class male, was being blocked by a Parliament consisting of precisely those men the Bill was designed to control. In re-working the journalistic traditions of sensationalism, Stead was involved both in redefining the role of the journal as social agent and in that redefinition of sexuality as a social/political issue which characterised the 1880s and crystallised in the passing of the Act (Gorham 1982; Walkowitz 1994).

The scandal of sensation as a quality of the New Journalism was part of a larger debate in which 'sensationalism' was linked either with the working class or with women. Both these groups lacked the objectivity and cool rationality of the middle-class male reader. The 'sensationalist' Sunday papers and cheap serialised fiction which had been available to the working class since the 1840s had been consistently defined as potentially dangerous. The novels which earned this title in the 1860s came to be defined as a sub-genre dominated by women writers and largely read by women (Flint 1993: 274–93; Helsinger *et al.* 1983 II: 111ff; Pykett 1992). 'Sensation' as a quality of literature was, therefore, a term loaded with meanings related to both class and gender. Much of the anxiety about the New Journalism centred on the fear that those characteristics associated with working-class reading would become general. Implicit was a related fear of another kind of deviant reading, that of the feminine. The description of the New Journalism as 'sensational' mobilised these anxieties as well as those around sexuality.

THE FEMINISATION OF THE PRESS

Arnold's account of it endowed the new democratic press with characteristics which were implicitly feminine both in its ambiguously good qualities – sensation, sympathy and generous instincts – and its clearly bad – being featherbrained. His argument about the erosion of standards and values explicitly invoked discussion of class but it was saturated with anxiety about the instability of the 'masculine' virtues of reason, detachment and seriousness. It was the feminisation of the press which Arnold feared as much as its democratisation.[10]

In some respects these fears were ill-founded. What is striking in reading the cheap press of the period, particularly that for women, is how determinedly unsensational it was. The new entrepreneurs of print were well aware of these anxieties associated with cheap print and consistently claimed that they were providing 'healthy' reading for the masses. Newnes shared Stead's Non-conformist Christianity but insisted that his secular mission was to provide anti-sensational papers, '"as clean as a new pin with stories as witty and humorous and brilliant as those unclean minds could invent" which were even then blighting the morals of the people' (Friederichs 1911: 54). Those who read a 'sex connotation' in the title *Tit-Bits* were angrily rebuked and, however trivial, the magazine was certainly not 'sensational' in any sense (Pound 1966: 21). Likewise, the penny magazines for women which I discuss in Chapters 12 and 13 were determinedly domestic and less sensationalist than the older-style fiction serials aimed at women.

However, the idea of 'feminisation' can still be usefully applied to New Journalism. Insofar as it stressed feeling rather than reason, the personal rather than the authoritative tone, the private or 'human' interest of its stories as against their public aspect, that press was indeed defined by features coded 'feminine' rather than 'masculine'. Likewise those changes concerned with lay-out and use of illustration worked not just to change the look of the periodical press but also to make the way it looked more important. Since femininity was always located in and defined by appearance, as masculinity was not, the stress on the visual character of the periodical was a further 'feminisation'. Moreover, the increasing visual importance of advertisement also located the reader as a consumer of commodities rather than as a worker or producer and one therefore with implicitly feminine characteristics.

The consolidation of a diverse but recognisable women's press and the general shift in the characteristics of the periodical, were not absolutely distinct. Just as women's papers were ensured a central place in the big new publishing houses, so they were a crucial nursery and testing ground for the development of the New Journalistic devices and qualities. The chatty tone, the tit-bitty article, the gossip column, the stress on illustration were all already well developed in that tradition of journalism which had defined its readers by their femininity and which now moved towards the centre of the New Journalism. Of course, these qualities of the new press which I have described as 'feminine' were sometimes associated also with other marginalised groups. Gossip, as Eve Kosofsky Sedgewick has pointed out, has culturally been associated with servants and gay men as well as women (Sedgewick 1991: 247). The construction of certain qualities as 'feminine' is part of the larger process of keeping cultural difference in place and is itself not stable.

During the period of the New Journalism, when the relationship between gender and sexuality was in crisis, the development of a 'feminised press' offered a threat to the norms of masculine reading but also the potential for some play, some exploration, in the gap between gender and the embodied, sexual self. In particular it opened up the possibility that the 'feminine' qualities of feeling, interest in appearance and the personalised appropriation of news which is called 'gossip' might become coded as 'human' and therefore also available to men. Individuals negotiated that process as they could, whether as writers or readers but always within unequal power relations in which not only was heterosexuality the norm but men relatively still had more power than women.

NEW GRUB STREET

The developments in the periodical press which I describe contributed crucially to the rise in numbers and in status of those who lived by writing. After a decade on decade increase, there were still only 11,000 'authors, editors and journalists' recorded in the 1901 census (Gross 1969: 220) but this could be doubled if one included the 'clergymen, lecturers, teachers of all kinds, lawyers, doctors, men in every branch of science, artists of all kinds, all of whom produce literary work' (Besant 1899: 1). Unlike other professions, new and old, which regulated their access, writing offered opportunities for the gifted amateur who might – with luck and practice – acquire full-time work. Arnold Bennett's career was paradigmatic. As an aspiring writer, he moved to London and sold odd pieces to the papers before escaping from his clerical job by persuading his father to buy him onto the editorial staff of a small women's magazine. Editing and writing for a range of papers while he produced novels, enabled him eventually to live as a freelance and concentrate on novel writing (Drabble 1975). The Berne Convention of 1885 and the American Copyright Law of 1891 ensured that writers like Bennett could claim copyright on books and articles reproduced outside Britain and so consolidate their earnings in an international market (Cross 1985: 210). The possibility for this kind of move from lower middle-class provincial life into metropolitan professionalism – even the international yacht set – made writing especially attractive to those whose gender, class or lack of formal education made access to other professions impossible.

But this same ease of access did little to enhance the status of writing as a profession, however much Walter Besant argued that writers were not mad geniuses but regular bourgeois: '[This modern man of letters] of whom there are many – or this woman, for many women now belong to the profession – goes into his study every morning as regularly as a barrister goes to chambers' (Besant 1899: 24). The creation of the Society of Authors in the 1890s with Walter Besant as its spokesman marked a new phase in the long and contested process by which writing became professionalised.

New Journalism not only provided the journalist/writer with the material basis for his recognition as a professional, it produced him discursively as a public figure, the prototype of the media personality. The early and mid-century traditions of anonymous journalism had been gradually eroded and by the 1890s the use of by-lines had become an element in the competition for readers except in newspapers. Cassells, for example, abandoned editorial anonymity when Oscar Wilde took over the editorship of their magazine, *Lady's World* in 1885 (Brake 1994: 128). The creation of stars, which characterised that other late nineteenth-century popular medium, the music hall, began more hesitantly in the press but celebrity interviews, portraits of writers and pictures of their 'homes' were soon a staple of the magazines.

The culture of the periodical press had always been narcissistic. Every publication relied on others for copy, either directly through the 'scissors and paste' method by which much provincial journalism was said to survive, or indirectly as one paper commented on or attacked another. New Journalism developed this self-referentiality. Periodicals reviewed each other, ran literary gossip columns and employed writers to interview each other. The 'Revolt of the Daughters' which I discuss in the next chapter began as a single article in the *Nineteenth Century* and was taken up and commented on in the search for good copy. The chatty column or *causerie*, which became popular in the 1880s, not only centred round a named writer as personality, but was inevitably biased towards the journalistic world with which the writer was familiar.

At one level Besant was right to argue that women were taking their place in this new professional world, a process signalled by the establishment of the Institute of Women Journalists in 1895. Women's magazines and papers routinely used female by-lines and built advertising campaigns around the name of female writers. *Causeries* and advice columns – even whole journals – were constructed round a named feminine persona, a practice 'Myra' Browne had pioneered with *Myra's Journal* and *Sylvia's Journal.* Pearson developed a series of magazines linked to 'Isabel' and one of the most popular middle-class magazine launched in the 1890s, *Woman at Home* was associated with the romantic novelist, Annie S. Swan. A handful of women journalists, including Mrs M. Beeton and Mrs Talbot Coke, Ada Ballin, L.T. Meade and – of course – Eliza Lynn Linton appeared again and again in different journals.

Yet these developments were always mediated through a gender politics of which Besant himself was representative. His assurance that women, too, could now be 'Men of Letters' failed to recognise how completely the role of writer – whether as 'genius' or as professional – was masculinised. Andrew Lang, the arch-professional journalist of the era, used his *Longman's* column to reproduce in print the masculine mateyness of the gentleman's clubs to which no woman could belong. Besant's own dystopic fantasy, *The Revolt of Man* (1882b) articulated an explicit hostility to the idea of a feminine society.

The ambiguity of the new professionalism for women was constantly evident in the illustrated interviews with women writers. This new journalistic genre became a staple of women's papers, where it merged with the long-established tradition of illustrated biography of a 'notable woman'. *Woman*, the penny paper, ran a series on lady editors in 1898 while the expensive the *Lady's Pictorial* and the *Gentlewoman* ran several on women writers (e.g. *W.* 25 Jan. 1898: 15; 22 Feb. 1898: 15; 20 April 1898: 15; 10 August 1898: 12). These consistently stressed the *womanliness* which marked even 'advanced' writers and New Women. Sarah Grand, whose novels dealt with the double sexual standard and venereal disease appeared in the *Lady's Pictorial* as

> slight and girlish in figure; the face a pure oval [with] . . . a broad, low brow, indicating spirituality and intellect; a complexion of a delicate colouring; large grey eyes that seem to deepen in hue while she talks; a serious, some-what sad expression [and] a smile of winning sweetness.
>
> (Black 1906: 321–2)

Besides, Grand was not 'too much "cultivated" to neglect such an important matter [as dress . . . and] has a very pretty taste of her own' as well as being in demand to advise friends on 'this or that gown, hat, fold or trimming' (ibid.: 322, 327).

The process of representing the writing woman as essentially feminine rather than professional, involved elisions and silences. The interview with Eliza Lynn Linton, which opened the series, not only produced her as tender, kindly and an excellent needlewoman, it also allowed her unhappy marriage and separation from her husband to disappear in the middle of a sentence: 'In 1858 the young writer married Mr. Linton, the well-known wood engraver, and in 1861 began again the interrupted series of fifteen novels . . .' (ibid.: 4). By obscuring the link between the breakdown of her marriage and her return to writing, the article obscured the common pattern of women writers' experience, that when their husbands died, or deserted, became bankrupt, ill, alcoholic or were simply incompatible, they took up the masculine role of breadwinner – as did Mrs Oliphant, Mrs Linnaeus Banks and Mrs Henry Wood as well as Eliza Lynn Linton (Cross 1985: 164ff; Mumm 1990).

The gap between the reader and the 'notable' subject of the article was bridged by the technique of the personal interview which promised to give readers direct access to the secret self of the interviewee, and by the emphasis on a femininity shared by the reader and the 'writer' – both as interviewer and subject of the interview. It is no wonder that writing for the press seemed to offer readers of these periodicals a way of solving the endemic problem of how to be economically independent *and* womanly.

However, contemporary women who sought to emulate Arnold Bennett's career were unlikely to be as successful. Certainly there was demand for writing by women but at least in part this was because editors paid them less well than men (Drabble 1975: 58; Smith 1900). While New Journalism did open up some jobs for women, particularly in the women's press, few could expect to be bought into an editorial position by their fathers as Bennett had been. The rapid growth in the women's press did not produce proportional editorial opportunities for women since most such magazines, including some purporting to be edited by women, were edited by men (March-Phillips 1894; see also pp. 188–9).

The creation of a feminised space in the press and particularly in the women's magazines opened up new opportunities but by no means only or mainly to women. Professionally it benefited men more than women. In the context of that gender disruption and re-inscription which I have described, some men were even able to use this space to explore questions of sex/gender identity. Oscar Wilde used his brief time as editor of *Woman's World* to question the gendering of femininity but also of masculinity (Brake 1994: 127ff). The male editors of *Woman* whom I discuss in Chapter 12 were not Decadents but they used female pseudonyms in a kind of journalistic cross-dressing. Writers on 'New Woman Fiction' have debated the anomaly that its production came to be dominated by men and that, while women like Sarah Grand or George Egerton were hailed at the time, it is Hardy,

James and Gissing who have remained in the literary canon. The question of literary value is not at issue. What is at stake is the way in which the gender instability of the *fin de siècle* gave even greater freedom to men exploring gender identity than it gave to women.

At the same time the institutions which governed access to print, the growth of professionalisation in journalism, the work of readers and agents in publishing houses, worked to privilege men as a group as against women (Tuchman and Fortin 1989). The process I have described as the feminisation of the press did produce new ways of writing and reading gendered identity in the 1880s and 1890s but economic and editorial power was still retained almost entirely by metropolitan, middle-class men and in this respect the New Journalism was the Old Journalism writ large.

9

REVOLTING DAUGHTERS, GIRTON GIRLS AND ADVANCED WOMEN

The true Advanced Woman is not at all that latch-key licensed, tobacco-tainted, gala contaminated Frankenstein, which . . . strides up and down the pages of modern literature. The veritable Advanced Woman is she who, pressed by necessity or touched by the conviction that to be a drone in a hive of workers . . . is unworthy, has bravely precipitated herself out of a pink miasma of sloth and stagnation into the wholesome daylight of self-dependence and effort.

(Dr Arabella Kenealy, *Idler*, IX 1894, 'Advanced Woman Number': 209)

Let women become senior wranglers, lawyers, doctors, anything they please as long as they remain mothers.

('The New Womanhood', Richard le Galienne,
Woman Literary Supplement, 1894:1)

The position of the woman writer has to be understood in the context of the demand for access to paid work which was a persistent theme of women and their magazines in the 1880s and 1890s (*W. at H.* V 1895–6: 67, 546–8 and passim). The demand was usually born of necessity. However, it was also born of the belief that work was a confirmation or even a creation of the self, and their exclusion from it deprived women of the potential for self-realisation. In seeking work which would be both economically rewarding and meaningful, women of the 1880s and 1890s unsettled not only the gendering of public and private politics but a gendered economic theory and practice.

The construction of paid work in terms of 'self-dependence and effort' was explicitly masculine and middle class. Throughout the century the idea of 'vocation' had distinguished bourgeois employment from the necessary labour of the 'working' class which encompassed women's work as well as men's. It was middle-class women for whom access to paid work was a radical demand. New Women sought to re-work or, in Foucauldian terms, to 'reverse' the discourse of vocation to make it gender-neutral in the same way as they sought to redefine 'citizenship'.

The radical implications of this unsettling of gender roles were recognised by at least one contemporary theorist, Thorstein Veblen in his *The Theory of the Leisure*

Class (1899/1970). Like the socialist theorists, Engels and Bebel, whose work was being translated into English and circulated in these decades, Veblen posited gender as the basis of the first class division. Unlike Engels he saw consumption, rather than production as the crucial marker of class. Veblen, therefore, deplored contemporary attempts to disrupt the economic division which prescribed women's role as that of 'conspicuous consumption' (Veblen 1899/1970).

Journalistic and fictional explorations of women's demands for 'self-dependence' and work were imbued with a different and specifically sexual anxiety. The absolute correlation of gender and sexuality meant that the powerful binary oppositions which linked masculinity with activity/production and femininity with passivity/consumption worked across the categories of the economic and the sexual. Women's claim to the 'masculine' roles of breadwinner and independent self therefore threatened not only men's economic power but their sexuality. This anxiety was evident not only in cartoons and jokes about mannish women but in New Journalistic symposia and in serious novels like Gissing's *Odd Women*, which made a devastating critique of the way economic dependence destroyed women but pathologised the aptly named protagonist, Rhodda Nunn (Gissing 1893; see also *Punch* 24 Feb. 1894: 90; 28 April 1894: 94–5; *W. Lit. Supp.* 'The New Womanhood' 1894; Gardner and Rutherford 1992: 1–7; Showalter 1991: 23–4).

The woman writer became a signifier of these threats to male sexual/gender identity as is clear in a Special Number on 'The Advanced Woman' in the *Idler*, a sixpenny weekly with an implicitly male readership. The demand for employment from advanced women posed a particular threat to such self-identified 'Idlers', who refused the masculine role of work for the print equivalent of a gentleman's club. The Special Issue made explicit that it was men's power in heterosexual relationships, symbolised by 'courtship' which was threatened by such demands (*Id.* IX 1894: 192–211). The discussion was framed on one side by one of Aubrey Beardsley's elegantly ambiguous female figures but on the other by a crudely drawn illustration of a tiny 'Man of the Future' crying 'I will be Good' as he cowers before the gigantic 'Advanced Women Writers' wielding their books (Figures 9.1, 9.2).

In the magazines which identified their readers as women, the figure of the Advanced Woman Writer was also a signifier of the instability of gender relations but she was a much smaller and less coherent figure. In *Woman at Home*, for example, Annie Swan regularly reported receiving letters from women 'trained to nothing in particular' asking how they could become independent. Some she dismissed as 'young ladies living in affluent homes asking how to earn pocket money or . . . simply asking for occupation to help them kill time'. Most, however, were 'sad cases of lonely women utterly unprovided for' (*W. at H.* V 1895–6: 546–8).

For many of them the professional woman writer was a figure of hope, the fantasised solution to the contradictions of a femininity predicated on the male breadwinner but which often left women 'utterly unprovided for' (ibid. and see Ch. 11). This, far more than the demand for access to political power or an end to

Figure 9.1 'The Man of the Future' from the *Idler* (IX 1894: 212)

the double sexual standard, disrupted the traditional femininity of the commercial women's magazines in the 1880s and 1890s.

In seeking to accommodate it, magazines re-worked their traditional strategy for dealing with female sexuality and gender contradiction, that is through displacement onto the young woman and the project of her education in control – of self and household. But in the 1880s and 1890s, the figure of the 'girl' acquired new meanings both within the magazine and in the wider culture. In the rest of this chapter I explore some of the 'girls' who appeared in the women's popular press, each marking a different line of fracture in the project of defining femininity exclusively in terms of the control of 'spending', both economic and sexual.[1]

133

How to Court the "Advanced Woman."

THE IDLER'S CLUB.

AUBREY BEARDSLEY

THE DEVELOPMENT OF THE "EMANCIPATED."

ANGUS EVAN ABBOTT.

THE development of the Emancipated Woman has been a gradual development, and, step by step, as emancipation has proceeded on its way to consummation, the conditions of courtship have undergone proportionate change. Looking into the subject, it will be found that originally women were Spoil. In earliest days, Man went courting with a club. He thirled the wood, and lurked in ambush

Figure 9.2 'How to Court the "Advanced Woman"' from the *Idler* (IX 1894: 192)

REVOLTING DAUGHTERS AND GIRTON GIRLS

> The rights of women what are they?
> The right to labour and to pray
> The right to watch while others sleep,
> The right o'er others' woes to weep . . .
> (Dr Kirton, *Happy Homes and How*
> *to Make Them*, 1882 edition)

The argument that met demands for women's social and economic rights with discussion of their moral responsibilities continued into the era of the New Woman and beyond. In seeking self-development and independence, therefore, women tried to capture the moral high ground on which femininity had been stranded by evangelicalism and to renegotiate the gendering of different moral qualities. If work and self-development were good for men, they must also be good for women and, by the same token, chastity and unselfishness were qualities to which men should aspire.

In 1894 this argument was re-worked in the press around yet another deviant female figure. When the *Nineteenth Century* ran an article by Mrs Crackenthorpe called 'The Revolt of the Daughters' it launched a journalistic catch-phrase. Mrs Crackenthorpe, whose article was sympathetic to the demands of young women for self-development, came to regret her title which was made the basis of the hostile tag 'Revolting Daughters'. Nevertheless, unlike the 'Shrieking Sisterhood' or the 'Girl of the Period', some young women publicly identified themselves with the idea of 'revolt' (*19th C.* XXX 1891: 455ff; *19th C.* XXXV 1894: 23ff, 424ff, 449ff; *W.* 24 Jan. 1894: 5; 28 Feb. 1894: 3 and 4, etc.). These 'Revolting Daughters' argued that the young woman of the middle and upper middle classes should be treated like her brother in terms of access to education and work. This did not mean she wanted to be like a man. On the contrary, she wanted

> her right to individual development, not merely for her own welfare and enjoyment or for that of her family but chiefly that she may become a more perfect instrument to perform her allotted part in the world's work.
>
> (*19th C.* XXXV 1894: 449)

Middle- and upper-class women's periodicals had, of course, sought to educate the daughters ever since the *Lady's Magazine* had represented itself leading young ladies away from the Temple of Folly. Such journals, up to and including the era of the 'Revolting Daughters', repeated Hannah More's attack on an education in mere 'accomplishments' but what should replace or complement 'accomplishments' was not so easily agreed (*EDM* I 1852: 2–3; More 1834; *19th C.* XXXV 1894: 424). As this book has made clear, women's education as good wives and mothers was harnessed to different ideas of family and the home, and could include self-development, involving serious reading. Ironically, More's demands that girls' education be taken seriously was potentially consistent with the establishment of the academic schools for girls of the mid-century and even the entry of women into higher education.

135

Nevertheless, the Revolting Daughters' appeal to self-development was perceived as a threat to woman's role as self-denying wives and mothers. 'Does Marriage Hinder a Woman's Self-Development?' asked the *Lady's Realm* in one of those symposia so beloved of 1890s magazine editors. Mona Caird was not alone in arguing that it did.[2] The complexities of this debate were focused in the late nineteenth-century popular imagination around some simple oppositions. Against the ideal of education for feminine dependence was posed the demand for access to the universities. The undergraduate woman acquired a symbolic power at odds with her statistical significance since higher education was only available to a tiny handful of mainly upper middle-class women by 1900 (Vicinus 1985: 127).

Among the female figures who appeared in the late nineteenth-century press as a symbol of the 'new' therefore was 'the Girton Girl'. Like the pun on 'Revolting Daughter', its alliteration no doubt gave it journalistic appeal, just as the visual image of the begowned woman became the object of satire in periodicals like the *Idler*. Annie Edwards's book, *A Girton Girl*, included the term but Grant Allen's *The Woman Who Did* was perhaps the most notorious fictional product of Girton even though she had left before taking her degree (Allen 1895).

Like the 'Revolting Daughter', whose plan to improve the world began with getting rid of the chaperone, the Girton Girl's class position made her more readily acceptable in the ladies' papers than was the suffragist.[3] The *Queen*, throughout its publishing history, not only reported progress on women's admission to higher education but as early as 1869 it welcomed the opening of the Cambridge examination to women (*Q*. XLV 1869: 191, see also 'Women at Oxford', *Q*. LXXXIII 1888: 669). Self-development, including access to higher education, was more easily accommodated with being a 'lady' than campaigning for political rights.

Even in the ladies' papers, however, 'the Girton Girl' was a deeply ambiguous figure. The *Gentlewoman*, which claimed its editor was 'an educated woman and not a milliner', carried cartoons of future women MAs and DDs (*G*. I 1891: 1, 151, 187, 223). *The Lady's* broadly sympathetic series on her 'experiences by a Girton Graduate' failed to convince its readers whose subsequent essays on girls' education stressed domestic skills and denounced higher education as 'a form of fashionable excitement' (*L*. I 1885: 184–5, 215–15, 1060–1).

In the magazines for the middle class the contested meaning of higher education for girls was worked out across the range of genres, in correspondence columns, competitions, articles and fiction. L. T. Meade's prolific contributions to such magazines were typified by a story called 'A Very Up To Date Girl' in which a Girton Girl gets into difficulties making an ill-advised solo ascent of an Alpine peak. Rescued by the Englishman whom she had dismissed as 'effeminate', she learns the limits of her education as she is clasped in his arms on the summit. The effeminate man and the graduate woman are thus restored to their proper places through the mechanism of the romance narrative.

'An Admirable Arrangement', a short story by Constance Smith, which appeared in the *Lady's Realm* for 1897, deployed the same narrative strategy to return the Girton Girl to true womanhood, that is marriage and maternity (*Wo. R.* I 1897: 76–81). A Cambridge don discovers to his alarm that the Girton graduate who is a fellow guest at a house-party has researched the primitive tribe which is his special study and produced a brilliant new theory which threatens his life-work and reputation. The threat of the Girton Girl beating the Cambridge Man at his own game is quite explicit. However, the true woman knows she is playing another game altogether. She loves and agrees to marry him on condition that her work be subsumed in the book he is writing to which only his name will be attached. As Richard le Galienne explained in yet another New Woman supplement, women might excel intellectually, even win the top award of Senior Wrangler at Cambridge, 'as long as they remained mothers' (*W.* Lit. Supp. 1894: 1).

The threat of the Girton Girl is defused here by a resolution which insists not only that the heterosexual romance is the only story for women but that heterosexual and national identity together provide the true telos of knowledge. The primitive 'other' becomes the ground for the 'Admirable Arrangement' of gender difference. 'True' femininity (and masculinity) are predicated here upon the distance of the white English middle-class subject from the 'primitive' object of knowledge. This connection between gender and national identity was central to Linton's regular column in the *Queen* in the 1890s and pervaded magazines like *Woman*, *Hearth and Home* and *Lady's Realm* in which this story appeared (*H&H* I 1891: 1; and see Ch. 12).

Favourable comments on higher education for ladies in the *Queen* remained isolated from the other models of femininity in its pages, which were themselves differentiated by distinct kinds of education/knowledge – of the heart, of manners, of taste. Stories like 'The Admirable Arrangement' suggested fictional strategies for reconciling these different and often contradictory discourses which were kept separate on the pages of the magazine and not allowed to interrogate each other directly. Readers, however, were free to ask themselves how they related to each other and to their own experience in the materiality of their lives.

GIRLS

The Girton Girl's threat to the social arrangements of gender/sex were defused in part by her class location but even more importantly by her youth. Still 'a girl', after all, her recuperation for marriage and motherhood could be readily assumed. But she was only part of a more general re-working of the concept of the 'girl' which the periodical press of the 1880s and 1890s both mediated and helped to create. Throughout the century, magazines for women had assumed that they also addressed the girl. Indeed she sometimes became a metonym for their entire readership, as in Beeton's castigation of his silly correspondents. In the 1880s and 1890s that metonymic relation began to be dissolved. 'Girls' began to be targeted as a specific readership group in their own right (Drotner 1988).

In 1868 – thirty years after Beeton launched his journal for boys – the *Young Englishwoman* (later *Sylvia's Journal*) had been launched. This owed much to the *Englishwoman's Domestic Magazine* both in its mix of contents and its elision of femininity and youth. The girls' magazines of the 1880s and 1890s, however, were pioneered by the *Girls' Own Paper* (1880–1927), a penny weekly published by the Religious Tract Society as a companion publication to their *Boys' Own Paper*. The *GOP*, as it was known, rapidly gained a circulation of 250,000 and soon outstripped the boys' paper (Forrester 1980: 14). It was followed by other papers for girls and young women including the *Young Woman* (launched 1892 as companion to the *Young Man*, with which it merged in 1915) and the *Young Gentlewoman* (1892).

The separation of girls from women readers was characteristic of the New Journalism with its ever more diversified target groups. In order to maximise sales, however, these categories were assumed to overlap. Girls' magazines also addressed other women in the household – the *GOP* was subtitled 'A Paper for Young Women and their Mothers' and magazines for women likewise continued to offer specific instruction to the young as part of their readership. The concept of the girl in the 1880s and 1890s magazines for women was thus given a more important but also a more fractured meaning. Besides the Girton Girl and the Revolting Daughter were a range of other girlhoods, very differently located, which the press simultaneously constructed and addressed: the mill-girl, the engaged girl, the working girl, the girl of the newly established Girls' Clubs, as well as the young woman interested in the traditional questions of fashion and romance. All these provided copy for the new magazines and models of femininity for new kinds of reader.

The commercial potential which the publishers recognised in the girl – however defined – was still most frequently addressed through the ideological project of education and control. However, the moral imperative of individual self-development continued to disrupt that project, as it had ever since Beeton established his prize essay-writing competitions. Prize competitions, whether for the best essay, poem, piece of needlework or portrait, were now a crucial element of the new magazines. They claimed to address the education of readers but were also, of course, central to a quite different competition between rival papers in which readers were the prize.

This double agenda produced a new kind of competition in the late century press: the 'magazine scholarship'. *Woman* was typical of these journals in that it offered educational bursaries to the girls nominated by the largest number of readers (see Ch. 12; *H&H* XVIII 1900: 21). Since a nomination paper was included in each copy of the magazine, the function of the competition as a sales booster was obvious. Editors and proprietors believed that the idea of education could be used to appeal to readers. The second and third competition for scholarships in *Woman* offered £25 for a girl to follow a commercial training. The acceptable aspect of education could thus too easily slide into the far more difficult question of how and whether girls should be trained for paid employment.

WORK: THE DILEMMA OF THE DAUGHTERS?

Throughout this period adult readers as well as Revolting Daughters asked how they could play their part 'in the world's work' and wrote to magazine columns like Annie Swan's to ask why they had been trained to 'nothing in particular' (*W. at H.* V 1855–6: 546). This question was, however, constantly recast as a young women's issue and specifically a problem about 'daughters'.

In the various 'What Shall We Do with Our Daughters' series which appeared in the woman's press in the 1890s, the mothers' dilemma centred not on their daughters' demand for intellectual independence but on their need for paid work (*LR* III 1897: 92–6, 105–6 etc.; *H&H* 1891: 223, etc.). The slipperiness of the term 'work' when applied to women remained. In 1861 the *Queen* had argued, 'Women do work (at home and in many cases at home and for a wage) but they must learn to transact business' (*Q.* I 1861: 51). The difficulties of that bracketed aside continued to disrupt the syntax of the women's magazines as they moved into the twentieth century.

These difficulties were addressed directly in the radical *English Woman's Journal* and in Emily Faithfull's *Victoria Magazine* (e.g. *EWJ* VIII 1861: 37–61, on women compositors). In their proto-feminist analyses, lack of economic rights was central to women's inequality and therefore access to paid work was crucial to any agenda of reform. Their editors, Emily Faithfull and Louisa Hubbard, also realised the potential of the periodical as a mechanism for spreading information on work for women, since it was already the medium through which workers and employers advertised for each other. The establishment of the Society for the Promotion of the Employment of Women grew directly out of the register of work in the *English Woman's Journal* (Herstein 1985: esp. 72). Faithfull's *Women and Work* in the mid-1870s and Hubbard's *Woman's Gazette* (1875–9) and *Englishwoman's Year Book* (1875–1916) provided practical information about work for lower middle-class women as part of a consistent project of analysis and reform (Rendall 1987). After 1900 a sub-genre of work-related magazines developed, stretching from the general *Women's Employment* (1900–74) to specialist journals like the *Nursing Times*, the *Business Girl* and the *Women's Farm and Garden Association*. Even when these papers were not firmly located in a feminist politics they assumed work as central to women's lives.

For Faithfull and Hubbard their own commercial success was secondary to their political campaigning. In the fully commercial women's press, the meaning of women's paid work was never located within a coherent model of the feminine. It was always marginalised by the emphasis on home as the site of true feminine labour. Nevertheless, the problem continually returned as a disruptive presence across the range of women's journals, disappearing completely only in the cheapest serials – the fantasy 'lady-land', of mill-girl fiction, whose readers most needed some escape from the work which dominated their lives.

Even in the ladies' papers, with their equation of femininity with consumption and leisure, the questions of productive work intruded. As with higher education, the *Queen* actively supported campaigns like that of Emily Faithfull to open up new kinds of paid work to women (*Q.* II 1861: 79). It advocated women's entry into male strongholds like the civil service and the factory inspectorate (*Q.* XLV 1869: 117; LXVII 1880: 2) and ran articles on women working in the new office jobs of telegrapher and short-hand typewriter (*Q.* LXXXIV 1888: 480–1). In the 1890s it began a regular series on 'Employment for Women' which in that year included typewriting and law-copying but also bee-keeping, writing, acting and being a private detective (*Q.* LXXXXIX 1891: 113, 151, 230, 399, 431, 871). 'Cassandra' in the *Gentlewoman* ran a column called quite baldly 'Money Making'. By 1900 employment for a wage was well established as a suitable subject for advice articles in the ladies' paper, constantly in tension with its other elements.

In the middle-class domestic magazines, like *Hearth and Home* and *Woman at Home*, it was frequently their readers who insisted that they deal with the problem of paid work at least in the correspondence columns. Annie Swan's readers complained constantly that their lives did not fit the models of domesticity which her magazine assumed (see Ch. 11). The heterogeneous form of the magazine had always allowed contradictory discourses to coexist. Potted biographies or illustrated interviews with women achievers were a staple of journals which defined women's work as necessarily domestic, unpaid and hidden. However, by the 1880s and 1890s demands for women's economic independence were persistent enough to threaten the dominant discourse of even the most thoroughgoing of the domestic magazines.

This was evident in a range of strategies of recuperation. One was the insistence that only a few exceptional women could combine work with femininity. The techniques of illustrated biographies and interviews, which had been used to represent women writers in terms of their 'womanly' qualities rather than their competence or ability, were extended to other women achievers. *Hearth and Home* emphasised, as did its title, that it did not represent 'the advanced or emancipated school of womankind' yet it opened its first number by simultaneously recognising that the working woman existed and seeking to forestall her disruptive potential:

> The conditions of modern life are such that many women must work and all honour to those who have found lives for themselves and opened up paths along which the rest of the sex may follow. But these can be fulfilled with sweet grace and without any sacrifice of those qualities which are sweet, beautiful and true belonging to the 'perfect woman nobly planned'.
>
> (*H&H* I 1891: 1)

A second strategy, which followed from the first, was the construction of certain kinds of (mainly middle- or lower middle-class) work as being compatible with sweet womanliness. Annie Swan's correspondents complained more than once that she never advised women to go into business or work in shops though her column carried a lively correspondence from working girls on the issue (*W. at H.* V 1895: 469). Her fiction sometimes showed women who preferred meaningful work to marriage but that work tended to be confined to writing, social work, and teaching and these roles were also central to her fictional series.

The most powerful strategy for dealing with the failure of the domestic ideal to fit women's lives was to deny that it was a problem for adult women. The denial of adult femininity to working-class women by naming them as 'mill-girls' or 'servant-girls' was a familiar rhetorical device for defending a purely domestic femininity. The adoption of the term 'girls' in discussion of middle-class women's work marked a significant shift. The demand for paid work was increasingly identified as coming from 'girls', which meant that, like Higher Education, paid work was a temporary solution to a problem marriage would resolve. The dilemma of paid employment was recast as the question of 'What Shall We Do with Our Daughters?'

By contrast, girls' magazines addressed the question of work directly. Even the conservative *GOP* carried careers advice alongside moralising stories of self-sacrifice (Gorham 1982: 32). In this respect it was like other serious papers for girls. The jobs advocated in the *Young Woman* in 1894 included the new white-collar jobs being recommended in the women's magazines: shorthand, teaching, press cutting agencies (*YW* III 1894-5: 426). The series on 'How I Can Earn my Living' by Miss Billington, was more ambitious and included civil service, nurse, teacher, doctor and the magazine ran articles including one by Clementina Black on 'The Condition of Working Women' (*YW* III 1894–5: 61, 166, 228, 265–7, 307, 412). The *Young Englishwoman* which was mainly concerned with fashion, fiction and a lively correspondence on romantic problems, told one correspondent seeking work in 1868 that the employment market 'is already overstocked' but later acknowledged the importance of work for girls and gave advice on earning money (*YE* III 1868: 557; *YE* N.S. V 1874: 55; N.S. VI 1875: 171, 218, 339, 390, 470, etc.).

Thus a range of very different kinds of magazine assumed that paid work threatened the femininity of the woman but was useful, even necessary, to the girl. Undoubtedly this did extend the opportunities for middle-class young women, who welcomed the chance to earn a living without incurring social disapproval. Indeed, the redefinition of girlhood opened a positive space for these women in many ways, although it was not until the twentieth century that adolescence became identified with the feminine physical ideal. Nevertheless, the costs of displacing women's work into girlhood were high and are still being paid in the material conditions in which mature women (as well as girls) work.

The opening number of *Hearth and Home* illustrated all these strategies in operation. Declaring its hatred of the 'Advanced Woman' and all her works, the magazine began yet another 'What To Do with Our Daughters' series by acknowledging:

> in these days every girl, whether rich or poor, should know how to earn her living. Misfortune may come at any time and even if it does not, she is none the worse for being able to make a little extra pocket money.
>
> (*H&H* I 1891: 1, 22–3)

The collapse of 'earning a living' into 'a little extra pocket money' still haunts the 'girls' at work.

10

ADVANCING INTO COMMODITY CULTURE

These papers live mainly by their advertisements.

('Women's Newspapers', Evelyn March-Phillips,
Fortnightly Review N.S. LVI 1894: 663)

[Advertising] enables us to give every week for one penny what without advertising would cost five pence to produce.

(*Woman*, 6 Jan. 1892: 2)

The periodical was a crucial site of the struggle over the meaning of women's work but it was also at the centre of an industry which gave employment to increasing numbers of women. Very few were able to make a living in journalism, though their number was growing as it became increasingly accepted that 'A press life need not disqualify a woman from home life' (*CR* LXIV 1893: 362–71; *H&H* I 1891: 22–3; Cross 1985: 164ff). There was also increasing demand for secretaries and typewriters in the offices of the press and its associated industries, such as advertising (Cross 1985: 166; Read 1979: 244). These were important gains. The periodicals' main economic role, however, remained – as it had been throughout the century – to position its readers as consumers of commodities. In the first instance these were the products of the print industry itself but, as press advertising became crucial to the distribution of commodities of all description, readers were defined as 'consumers' in a more absolute sense.

Advertising had always had a dual role in the press; underpinning its finances and entering into the meanings publications constructed for their readers. In the new press of the 1880s and 1890s both the material and symbolic importance of advertising grew. This was especially true in the women's press where consumption and the control of spending were inseparable from the ideological project of defining the female reader.

ADVERTISING IN THE
FIRST HALF OF THE CENTURY

In 1759 Samuel Johnson's complaint about the extent of advertising instituted a critical tradition which has persisted ever since (Turner 1965: 27). For Thomas Carlyle, writing in the 1840s, advertisers with their promises of easy solutions to every problem were symptomatic of a nation in crisis. He singled out for attack the 'quack' doctors – specifically Morrison – who were among the first to realise and exploit the potential of large-scale advertising (Carlyle 1843: 20ff). Even Morrison with his 'universal pill' was surpassed by Holloway who built a huge commercial empire on the sale of pills and ointments and, in turn, was overtaken by others who became household names, like Beechams and Enos. The success of these patent medicine men continued to arouse critical comment throughout the century, but this did not prevent them from 'infiltrating every layer of social life' from the street with its billboards to the drawing rooms where the *Lady's Museum* or *La Belle Assemblée* lay on the table (Richards 1990: 70).

Though advertising in some form preceded the emergence of the journal, from the seventeenth century onwards their development was intertwined. In Britain they sustained each other through the years between 1712 and 1853 when puni-tive taxes on advertisements were levied by successive governments as part of the general tax on print.[1] Despite these financial and ideological deterrents, adver-tising continued to grow in importance during the period of the 'taxes on knowl-edge'. Publishers from the first had been aware of the advantages of 'puffing' their books in the papers, especially in their own journals. In fact, since the review was a staple of the periodical from the start it had sometimes been difficult to distin-guish editorial copy from advertisement.[2]

Where publishers and medicine men went, others followed. In 1851, just before the repeal of the tax, there were more than 2 million advertisements recorded in newspapers (Hindley and Hindley 1972: 62; Lee 1976: 85–7; Wiener 1969: 9–12). Much of this continued to be small scale, what we would now call 'classified', but awareness of the periodical's potential as a commercial medium was growing. Financially, the periodical press was heavily dependent on adver-tising by the time the tax was lifted in 1853. Lee argues that newspapers in the 1850s and 1860s had to earn at least as much from advertisements as sales to remain financially viable (Lee 1976: 87).

Researching the finances of other kinds of periodical is fraught with problems (Shattock and Wolff 1982: 145–257). However, most were – to varying degrees – dependent on advertising. There were few political and philanthropic journals which – like Jessie Boucherett's *Englishwoman's Review* – could rely on wealthy individuals or sponsoring groups to finance them completely (see Ch. 12).

The relationship between advertising and editorial copy was thus potentially even more fractured than between other elements of the magazine. The practice of placing advertisements together, either on the covers or just inside them, made an obvious visual line of demarcation. It also made it easier to strip the advertise-ments out before binding, a practice which has made research in this area extremely difficult.[3] Even where copies of nineteenth-century periodicals have been preserved complete with advertisements, they present particular problems of reading.

This is most dramatically apparent with publications whose main aim was not commercial, like the very high-minded *Female's Friend*. This 'organ of the

Associate Institution for Improving and Enforcing the laws for THE PROTEC-
TION OF WOMEN' still made a hard sell of its space to would-be advertisers:

> As this magazine will circulate in families of the middle and upper classes, it
> will be found a most advantageous medium for advertisements of books,
> schools, charitable institutions, apprentices, servants or situations wanted as
> well as general business.
>
> (*Fem. F.* I 1846: 4)

While the magazine in general assumed a masculine readership dedicated to
saving lower-class women from the snares of the flesh, some of these advertisements addressed the middle or upper-class woman eager to enhance her physical
appearance with such products as 'Rowlands' unique preparations for the Hair!
the Skin! and the Teeth! as used by the Queen and several sovereigns of Europe'
(ibid.).

Advertising developed in sophistication as well as scale during the nineteenth
century. By the 1840s the trade of the advertising agent was emerging from the
newspaper agents and coffee shops. Mitchell – one of the first such agents in
Britain – launched an annual *Newspaper Press Directory* in 1846 which continued
and expanded throughout the century. Publishers had throughout the century
described their readership in terms they hoped would entice potential advertisers,
as did the *Lady's Museum* when it claimed thousands of readers in the drawing
rooms of Britain, but the directories allowed advertisers to locate periodical readerships more precisely in terms of class, region, religion and gender (Hindley and
Hindley 1972: 20–1).

This was a slow development and even where the disjunction is not as striking
as in the *Female's Friend* we may still find that the advertisements fit uneasily with
the rest of the copy. Sally Shuttleworth has pointed out that provincial newspapers
like the *Leeds Intelligencer* in the 1840s and 1850s implied a masculine readership
but carried a substantial proportion of advertisements for medicines, including
those for 'female complaints' which specifically addressed women (Shuttleworth
1990). Her suggestion that the advertisements were read by different members of
the family from the rest of the paper is not entirely satisfactory, though certainly
different members of the family would read the same pages differently
(Shuttleworth 1990: 48).

The concept of targeting advertisements towards specific readerships was still
relatively undeveloped in the middle of the nineteenth century. However, the
technique of repetitive advertising across a range of different kinds of publication,
or even different media, was already well developed and continued to be
throughout the century. The advertisements for female complaints in the pages of
the *Leeds Intelligencer* were symptomatic of this practice and also made sense
within the publishing and reading conventions that tolerated a radical disjunction
between advertising and the rest of the paper.

This is not to deny the disruptive power with which the female body appeared
in advertisements in the general press. Advertisements do not only mobilise

already existing cultural meanings to sell commodities, significant though this is. They actively enter into negotiations over the meanings which they then return to circulation. Advertisements are therefore, as Shuttleworth rightly argues, indispensable to understanding the circulation of symbolic meanings in the periodical press. The extensive advertising of powders, ointments, pills, lozenges and other cures for female complaints in the local papers was important in the struggle over gender definition and the meaning of the female body in that press.

In addressing women rather than men as potential buyers, such advertisements drew on a range of constructions of femininity already prevalent: that women were physically more fragile than men; that women were responsible for the health of their families; perhaps that women were particularly susceptible to utopian promises, whether those of priests or the new priesthood of medicine and science, and that women controlled household expenditure and were buyers of commodities for themselves and others (Richards 1990: 206). Crucially, however, these advertisements drew on the pervasive identification of femininity with the body, a body both potentially pathological and in need of regulation.

The female body in the mid-nineteenth century was the object of study and prescription by male doctors. As medicine became increasingly professionalised, so the female body became increasingly pathologised in medical discourse. Endemically ill, perpetually in crisis, the 'health of females depended on circumstances more complicated and uncertain than that of the other sex' (Shuttleworth 1990: 50). Advertisers used and validated this medical discourse. Since the female frame was so liable to 'general Debility of the Constitution . . . obstructions . . . fainting fits . . . nervous giddiness' and other vaguely defined and gender-specific ills, the advertisers offered solutions in terms which matched. The female body could only be cured, rendered beautiful and freed from unwanted elements (whether 'female obstructions' or facial hair) through the consumption of their products. Femininity was identified, therefore, not just with economic consumption in an abstract sense but with a female body constructed by and through commodities.

ADVERTISING, THE NEW JOURNALISM
AND THE NEW FEMININITY

The new kind of femininity created through the advertisement was evident well before the 1870s. However, after 1875 this discourse of the commodified female body acquired a new power, produced at the intersection of those two discursive practices which are my subject: the new woman and the new journalism.

In the last quarter of the century advertising in British periodicals was transformed. Newspapers in particular had been slow to take advantage of the repeal of the tax on advertisements in the 1850s, and continued to lag behind the press in America, where there had been no such restrictions. But in the 1880s all this changed (Lee 1976: 87). Financially journalism was being transformed, not only by the lifting of local restrictions but by major international shifts towards larger

145

units, cartels and monopolies. Brand-name products sold on a national basis began to take over from small-scale locally produced goods, whether these were shoes, soaps or magazines. As a consequence, industrialists and producers began to perceive control of the market as important.

This meant a shift of interest which affected both economic theorising and practice. Veblen and the marginal utility theorists represented a new theoretical emphasis on consumption rather than the production of goods. The development of market research mechanisms was central to an increasing emphasis in business practice on manipulating desire as against satisfying already existing needs. In individual firms this led to clashes between the older generation and the new about the place and scope of advertising. The triumph of the new thinking in the person of T.J. Barratt at Pears, for example, made Pears Soap a national by-word through extensive advertising in posters and in the press (Hindley and Hindley 1972: 42–3, 57–8; Turner 1965: 100).

The periodical press was doubly affected by these changes; directly as an industry and indirectly as the medium through which others sought to market their products. As I have already argued, advertising became integrated into the publishing houses (see pp. 123). They competed with each other for advertising revenue, not only through the production of properly audited sales figures but through advertising in the press directories where they promised 'results' and made special offers of key positions and strategic placing to prospective buyers of their space.

The visual importance of advertisements in the periodical became a visible sign of the invisible role played by advertising revenue in financing the press. The relative proportion of space given to advertisements in magazines like Newnes's *Strand* with its 100 pages of ads to 120 of text was itself striking testimony to this (see also Turner 1965: 140). Moreover, under pressure from advertisers, the editorial tradition of segregating advertisements on separate pages and confining them to the endpapers began to be eroded. Advertisements thus not only took up more space in the magazines, they were harder to distinguish from the editorial text.

If advertising was essential to the press, the reverse was equally true. Despite the explosion of poster and billboard advertising, especially in the 1890s, the periodical remained the crucial site on which advertising developed its new discourse. That discourse was inevitably concerned with commodities not simply as made objects but as objects with 'value'. This value was not intrinsically related to the function of the product but was a measure of its cultural and symbolic worth; hence, advertising not only represented but produced the value of the commodity.

In the period of the new journalism the desirability of commodities was increasingly linked to their visibility. The interrelationship of desire and visibility for commodities had begun to develop in other aspects of Victorian culture, notably through the mechanism of the 'Great Exhibition' of goods, as early as the 1850s (Richards 1990: esp. 17–72). From mid-century onwards it was manifest also in the development in urban centres of the great department stores with their plate-glass windows and interior displays. Writing in 1895, Lady Jeune recalled how twenty-five years earlier

> There was little or no display in the windows . . . . An afternoon's shopping was a dreary affair, when one was received at the door of the shop by a gentleman in black, delivered over to another gentleman . . . who found one a chair and in a sepulchral voice uttered some magic words such as 'Silk, Mr. Smith' or 'Velvet, Mr. A' and then departed to seek another victim.
>
> (Jeune 1895: 123–4)

By the mid-1890s, this old style of shopping was giving way to a new emphasis on display and on allowing the shopper to wander round 'just looking' (Bowlby 1985, but see Adburgham 1964). This looking eroticised the commodity and produced an entirely new pattern of consumption and desire:

> It is not that we need so much more . . . but we are not able to stand against the overwhelming temptations to buy which besiege us at every turn. We go to purchase something we want; but when we get to our shop there are so many more things we never thought of till they presented their obtrusive fascinations on every side. We look for a ribbon . . . and find ourselves in a paradise of ribbons without which our life becomes impossible.
>
> (Jeune 1895: 124)

It was through advertising that this eroticism of the commodity was displayed. By the mid-1880s the discourse of visibility and desire dominated representations of the commodity on posters, billboards and the advertising pages of the women's magazine. This development was bound up with the changes in print technology which made possible better quality picture reproduction whether in posters or in the magazines. The print tradition of the eroticised female body, which had persisted in magazines for women since the Books of Beauty, entered a new stage of its relationship with technology and consumption. That relationship was dramatically enacted when shops in the 1890s put pictures of aristocratic beauties in their windows as part of their display (Asquith 1920: 58).

Advertisers were well aware of the new importance of the visual in their discourse and stressed the relationship between advertisement and High Art. In the 1880s and 1890s the poster began to be regarded as an art form instead of an urban excrescence. The first Poster Exhibition was held in London in 1894 (Hindley and Hindley 1972: 69), well-known artists like Beardsley designed them, and advertisers bought or commissioned work from members of the Royal Academy. When Pears Soap bought Millais's painting of *Bubbles* for their advertising campaign in 1887 there was a public outcry, but the close relationship of Art to advertising was routinely assumed, not least in the advertisements in the ladies' papers (Hindley and Hindley 1972: 43–4; Turner 1965: 100). Beecham's pills, for example, offered the readers of *Queen* in 1880 a vaguely classical pair of draped female figures with the modest claim, 'This exquisite illustration, which is perhaps the most artistic study yet produced in the form of an advertisement depicts HEALTH CROWNING BEAUTY' (*Q.* VII 1880: unnumbered page).

Visual and verbal references to classical art suggested the value or 'worth' of the pills, underlined in Beecham advertisements by payment in guineas rather than the pounds, shillings and pence of everyday transactions. But classicism also provided an acceptable model for the representation of the female body, not unclothed, but certainly with its 'natural' shape revealed through the clothing. Semi-clad female figures were routinely used – particularly but not exclusively in the ubiquitous corset advertisements – where they would not have been allowed as illustrations to the editorial text.

These advertisements constructed a femininity in which desirability was linked to visible beauty. The association of the feminine with the pleasures of looking was endemic in the culture and central to the tradition of the woman's magazine. The importance of visibility or spectacle for the meaning of the commodity linked it to the feminine in a closed circle. Femininity both defined and was defined by its likeness to the commodities with which it became associated. As the new advertising became more important, the commodified female body loomed large in the pages of the women's magazines.

ADVERTISING IN THE NEW WOMEN'S PRESS

This kind of advertising worked through repetition across a range of different publications but its appearance in the *Queen* is particularly significant. The changes involved in new journalism, I have argued, had a particular resonance in the women's press, where the association of femininity with consumption had long been axiomatic. Mitchell's *Press Directory* for the 1880s and 1890s was clear that women's periodicals presented a particularly lucrative outlet for advertisers because, as the *Gentlewoman* argued, it was common knowledge that 'Women spend 90% of what men earn' (White 1970: 66). This assumption, explicitly spelt out in the press directories, shaped the new journalism at every level.

In quality papers like the *Gentlewoman* and the *Queen* which promised advertisers access to 'the Upper Ten Thousand', the new advertising was developed. Though expensive at sixpence, their costs were reputed to be such that a shilling would barely cover them, let alone make a profit. 'It is from the high prices charged for advertising space that the harvest is reaped', one contemporary wrote (March-Phillips 1894: 663). Another argued not only that 'The advertising firms even more than purchasers of papers are the greatest supporter of the press' but that these advertisers were the 'philanthropists' and 'true socialists' of their age since they ensured continuing publication for so many magazines each of which employed 'hundreds of persons' (*G.* I 1890: 370). Others took a less sanguine view of the relationship between advertisers and these papers and accusations of bribery occasionally erupted into the press (*W.* 17 Jan. 1894: 5).

The ladies' papers as a group were immensely successful in attracting the personal and occasional advertisements which remained an important source of revenue and for which *The Lady* is still famous (White 1970: 70). The *Queen* also drew hundreds of small advertisers for its 'Exchange' or 'Exchange and Mart' sections. Here, in columns crammed with minute print, notices for sale of 'antique oak furniture', 'beautiful angora rabbits' and 'very pretty small garnet earrings' were squeezed between requests for cut flowers, old bureaux and offers to exchange 'The *Queen* complete for the *Illustrated London News*, each posted Tuesday after publication and kept' (Q. LXVII, 28 March 1885: 338).

This proved so lucrative that in 1868 the proprietor, Cox, launched *Exchange and Mart*, a magazine dedicated entirely to such advertisements, offering, 'to enable anyone who wishes to dispose of any article to do so at a very cheap rate'. In case its readers 'wish[ed] to keep secret' their part in such transactions, the paper offered something new, the anonymity of box numbers.[4] The success of *Exchange and Mart*, which flourished into the late twentieth century, did not detract from the *Queen*'s 'Exchange' column, an indication of the potential for a press funded more or less completely by such advertising.

It was not, however, from the occasional advertiser that women's periodicals in general and the ladies' papers in particular reaped 'the harvest of their profits'. It was from those with products to sell on a regular basis, companies who marketed on a national scale and across all forms of print media. Advertising of brand-named products gained in importance in every kind of women's magazine from *Hearth and Home*, which claimed it was read by the Queen, through *Woman at Home*, cheaper fashion journals like *Myra's* and the penny papers, *Woman* and *Home Chat*. *Woman* told its readers that without advertising it would have cost, not a penny but fivepence, which suggested it was even more dependent on advertisers than *Queen* (*W*. 6 Jan. 1892: 2).

The importance of commercial advertising was immediately obvious to the reader of any of these publications. In the 1880s, before the *Strand* was even a gleam in the eye of Newnes, *Queen* routinely devoted half or more of its pages to advertisements.[5] The bulk of advertising in most women's periodicals where I have been able to see it continued to be carried on separate pages from the editorial copy and was probably still arranged in blocks on the endpapers each side of the covers. However, advertisers were recognising the disadvantages of a system which enabled readers to skip their messages completely. Though the full-page ad remained – as it still does – a staple, particularly of the up-market papers, the middle and cheaper papers began to carry pages which mixed editorial copy and advertising. When Harmsworth and Pearson entered the penny women's magazine market in the 1890s, advertisements began to be interleaved and even to appear along the side and facing the editorial copy.

As well as occupying more space and more commanding positions in the text, the visual impact of advertising was enhanced by changes in presentation. The use of different kinds of type was not new but it was now accompanied by the breaking up of the page, the development of a more exciting – sometimes frenetic – graphics and, above all, the use of illustration. Not all were as sophisticated in their grasp of the new medium as Beecham's, and the artist who tried to sell Carter's Beautiful Flower Seeds by drawing a picture of a box of seeds clearly had a good deal to learn (*Q.* LXVII 1885: unnumbered). Increasingly, however, the pleasures of the visually exciting page were offered as preliminary to the pleasures of the commodities they represented. The details of particular images were less important than the construction of the reader as a consumer, defined not in abstract terms but in terms of the commodities she looked at as well as purchased.

The consumer was visible to herself in the advertising's recurrent images of the female body. Sometimes the whole body was represented: in mourning wear, on horseback and endlessly displaying the latest fashions (Figure 7.5, p. 108). But as often the body was fragmented or truncated; hands, feet, heads and female torsos littered the advertising pages of *Queen* (Figure 10.1). All these images constructed the female body out of commodities (the hair-dye, the hand cream, the dress, the shoes). The corset advertisements, which were crucial to the women's press from most expensive to cheapest level, often showed a woman's head and arms emerging from the garment. Frequently, however, the corset stood miraculously by itself, symbolically containing and replacing the exaggeratedly female body of these advertisements.

The dissolution of that body into clothing had of course been central to the discourse of fashion in the women's magazines throughout the previous century (as it was to be in the next). As I have argued, these magazines located a new kind of femininity in the visible codes of dress specifically through their use of the fashion-plate. In the magazines of the 1880s and 1890s, the female bodies represented in the advertisements gave back an echo of the fashion pages with their complex meanings and ambiguous pleasures. In addition they promised that the threatened rift between the woman reader and the visible and desirable female body could be healed through the purchase of commodities. Even more insistently than the fashion page, they offered her a model of the desirable woman to whom she related both as object of desire and potential desiring self. The fashion-plates were usually full-length figures but the advertisements often fragmented this figure into its component parts, showing here the waist, there the foot, the torso or the hair (Figure 10.2). The task of retrieving the completed self from these fragments was always unfinished. Each week or month the reader was confronted yet again with the scattered images on the advertising pages which had to be re-made through the labour of informed consumption.

Along with the visual fragmentation of the female body, advertisers deployed the now familiar discourse of female pathology. The same claims to restore the inherently unsound female constitution were recycled in terms almost identical with those of the 1840s pill merchants. An 1890s electric corset, for example, offered to deal with 'Female Ailments, HYSTERIA, internal complaints, Loss of Appetite, DYSPEPSIA, Kidney Disorders, RHEUMATIC AND ORGANIC AFFECTIONS etc.' (*Q.* 1892, quoted in de Vries and Laver 1968: 36). Such commodities were always designed 'by a physician' or 'on scientific principles' as they had been since the early Victorian era.

These representations of the female body both produced and depended on a contradictory discourse of the 'natural'. Womanly beauty was simultaneously

Figure 10.1 Advertisements from *Queen* (LXXVII 28 March 1885)

guaranteed as natural and – like her health – always threatened and dependent on the constant work of construction and artifice. The 'Be natural but' which marked femininity was taken up and echoed through the advertising pages. Products were always 'Aids to Nature', designed to restore the lost hair colour, healthy skin or beautiful figure which was 'natural but' . . . somehow mislaid or lost. The corset controversies (see Ch. 6) had epitomised this 'natural but' of feminine beauty and it was in the recurrent corset advertisements that the fragmentation of the female body and the eroticisation of the commodity continued to be most clearly demonstrated (see Figure 6.3, p. 85).

In using these discourses of the feminine, advertisers re-worked their meaning. So completely did they succeed in identifying femininity with commodities that the female body began in the 1890s and early twentieth century to become a

Figure 10.2 Advertisements from *Queen* (LXXVII 28 March 1885)

general and pervasive symbol of consumption. The body of the 'sea-side girl' began to move from advertisements for specifically feminine products like 'Beetham's Glycerine and Cucumber' into posters for sea-side resorts and more general advertising including cigarettes, fountain-pens and cocoa (Figure 10.3). As Richards argues, 'The [female] body had become the prevailing icon of commodity culture and there was no turning back' (Richards 1990: 205).

As the female body became the symbol of the new commodity-centred

Figure 10.3 Advertisement from *Queen* (LXXXVI 7 December 1889: xxi) © Manchester City Art Galleries

153

economy, it prefigured a new kind of self identified by what it consumed rather than by its work. In the twentieth century the traditionally feminine role of consumer was to be redefined so that it became a mark of modernity rather than the mark of gender. However, just as the discourse of femininity in the editorial pages was disengaged from the position occupied by historical men and women in publishing, so the symbolic femininity of the modern consumer as it emerged in the 1890s was disengaged from the economic realities of historical women's lives.

The new woman of advertising culture, identified with the pleasures of consumption, represented a challenge to the New Woman who had demanded access to paid employment and productive labour. One of Beecham's advertisements made this challenge directly with a picture of the smoking, knickerbocker-dressed virago of popular imagination claiming 'Since taking Beecham's Pills I have been a New Woman'. The joke was certainly against the New Woman here. Despite her limited successes in gaining access to education and some white-collar jobs, she had not dismantled the gender identities which still effectively made true femininity incompatible with economic independence. Moreover, in the new commodity culture these limitations were constantly redefined as pleasures – the joys of 'looking' and 'shopping' – on the assumption that 'women spend what men earn'. In a further irony, it was the 'true' woman who had constantly to re-make herself from the body-parts offered in the pages of the magazines and not that 'tobacco-tainted, gala contaminated Frankenstein' who was popularly construed as her opposite (see Arabella Kenealy, *Id.* IX 1894: 209).

Part IV

THE REINVENTION OF THE DOMESTIC ENGLISH WOMAN: INTO THE TWENTIETH CENTURY

11

WOMAN AT HOME:
THE MIDDLE-CLASS
DOMESTIC MAGAZINE
AND THE AGONY AUNT

'Nothing Lovelier can be Found in Woman than to Study Household Good.'
(Milton)

(Mrs Beeton's motto, *Hearth and Home*, passim)

I am more than pleased to number LITTLE AFRICANDER among my
friends and correspondents overseas. She sends me a most delightful letter
with a brightly written and amusing account of family life in a doctor's house
in Cape Colony. It does not differ so very much from life at home – that is
family characteristics are the same everywhere . . .

('Over the Teacups', Annie S. Swan, *Woman at Home* VI 1896–7: 711)

The new femininity of consumption was located within the dominant ideology of
the domestic. The 'True Woman' whom the New Journalism addressed and
sought to bring into being was still defined by the motto from Milton used every
month in *Hearth and Home* by its household adviser, 'Mrs Beeton'.[1] The tradition
of the domestic magazine therefore proved even more productive in the 1890s
than that of the ladies' newspapers. The well-established form of the sixpenny
middle-class monthly was revitalised in titles like *Woman's World*, *Woman at Home*
and the threepenny *Hearth and Home*. Even more significant in terms of readership and circulation figures was the re-working of that form in the new penny
weeklies. All these journals renegotiated the meaning of the English Domestic
Woman in terms of the New Journalism and the era of the New Woman.

This last section of the book deals with the reinvention of the domestic in both
the monthly and the cheaper weekly magazines of the 1890s. This chapter is a case
study of the sixpenny monthly *Woman at Home* whose sub-title, 'Annie S. Swan's
Magazine', identified it with a popular romantic novelist. In the next chapter I
discuss *Woman*, an attempt to produce a purely commercial penny magazine for
'the advanced woman' but one whose motto, 'Forward but not too Fast' proved
only too apt. The last chapter deals with the penny magazines, especially *Home
Chat* and *Woman's Weekly*, which carried the domestic magazine into the centre of
twentieth-century women's reading.

157

WOMAN AT HOME:
THE DOMESTIC ENGLISHWOMAN IN THE 1890s

Woman at Home (1893–1920), like the other sixpenny monthlies, used the ingredients by now established as essential to the genre: fiction and poetry; reviews; fashion news, needlework patterns and tips on shopping; illustrated biographies or interviews with celebrities; advice on health, beauty and domestic management; and the correspondence columns. Within this mix, it stressed precisely those elements which *Queen* down-played; the fiction, the exemplary biography, advice on cooking and the details of family management. Above all it reinstated the confessional letter at the centre of the magazine. Annie Swan, like the early Beeton, developed a dialogue with readers through two separate letter-columns, 'Over the Teacups' and 'Love, Courtship and Marriage'.

Its title, its price and its mix of ingredients made clear that *Woman at Home* situated its readers in a space defined by the overlapping circles of the domestic, matrimony and the middle class. Its editor had conceived it as 'a popular sixpenny monthly which should concern itself first and foremost with domestic life and should be written for women who were married or expected to marry' (Darlow 1925: 111). Yet that confident statement was immediately undercut by his recognition 'that numbers of the best women now live independent lives and that their tastes and needs must also be taken into account' (ibid.). His biographer's explanation that 'He refused the false doctrine that a "domestic woman is a woman like a domestic"' (ibid.) only highlighted the slipperiness of the term 'domestic', with its confusion of class and gender relations.

It was to this tangle of definitions, compounded by the historical shift towards a New Womanhood, that Annie Swan specifically addressed herself when 'her' magazine was launched. Annie S. Swan was the pen-name of the popular novelist, Mrs Burnett Smith. Both the magazine's sub-title and the 'Over the Teacups' advice column, which acted as an editorial, positioned her as the voice of the magazine. She spoke with this authority when in the first number, she defined its readers as middle-class 'women' rather than aristocratic 'ladies':

> I have no hesitation in saying that it is the middle class woman who is the reader of today among her sex. She is less harassed by the claims of fashions . . . and therefore has more leisure than her wealthier sisters to devote to mental culture.
>
> (*W. at H.* I 1893: 62)

She was less confident, however, about what kind of reading to supply and characteristically invited her correspondents to help in the task of defining appropriate reading for the domestic female readers of the 1890s. Even women who were not 'New' rejected

> the old pabulum, the goody-goody tales no longer find favour in their eyes. The reader of today no longer sympathises with the heroine who melts into

tears on the smallest provocation but prefers a more robust personality who strikes out a path for herself.

(ibid.)

Annie Swan knew her readership. The magazine was an immediate success and sold 100,000 copies of its first number when its publishers, Hodder & Stoughton, calculated 30,000 would make it viable (Darlow 1925: 111). It continued publication until 1920 when it merged with *Home Magazine*. As a publishing venture it was proudly New Journalistic, intended by its publishers to 'catch the masses'. They took as their model Newnes's the *Strand*, launched in 1890 as a sixpenny monthly with a picture on every double spread and good fiction. When Hodder & Stoughton determined to produce a '*Strand* for Women', they were thinking of a 'mass' magazine aimed, not at the working class, but at the expanding middle-class readership. However, they adopted techniques familiar from Newnes and his rivals; they spent £1,100 on the launch of the first number and they continued to advertise, for example in other journals for women, specifically exploiting Annie Swan's popularity as a novelist (ibid.; *W.* 31 March 1897: advertisement). They must have imitated Newnes, too, in making the magazine itself a vehicle for advertising, but I have been unable to find any copies which retained these.

They certainly deployed the new technology to create a quality periodical. Printed on glossy paper and 'profusely illustrated' with a half-tone plate or some other picture on almost every page, it compared favourably with the sixpenny weeklies, like the *Gentlewoman* and *Queen*. It was magazine – rather than newspaper size (at 9½ × 6½ inches), but then it had more than 80 pages in every number, thus making up in thickness for its smaller page size and less frequent publication.

Obviously *Woman at Home* was aimed at a much less wealthy readership than the *Queen*. The difference was not only a matter of economics. It was also a struggle over values. *Woman at Home* did not simply locate its readers in the middle class; it set up an opposition between them and their aristocratic 'sisters' where all the advantages were perceived to lie with the middle-class woman. Significantly, it was 'the claims of fashion' which were construed as preventing the wealthy from inner development. This opposition between concern for the outer as against the inner woman continued to be given a class dimension, as it had in Sarah Ellis's work or the mothers' magazines of the 1840s with their attacks on aristocratic values. Here, however, it was complicated both by the economics of the New Journalism and by the new politics of gender.

Woman at Home had to acknowledge that appearance, as represented in the fashion column and plate, was central to the genre of the woman's magazine and to the femininity which it both signified and addressed. Even Oscar Wilde, in his attempt to make the *Woman's World* more serious, did not banish fashion completely, only sent it to the back of the magazine – a place it also occupied in *Woman at Home* (Brake 1994: 132–3). Its illustrations of gowns were there but they were small figures set in the text, rather than the crisp full-page spreads in *Queen*.

Crucially, *Woman at Home* sought to capture fashion and the ideal of physical beauty – as it sought to capture the delights of the photographic illustration – for the elegant economy of bourgeois virtue. The mark of this virtue was the discrimination which accounted for every penny in advising 'How to spend a Dress Allowance' and extended to the 'simple but refined' dinner menus (*W. at H.* V 1896: 68–70, 76). Deciding between a 'safe' choice of dress and one which was a sign of extravagance was a necessary task. However, it was made difficult because within the discourse of fashion journalism both were likely to collapse into the category of 'the novelty':

> By the beginning of October all the shops are full of autumn novelties and it is quite safe to select among the pretty stuffs on view a best autumn dress for nothing very particular will appear later on, excepting a few novelties which will be very expensive and only within the reach of wealthy people.
>
> (*W. at H.* V 1896: 73)

The greater freedom of the 1890s woman and her search for more robust heroines gave the problem of dress and appearance a new twist. 'What is the best cycling dress for Women?' was a question which divided those who believed 'women's participation in sports and outdoor amusements should be limited to those in which they can wear a skirt' from those who maintained that 'for cycling, a skirt is impossible' (*W. at H.* VI 1896: 620–3). What was never in dispute was that women's dress mattered, whether on her cycle or on the tennis court.

Acknowledging the importance of appearance produced within the magazine the intractable problem of the female body with all its tendencies to vanity on one hand and pathology on the other. It appeared not only in the fashion-plates and in the two fashion columns but in the illustrated 'Brides and Grooms', in numerous other illustrations, in biographies and interviews and in the fiction, which was almost always romantic. To deal with this the magazine offered, beside its column on 'Love, Marriage and Courtship', advice on 'Health and Personal Appearance'. Here 'beauty' and 'health' became linked both functionally and by analogy. Both were simultaneously natural and the product of women's careful diet, cleansing rituals, 'perseverance' and the application of certain specifics (Jaborandi hair tonic, Juno's bath salts, or the mixtures whose ingredients readers were given to have made up by the chemist). The double appeal to the natural and women's work, which alone could realise the natural, was a familiar strategy.

Here it was mobilised to equate 'Beauty' and 'Health'. Advice on diet, exercise and habit of life was indistinguishable from advice on hairstyles and complexion ointments. 'Scientific' explanations of the physiology and chemistry of the body were produced in answer to enquiries about open pores or greasy hair (*W. at H.* VI 1896: 718). This construction was, in turn, linked not to the agnosticism of modern science but to a religious faith in the natural as God-given. 'Beauty [was] God's gift' and this gave a theological force to the injunction that it was 'the right and duty of every woman to look as well as nature meant her to look for as long as she can' (*W. at H.* V 1895–6: 156).

It was typical of Annie Swan's Christianity that human nature, even at its most sinful, was identified as 'God-given'. Although she owed much to the tradition of evangelicalism which shaped the mothers' magazines, she did not share its condemnation of humanity as inevitably fallen, stressing instead a more humanist faith in natural goodness. This even made possible the incorporation of the unruly or unhealthy female body back into the femininity of domestic duty and non-sexual love.

The dynamic of these links between the outer and inner woman needs to be understood in the context of other elements of the magazine. Those which occupied the most space were the biographies, especially of royalty, Annie Swan's correspondence columns and the fiction. I discuss each in turn in the rest of the chapter.

THE BIOGRAPHY AND THE NEW ROYAL FAMILY

The illustrated biography was not only given a substantial space in most numbers of *Woman at Home*, it was usually the lead item, a revival of the tradition of the early ladies' magazines which had placed the portrait and life of a notable woman first. Subjects in the 1890s included notable men as well as women and articles varied in length from the serialised book-length biography with illustrations on every page to the brief, even single-column, articles with small inset photo of Sarah Tooley's series on the ladies of various cities (*W. at H.* V 1895–6: 1, 81, 321, 401, 481, 585, 826, 981, etc.).

Whereas the fashion was illustrated with sketches, the technology of the half-tone photograph was crucial to the biographical articles. Here it promised not visual pleasure but sober truth. But that promise encoded a variety of different meanings. The likeness of the famous individual produced the truth of their appearance so that they became recognisable, even familiar to the reader. This, of course, was also the meaning of the new journalistic emphasis on the interview and the personalised reporting of news. The numerous photographs and portraits which accompanied these biographies promised more than an outward likeness; they became coded messages from which the reader was invited to know the true – that is the inner – character of the subject.

Although the subjects of these studies were chosen because of their extraordinary achievement or position, they appeared in *Woman at Home* as both unlike the readers and like them; the truth about them was that they were women or men first and princesses, writers or politicians second. This common humanity was located by Annie Swan's magazine in their moral and spiritual life, but that life was essentially shaped by their gender. The quality of womanliness (or occasionally, manliness) were elements of the true self which appearance reflected.

This tradition of the biographical article and the photo-portrait were harnessed in *Woman at Home* to the radical reshaping of the meaning of royalty in the last years of Victoria's reign, a larger process in which women's magazines like this played a small but important part (Cannadine 1983). Though it assumed that pictures and accounts of ceremonial events and dresses would interest its readers, *Woman at Home* represented royalty through the illustrated biography and the organising trope of the family which had been so crucial to Victoria's meaning in the iconography of popular print throughout her reign (Homans 1993). It therefore sought to redeem royalty, as it did fashion, for a bourgeois concept of femininity.

The constant reinvention of the monarch as domestic woman entered a new phase in the 1890s in which Victoria's meaning was created in the tension between her position as Empress and as widowed mother. This process is well demonstrated by the 'Life of Queen Victoria' which *Woman at Home* serialised between 1895 and 1896 (*W. at H.* V 1895–6: 1, 81, 321, 481, 585). The negotiations between Victoria's 'womanliness' and her public role were its theme, usually implicit, sometimes explicit, as when her decision to marry was welcomed by Lord Melbourne since 'a woman cannot stand alone for any time, in whatever station she may be' (*W. at H.* V 1895–6: 81). Victoria was shown resolving the problem of her position in two complementary ways. First, she rejected a purely decorative role for herself, choosing instead the bourgeois ideal of work and, second, she made her family relationships central to her life.

From the start of the serial, Victoria was described as having 'made her choice in favour of being a working, rather than a show monarch'. Every moment of her day was 'regulated with due regard to her many duties' (*W. at H.* V 1895–6: 7, 10). This biographer was not very interested in the Queen's constitutional role, but in her habit of life and adherence to the Protestant ethic. The opposition between 'work' and 'show' recalled the formation of middle-class gender identity earlier in the century but that formation was being thrown into crisis in the 1890s, especially by the problem of the nature of 'work' for women, which was a persistent theme of the letters from readers.

The royal 'Lives' in these magazines reiterated that even royal 'work' must be subordinate to the primary demands of 'the family'. Victoria was a true woman because she placed her domestic and familial relations' ips before her public role. Much of the biography was taken up with her marriage, her concern for her children and her care for her domestics and the poor. Her marriage to Albert was represented as an ideal one, not least in her insistence that she take the vow to obey, since 'she wished to be married as a woman not as a Queen'. Albert's devotion 'during his wife's seclusion' after the birth of their first child and their joint concern for their children's education were exemplary (*W. at H.* V 1895–6: 88, 91, passim).

Victoria's active involvement in the moral and emotional education of her children was specifically posed against the practice of giving the task entirely to servants, which was common among the aristocracy (*W. at H.* V 1895–6: 405). It was a persistent theme of middle-class women's magazines in the 1890s, which took up the argument of maternal associations of the 1830s and 1840s. In *Hearth and Home*, for example, 'Candida' argued in an article on 'unmotherly mothers' that there was 'more of a threat to maternity from society ladies than from

THE QUEEN IN WEDDING DRESS.

Figure 11.1 Queen Victoria, from *Woman at Home* (V 1895: 85)

working women' (*H&H* I 1891: 207). The debate on revolting daughters frequently turned round the question of whether the revolt was caused by *mothers* who failed to establish close bonds of love and trust with their children.

The magazine could not entirely ignore the place of ceremony and display in the modern monarch's role, any more than it could discount the importance of illustrations and court events in women's journalism. The 'Life' was generously illustrated and gave detailed descriptions of her wedding dress and her coronation robes. Victoria's early delight in balls and dancing was described, but the reader was assured that it was always consistent with purity. Indeed under her influence 'the Court became as pure as a good woman could make it', an example of the redemptive power of true womanliness (*W. at H.* V 1895–6: 325; Figure 11.1).

Just as the ghost of domestic womanliness lurked around the *Queen's* representation of royal femininity, so the shape of the fashionable lady fell across the page of *Woman at Home*. The reinvention of the monarchy in terms of public display and imperial visibility coexisted with that other creation of royalty as 'a family on the throne' (Cannadine 1983). At the Jubilee the Queen had 'waived ceremony' to draw the members of her family in turn into her 'motherly embrace', thus turning 'the grand pageant into a family re-union' (*W. at H.* VI 1896–7: 594). This strategy recalled that of the *Queen* in transforming the pageantry of royalty first into a private family event and then – through the medium of the magazine – into a public display of family virtue. Here Victoria became the signifier neither of the aristocratic, nor the erotic, but of the maternal body. The insistent displacement of female sexuality into the maternal pervaded these biographies and produced even the notorious relationship with John Brown as testimony to the Queen's 'beautiful' and essentially womanly concern for her household (*W. at H.* VI 1896–7: 591–2).

The interest in the royal 'family' extended to all the ramifications of Victoria's progeny who were produced in this magazine in endless biographical articles and studio photographs.[2] The fact that the Queen was mother to a numerous family gave added force to the restatement in an imperial context of the cliche that she was a mother to her people. Characterising Victoria as a virtuous and loving mother enabled *Woman at Home* to claim a universal validity for womanhood defined as 'a regulated life' with family relationships at its centre. More importantly, in the context of Britain's imperial role, the magazine assumed that 'family characteristics are the same everywhere' (*W. at H.* VI 1896–7: 711).

In her correspondence columns Annie Swan almost every month referred to letters from readers in Australia, Africa, India and other parts of the empire, where *Woman at Home* was welcome, 'remote places to which few voices from this side of the great waters ever penetrate' (*W. at H.* V 1895–6: 461). It was general practice across the empire well into the twentieth century that Britain was called 'home', even by those who had no memories of it or had never been there. The contradictions of defining the place and people among whom you live as simultaneously of the imperial family but not of the imperial home were evident in these letters. Like the editors of the 1840s mothers' magazines, Annie Swan both assumed a

universal model of womanhood in the family and also took as norm the experience of her British readers. Domestic femininity both validated the empire and
was validated by it.

The mechanism for the reinvention of Victoria as Empress/mother in this
magazine was the biographical narrative. The middle-class domestic woman was
likewise reinvented through the biographical or autobiographical narrative.
Unlike *Queen*, which produced femininity as a visible text, *Woman at Home*
produced it as a life story. Readers' own life stories were central to the reinvention
of the middle-class woman enacted in Annie Swan's letters columns, to which I
now turn.

ANNIE SWAN AND 'OVER THE TEACUPS'

Annie Swan was well-known as a novelist when the magazine associated with her
name was launched. By her account, she devised it as a medium through which to
deal with the overwhelming number of letters from readers asking her advice,
especially on how to become writers (Black 1906: 319; see also *The Times* 19 June
1943, obit.). However, there is another version of how *Woman at Home* came into
being. According to his biographer it was the brain-child of the Presbyterian cleric
and journalist, Robertson Nicoll, and he brought his friend Mrs Burnett Smith
(Annie S. Swan) into the venture (Darlow 1925: 111).

This dual story is significant not as a post-structuralist joke about the impossibility of defining origins. The joke of this story lies rather in the game of hide-and-
seek played around the question of gendered authority/authorship. Though
Robertson Nicholl was the editor, he remained entirely invisible in the magazine
which not only carried the name of Annie Swan, but was dominated by her
persona. Her fiction appeared in most numbers and of her two by-lined correspondence columns, 'Over the Teacups' was regarded by readers as 'the titbit' of
the whole (Black 1906: 319). No wonder contemporary readers and later scholars
have assumed that she was indeed the magazine's editor.[3]

The figure of the male editor concealed behind the skirts of a female editorial
persona was not unique to *Woman at Home* in this period, as I have already
suggested. Apparently the overtly masculine editorial voice which Beeton had
used so successfully in the *Englishwoman's Domestic Magazine* of the 1860s was less
acceptable to women readers of the 1890s. The reasons for this probably included
the rejection of the 'goody-goody pap' of mid-century female reading, even by
women who labelled the New Woman as deviant. Developments in New
Journalism also represented the writer as the reader's intimate rather than a distant
authority figure. Whatever the reasons, as I have argued throughout, it makes
impossible any simple correlation between the feminisation of the editorial voice
and the position of women as writers or readers.

What is significant in this magazine was the authority with which Annie Swan's
persona was endowed and the specifics of how 'she' and her editor used it to
produce the femininity of the magazine. Although the tradition of advice on

personal problems went back to the eighteenth century, Annie Swan was the first 'agony aunt' in the modern sense, a female figure who was mature but not 'old' and who treated her correspondents' problems with the attention due to equals. Like Beeton, she encouraged readers to write in, using the confessional mode to discuss their personal relationships, especially the romantic and marital. However, instead of a jovial masculine authority, she offered sympathy and moral seriousness in a thoroughly feminine persona.

This persona suffused all the advice columns but was most fully developed in 'Over the Teacups'. Afternoon tea, which hardly ranked as a proper meal, was the occasion at which the woman of the house presided directly. Pouring tea was imbued with femininity, an association played upon by many novelists and still maintained in the jokey 'Will you be mother?', meaning 'Will you pour the tea?'. The title, 'Over the Teacups', thus represented Annie Swan's column as a place where women could exchange confidences as equals and friends. This was reinforced by the illustration. The detail varied from season to season but it always showed a group of seated women facing each other with no obvious authority figure (Figure 11.2). Female correspondents to the magazine always outnumbered men – as we might expect – but in 'Over the Teacups' the preponderance of women was greater even than in the 'Love, Marriage and Courtship' column, establishing this as an almost exclusively female space.[4]

To sustain the character created by her title and illustration, Annie Swan took up and carried further Beeton's policy of printing extracts from readers' letters rather than simply her replies. Long apparently verbatim quotations and detailed synopses created a sense of dialogue, which was also maintained by her practice of inviting and printing follow-up letters. Unlike Beeton, she presented herself as essentially like the readers in her joys and perplexities and they reciprocated with affection. When her son was born in 1896 she thanked

> the many kind friends among my readers who have expressed sympathy and congratulations. It is very precious to me to know that so many whom I have no likelihood of meeting face to face feel so kindly disposed to me and mine and it will be my aim when my children are old enough to explain to them what a precious and powerful bond is this sympathy which makes bands of love enough to go round the world.
>
> (*W. at H.* VI 1896–7: 711)

Her column thus enacted a feminine dynamic of mutual support and created, as had the mothers' magazines, a community of like-minded readers who encouraged each other in the difficulties of everyday life. That community, however, did not extend beyond her column and her persona was its signifier and its only embodiment.

In 'Over the Teacups' womanliness was the subject of debate but womanliness was also what made it possible. Annie Swan's writing enacted the qualities which she recommended to her readers. Central to it and the source of her authority was the capacity to *feel* for and with her readers:

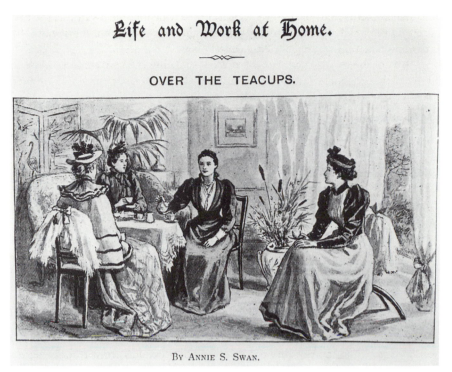

Figure 11.2 'Over the Teacups', from *Woman at Home* (V 1895: 387)

The letter of a lonely woman has touched me very much. It is indeed, as she says, difficult for one past middle age to find anything acceptable to do and this keeps her in a situation which is both hard and uncongenial . . . . What can I say but send her my sympathy? The burden of the middle-aged woman for whom there appears to be neither calling nor room in this great world lies heavy on my soul.

(*W. at H.* VI 1896–7: 949)

Each page was dotted with feeling responses to her letters: 'I am more than pleased . . . I am much touched . . . I send my heart-felt thanks to A Celt for her kind, helpful and comforting letter' (*W. at H.* VI 1896–7: 710–11). But feeling sprang from an awareness of responsibility for oneself and others and was not an end in itself. Above all, it was the basis for women's domestic duties and, therefore, each woman's conscience and 'heart' were her own best advisers.

After TROUBLED ALICE reads the above, she may feel more disposed to remain at home as housekeeper to her brother . . . . I do not see that she need worry her head more about her independence . . . . So far as her *duty* is concerned it is not so binding, of course, to a brother as a father and I should be inclined, were I in her place, to act upon my own feeling and responsibility concerning the disposal of my life.

(W. at H. VI 1896–7: 630)

Inward femininity was not about worrying 'your head' (it never had been); it was about the 'heart', here defined as the seat of love, not in the romantic sense but as the foundation of moral and spiritual life.

Like Robertson Nicholl, Mrs Smith came from the Scottish Non-conformist Christian tradition with its emphasis on individual salvation and she drew on this in her column. Although *Woman at Home* was ostensibly modelled on the *Strand*, it owed a good deal to the tradition of the quality religious magazines, produced for Sunday reading, like *Good Words*. These did not specify a female readership but were always aimed at the woman-centred family. Within that tradition, hierarchies of class, race and gender were both assumed and contested by the radical claims for sameness – if not equality – before God.

As a Non-conformist Scot in the imperial capital, Smith/Swan was sensitive to the differences of region and religion within Britain. The work of folklorists and the development of dialect journalism in this period constructed a British identity in which regional difference was confirmed as part of being British (Dorson 1968). This process, which *Woman at Home* enacted in its fiction and articles, was also central to Swan's persona, since she represented herself at once as an ex-patriate Scot and as essentially a metropolitan.

The hierarchies of class and race were more difficult to deal with. Swan assumed the middle-class woman was not only her reader but represented the best kind of femininity. The mill-girl who wrote asking how to escape from relentless labour into a life as a lady's companion was advised that it was better to be content than aspire to change her class position (*W. at H.* VI 1896–7: 950). Swan read her letters from across the empire, as evidence of the power of love around the world but they consistently assumed that the 'natives' were not fully human. Whether 'aborigines' or 'Kaffirs', they were represented either as part of the exotic scenery or as objects of charity but never as the potential friends or sisters which other 'white women' in the same place were presumed to be (*W. at H.* VI 1896–7: 788–9).

This casual racism which Annie Swan never disputed was linked with an implicit elision of Christianity, whiteness and the capacity to be a self. Yet in her fiction Swan addressed the issues of racial prejudice in the West Indies with some sensitivity to its destructive power (*W. at H.* III 1894–5: 92–100). Similarly her Christianity was not sectarian; she had no time for inter-church rivalries and theological disputes. But she did assume a consonance between Christianity and the highest morality which posited inclusiveness but excluded those who did not share her position.

Readers complained that it was impossible to fit the ideal femininity of the magazines with end-of-the-century female experience but it was not these differences which were their concern. Few working-class women appeared among the correspondents and none of the non-white women from around the world.[5] The letters came from middle-class women, usually married or expecting to be, living at home – precisely the target group of the magazine. The problem of how to find a suitable partner, which had been the stuff of novels and correspondence columns for decades, was only one – and that not the most important – of the recurring motifs. Much more important were the letters from those already married or in families who were, nevertheless, unhappy, 'lonely' or even 'desperate'.

There were letters from unhappy wives whose husbands locked them into 16-inch corsets, embezzled their money, neglected them for younger women or were simply 'bad' (*W. at H.* V 1895–6: 316, 477, 556). Annie Swan did not condemn the wives who complained; she offered her sympathy and her prayers. More remarkably, in the case of the 'bad' husband, she suggested that:

> When a woman conscientiously feels that [her personal dignity and self-respect] are constantly degraded by the relations of her married life, then I think it is her duty to end it . . . . We know how the world treats the woman who lives apart from her husband. It is this which keeps many women in the house of bondage when their outraged spirit would be free.
>
> (ibid.: 556)

Annie Swan was no radical or New Woman. She challenged the double sexual standard and argued for reciprocity in marriage but her grounds for doing so were that 'the divine spark' was present in each individual. She strongly condemned the 'spirit of unrest, the desire to kick against authority, the cry for liberty which is no liberty at all', which she perceived as undermining contemporary society. But the space given to letters from unhappy wives created anxiety in other readers. Some contributed letters on 'How to be Happy though Married'; happy wives suddenly decided – sometimes at their husbands' request – 'to write and tell you how happy I am'. Some contemplating marriage wrote in because they were 'anxious to avoid the apparently unhappy existence of some of your correspondents' (ibid.: 476, 556). Contented spinsters wrote in to say they were too busy with 'womanly pursuits' to bother with falling in love (ibid.: 556).

Such complaints from those at the very centre of the society rather than its margins, posed a radical threat to the equation of woman with home and marriage on which the magazine was based. Annie Swan's faith in woman's 'conscientious feeling' as a guide to her 'duty' sometimes made her suggest the inadequacy of social codes, which elsewhere she upheld. More radically, she began to identify the 'bitter cry' of the middle-class woman not as an individual but as a social problem. However, within the moral and individual discourse of the magazine, an analysis on these lines could not be entertained. This becomes apparent in that most persistent problem of her correspondents, how to earn a living as a middle-class woman.

WRITING AND THE NEED
FOR ECONOMIC INDEPENDENCE

Annie Swan regularly complained that she was beset with letters from women needing to earn a living and specifically from aspiring writers:

> SPIGA'S case is one of which I hear so often that I feel oppressed by a great sadness. The bitter cry of the single woman without means or lucrative occupation seems to me one of the most pressing problems of the age. She proposes to write, if I can give her any hint as to the best way to succeed. I do not think that even with the most careful guidance the writing of stories and poems can meet 'Spiga's' present pressing need.
>
> (*W. at H.* V 1895–6: 67)

Instead she suggested Spiga try and obtain a situation in a household 'where, if she has any leisure, she may cultivate her talent' (ibid.).

Two aspects of her response to Spiga were typical of Swan's column. First, although she defined the problem of the odd woman as a – indeed *the* – pressing social problem of the age, she could only offer sympathy. Her solution was to thrust Spiga back into the role of the woman who was 'merely a domestic'. The chance of having leisure to write disappeared in parentheses. Her refusal to recommend writing, like her silence on shop-work or other 'business' employment, was bitterly attacked by one correspondent who 'suppose[d] you, like too many ladies, feel the occupation is *infra dig*' (*W. at H.* V 1895–6: 469). Though she rejected the charge, Swan was caught in the dilemma of recognising the problem, feeling for the victims but offering as solution a restatement of the problem.

Yet she herself, as a professional writer, was visible proof that there was a way of reconciling the roles of 'woman at home' and 'professional writer'. The very public persona of Annie S. Swan had inscribed within it another, more shadowy, but also more solid – that of Mrs Burnett Smith, the 'real' woman, wife and mother. Unlike the figure of the 'real' editor, Robertson Nicoll, the figure of Mrs Burnett Smith was regularly brought before readers. References to her Scots childhood, her happy marriage, her children, her household were delicately interwoven into all Annie Swan's columns.[6] Her double persona (Smith/Swan) enabled her to present herself simultaneously as an ordinary woman, just like her readers, and as extraordinary, having escaped the problems which her columns revealed as endemic to womanhood. In addition, the magazine regularly ran the usual illustrated interviews with writers and, in the new century, a regular series called 'Journals of a Literary Woman in London' (*W. at H.* II 1894–5: 118–23, 247–52; XIII 1901–2: 42, 130, etc.).

No wonder that for Spiga and many other of Swan/Smith's correspondents, writing seemed to offer an escape. Annie Swan's steady unwillingness to offer any encouragement to these would-be-Annie-Swans probably sprang partly from a professional's resistance to the idea that anyone with a modicum of education could be a writer and partly from her knowledge of the substantial difficulties facing women who wanted to earn a living by 'stories and poems'. However, she was also caught up in a dilemma: how could she make a space for her own achievement within the ideology she inhabited? She continued to represent the role of professional writer as both impossible for women and important to them. She returned again and again to this, not only in her columns but also in her own and other's fiction.

ANNIE SWAN'S FICTION

Up to half the space in *Woman at Home* was given to fiction, and it regularly carried at least one serial as well as complete short stories and, at various times, series of stories by Annie Swan. The pattern of a series of short stories linked by a central figure was a periodical format which combined some of the advantages of the serial, especially familiar characters, with those of the short story. In the publishing turmoil of the 1890s, magazines began to adopt this format, most famously in Conan Doyle's Sherlock Holmes series in the *Strand.*

Swan's major series also used a connecting character: in one the school teacher, Margaret Grainger, and in another the woman doctor, Elizabeth Glen.[7] Like Conan Doyle, Swan located her Doctor series in London but instead of the detective genre, she used naturalism to explore a range of social problems, especially as they affected women. Stories of alcoholism, the plight of young women workers in London, race prejudice, adoption of working-class children by the middle class, all centred round the activities of her protagonist, the young and beautiful Elizabeth Glen.

Again like Conan Doyle, Swan constructed this series round the interplay between a protagonist and an observer/narrator. In her story, both were professional women. Elizabeth Glen, her heroine, was a doctor but, unlike Dr Watson, her practice provided the impetus for the various stories. Her unnamed narrator was obviously Annie Swan herself. The contradictions of what it meant to be a professional woman in the 1890s become evident in the turns the series took along its time-span, since Annie Swan developed an overarching narrative as well as a central character. The story of Elizabeth Glen MD seemed at first to be both a vindication of the New Woman and a model of that more robust 'alternative to the heroines of fiction' which the 1890s needed (*W. at H.* I 1894: 11). Trained as a doctor, despite the resistance of her family and society, she was not at all the mannish woman of the stereotypes. Her femininity was both outward and inner; visible in her beautiful eyes and sweet face and evident in her compassion and concern for the moral as well as the physical well-being of her patients. In her womanliness and professionalism – even in the disputed area of medicine – were compatible.

But the original project could not apparently be sustained. The trajectory of the story began to follow the line of Annie Swan's other romances. Elizabeth Glen married a childhood sweetheart, who was rich, handsome, and alternated living in his castle in Scotland with the fashionable London residence necessary to a rising

MP. In a second series she retired from practice and, as Mrs Keith Hamilton, struggled with how to employ her energies, falling back eventually on charitable works and trying to produce an heir. The return of the heroine to her traditional place is the result of two related forces, the demands of the romance fiction formula and the need to reassert the domestic nature of woman.

Much of the fiction in *Woman at Home* remained within the territory marked out by this second series. Other kinds of narrative occasionally appeared with alternative heroines who chose work rather than marriage, as in Annie Swan's own short story, 'Independent Woman' (*W. at H*. VIII 1899–1900: 265–74). More frequently serials and short stories ended with the recuperation of both heroine and narrative to the traditional fictive and social order.

The role of the other professional woman, the narrator of the series, was less well developed. However, it reinforced the importance of 'the woman writer' as a symbol in the magazine. In particular, she represented the recurrent fantasy that professional writing could be both financially rewarding and consistent with women's traditional role. The winning entry to a 'storyette' competition held in 1899, reverses the usual narrative pattern and has the heroine rescuing her husband. In 'The Disillusionment of Allan Upton' the wife has earned enough through her anonymous writing to save them both from ruin and his ailing magazine from collapse (*W. at H*. VIII 1899–1900: 64–6). However, this outcome followed from her decision when she married to bury 'the old ambitions, the dreams of an independent career' so that 'out of the ashes springs another woman more useful than the old – perhaps happier . . .' (ibid.).

The woman forced to write by the bankruptcy, death or illness of her father or husband was a common figure in the literary world of the 1890s (Black 1906: passim; Cross 1985: 164–203; Mumm 1990). In this storyette she became a heroine. The challenge presented by the professional woman to the ideology of the domestic was defused through the benign power of writing-in-the-magazine, which was both the subject and the medium of the story.

The Annie Swan of the Elizabeth Glen series was the signifier of this power. As the heroine's friend she represented that ideal of female solidarity which Swan also enacted in her letters columns. However, the Swan of the series was also the complete professional journalist, described by her friend's husband as 'insatiable for copy', always ready to display the intimate details of her friendship in public, eager to make a story out of the suffering which her friend sought to relieve (*W. at H*. V 1895–6: 32). Not only was she a woman whose identity was defined by her profession, rather than her domestic situation, that profession meant destroying the private/public divide and bringing the most private aspects of women's lives under the public gaze.

The fictional transformation of domestic life into public performance, which was the writer's role in the Doctor Glen series, echoed the process involved in the serialised life of Queen Victoria and in Annie Swan's letters columns, where the power of published writing to transform the private into the public truth was most apparent. The promise that the woman's magazine can transform the female reader is endemic in the genre. In the late twentieth century the readers of one journal can volunteer to be 'made-over' with a new haircut, clothes and make-up. Annie Swan resisted readers' demands that the magazine transform their material circumstances by giving them access to the world of journalism through writing in the magazine. Instead, it was the process of *writing* itself which promised to make over its correspondents, transforming their private selves into public narratives through the power of print.

12

'FORWARD BUT NOT TOO FAST': THE ADVANCED MAGAZINE?

> 'WOMAN' is intended to be neither a fashion paper, a 'Society' Journal nor the organ of the 'Anti-Man' or 'Blue Stocking' Schools. We intend to do our best to cater for modern woman, not as she might be, but as she actually is. While sparing no trouble or expense to make our paper readable, we shall avoid pandering to unwholesome appetites or appealing to those who are 'women' in name only.
>
> (*Woman* 11 Jan. 1890: 2)

> We recognise not only the progressive tendency of the age but also the ever-growing demand among all classes for cheap journalistic literature.
>
> ('Opening Editorial', *Woman* 3 Jan. 1890: 1)

In 1890 it was easier to define 'the modern woman's' reading by negatives than to offer positive models. Belief in the 'progressive tendencies of the age' left open the question of what a progressive woman's paper might look like. Apart from the publications of political and campaigning groups, there had been, from mid-century onwards a few journals which explicitly advocated a programme of women's rights. It was a thin trickle which became a stream, if not a torrent, of words between 1900 and 1914 when, for the first time ever, there was a lively and diverse periodical press which spoke to and for women in terms of their rights, especially the right to vote (Doughan and Sanchez 1987). However, even at the height of the suffrage campaigns, this was a relatively small part of the women's press and most papers still refused to have anything to do with what they described as 'strong-mindedness' or 'women's rights-ism'.

In the 1890s, 'the Woman Question' continued to provide subject matter for debate but, in the dynamic between the economic and the ideological in which magazines were made, addressing the strong-minded woman seemed incompatible with selling copies. I begin this chapter with a brief survey of some of the radical or progressive journals of the latter half of the century but its main focus is *Woman*, a strictly commercial, 'advanced' penny paper founded in 1890 to provide for a readership it defined as neither strong- nor weak-minded but 'intelligent womanly women' (*W.* 1 Jan. 1891: 1).

RADICAL EXPERIMENTS, 1850–90

In the late 1850s, as Beeton's *EDM* established itself, two very different – though similar sounding – titles were launched which specifically addressed women's social and political position. The *Englishwoman's Review (and Drawing Room Journal of Social Progress, Literature and Art)* (1857–9) claimed 'to address the women of England from the woman's point of view' and defined women's lack of occupation as a pressing social problem. Categorically refusing to 'prate of "women's rights"', it deployed the well-worn strategy of redefining 'rights' and 'occupation' in terms of 'usefulness and kindness' (*EWR* I 1857: 1). It carried political news but only to enable women to shed their 'softening influence' more widely and its refusal to give space to fashion or the 'London Season' sprang from its anti-aristocratic sentiment. It thus reproduced the now familiar identity of the English Domestic Woman as moral agent.

By contrast the *English Woman's Journal* (1858–64) explicitly addressed women's rights in relation to paid employment, education and legal status. Edited by Bessie Parkes and Mary Hays, it continued every month until 1864, offering its readers a forum for discussion of the theoretical and practical problems of early 'feminism' (that is the middle-class, liberal feminism of the Langham Place Circle)[1] (Horstein 1985; Nestor 1982; Rendall 1987). It merged with the *Alexandra Magazine* (1864–6) in a cheaper format but this new journal did not last. It was followed by the *Englishwoman's Review* which lasted until 1910 (Doughan 1987; Nestor 1982).[2] This journal sustained the political commitment to women's rights pioneered by the *Journal* but tended towards being 'a log-book' and notice board of political activities rather than a true magazine (Walker 1974: 3).

Important as both the *English Woman's Journal* and the *Review* were in terms of the development of feminism as a theory and practice, their circulation remained tiny (probably no more than 500 in the case of the *EWJ*, possibly 2,000 for the *EWR* by 1910) and they deliberately did not compete with commercial publications for women (Rendall 1987; Walker 1974). Jessie Boucherett not only edited the *EWR*, she sustained it financially. She was convinced that the project was incompatible with commercial publishing and the intrusion of 'active pecuniary interest' into the venture would mean

> . . . goodbye to the advocacy of any subject which would have entailed a breath of ridicule; goodbye to any thorough expression of opinion, goodbye to the humble but ceaseless struggle of all these years and to the results which have sprung up around the small office where so many workers collected together because the purpose and the plan were *honestly conceived and carried out.*
>
> (quoted in Nestor 1982: 97 and Walker 1974: 20)

This analysis of the connection between the ideological and commercial formations led her to refuse any concessions to the market. In the absence of a broadly based political movement to give financial support, this position was only possible to those, like Boucherett, who had substantial private means. It was not available to or, perhaps, even shared by, others who wanted to use the periodical press to advance the cause of women as a group or class.

Between the 1860s and the 1890s a handful of editors and proprietors tried to find a way between the stark alternatives of the small circulation, non-profit-making paper and the commercial venture which refused any taint of 'women's rights-ism'. These journals were mainly short-lived. *Women's World* (1866–8) became the *Kettledrum* in 1869 but this 'woman's signal for action' sounded only until 1870, which seemed to endorse the argument that a feminist position was incompatible with the market (Braithwaite and Barrell 1988: 8). Amelia Lewis adopted a rather different tone but was no more successful in establishing a radical commercially viable magazine for women in the 1870s. She was involved in at least two separate ventures which each lasted less than a year; *Woman* (1872) which claimed to speak for women 'as a class' and *Woman's Opinion* (1874), representing the social, domestic and educational interests of women.

There was, however, one successful periodical of the 1860s and 1870s which was produced by women and which dared the 'breath of ridicule' by espousing women's rights and which shared the position and was produced from the same group as the *Journal*. It was the *Victoria Magazine*, a shilling monthly launched in 1863 which continued until 1880, carrying fiction, poetry and general articles. Edited by Emily Faithfull of the Langham Place Circle, dedicated to a female monarch, produced on the Victoria Press, which was run entirely by women, and committed to attacking the unjust social prejudice which constrained all the female sex, it was a women's magazine in every sense, except that it did not define its readers exclusively as women – aiming instead for a general if sympathetic readership (Nestor 1982: 103). This important venture in female publishing deserves a book of its own but is outside the scope of this one.

Other 1870s radical magazines aimed at women which survived, tended to be more specifically focused either on employment issues, like Louisa Hubbard's publications, or on specific campaigns, especially the vote. The *Women's Suffrage Journal* (1870–90). which Lydia Becker edited and produced in Manchester, was a log-book for the movement and the forerunner of the feminist press of the years between 1900 and 1914 (Doughan 1987).[3]

Although it, too, is outside my scope, the feminist and especially the suffrage press is significant for my study because it did not eschew everything about the commercial press. Not only did *Votes for Women* and other journals use the techniques of New Journalism to good effect, deploying headlines, pictures and lively writing, they also followed commercial practice in taking advertisements as a method of finance. Boucherett's fears that such concessions would mean 'goodbye to any thorough expression of opinion' proved too pessimistic – or perhaps did not take account sufficiently of the radical heterogeneity of the periodical. Nevertheless the problem of reconciling political radicalism and the strategies of commercial journalism continued – as they still do a century later.[4] The potential contradiction in the suffrage press between the woman reader as constructed in the editorial copy and addressed in the advertisements was only the most visible sign of this problem.

The suffrage journals of the early twentieth century were building on the developments of the 1890s, a decade in which particular groups, parties or organisations increasingly produced their own journals for members but which also saw various attempts to find a way of sustaining a commercially viable but radical press for women. One of the liveliest of the new wave of papers which openly espoused women's rights was the *Women's Penny Paper* (1888–90), which became the *Women's Herald* (1891–3). This, like the *Victoria Magazine*, was produced entirely by women and advertised itself as 'the only paper in the world conducted, written [printed and published] by women'. Unlike the *Victoria* this adopted a newspaper rather than a magazine format and, as a penny weekly, aimed at a more popular readership. It was succeeded by Mrs Fenwick Miller's *Woman's Signal* (1895–9), another radical penny weekly which eventually flagged and failed despite the prodigious energy and journalistic skills of its editor/proprietor (Van Arsdel 1982). A rather different but also important radical paper was *Shafts*, launched in 1892 as a paper 'for women and the working class'. Neither of these papers had a simple or stable position over the course of their publication history, but both sought to combine a more or less radical politics with elements of commercialism.

Though none of these lasted for long measured against the new magazines launched in the 1890s by Pearson, Harmsworth or Newnes, they survived at least as long as many smaller ventures with a purely commercial aim. The apparent success of the radical penny papers in particular must have raised the question of whether there were now enough 'advanced' women to make it worth running a progressive journal on a purely commercial basis.

WOMAN, A CHEAP PROGRESSIVE MAGAZINE?

Woman promised to be a paper addressed, not to the 'new', but to the 'modern' woman. Its first editor and founder, Fitzroy Gardiner, declared that it was providing something 'never before attempted', a penny weekly for 'intelligent but womanly women' (*W.* 2 Jan. 1891: 1). Claiming an imprecisely large circulation after a year, he attributed this success to the support of 'young women of the middle and upper classes who are intellectually outgrowing the namby-pamby milk-and-water-style of literature with which they have hitherto been provided by most papers devoted to their sex' (ibid.).

Woman from the start distinguished its kind of progressiveness from that of the early feminists. Its second number claimed it would address 'women who do not fight for rights but are womanly without being dolls' (*W.* 11 Jan. 1890: 13). A year later it repeated that:

The aggressive type of strong-minded woman who insists upon doing everything that men do and displays a morbid love of discovering grievances and disadvantages – frequently imaginary and occasionally real – under which women exist is, we are told disgusted with us . . . . For her we have never intended and never wish to cater.

(W. 1 Jan. 1891: 1)

Positively defining the female reader for this new kind of magazine proved much more difficult though the editors tried:

> Our *raison d'être* is neither politics, dress, the doings of 'society' . . . the ventilation of imaginary grievances of the sex, the school of sickly sentimentality nor the advertisement of vice and viciousness but simply to inform and entertain modern woman – not as she might be, but as we find her.

(W. 3 Jan. 1890: 1)

Arnold Bennett looking back on his period first as an assistant editor and then as editor of *Woman* in the 1890s recalled how the 'editorial belief that the status of women ought to be raised and enlarged' was tempered by such a powerful determination to 'offend the feelings of nobody that our columns almost never indicated in what direction feminine progress ought to be made' (Hepburn 1979: 34). However, the struggle to define the modern woman, which was evident in *Woman*, and which makes it a useful case study was not located only in the editorial consciousness. Nor was it confined to gender politics, fraught though these were in the 1890s. It was also about the new press.

In its address to the modern woman as magazine reader, *Woman* situated itself at the intersection of gender politics and journalism, each going through its own crisis of the 'new'. It specifically linked the 'progressive tendency' of the age not only with the advance of woman but also with the 'ever-growing demand for cheap journalistic literature' (*W.* 3 Jan. 1890: 1). It thus prefigured the processes by which in the mid-1890s, the New Woman was to become increasingly identified with the New Fiction, not least in the pages of *Woman* itself. Indeed Arnold Bennett, who was assistant editor from 1894 to 1896 and then editor until 1900, claimed the magazine as a 'progressive organ', more for its sympathetic treatment of 'advanced fiction' than its support for 'advanced woman' (Hepburn 1979: 35). He thus elided fictional style and gender politics through the connecting mechanism of the epithets 'new' or 'advanced'.

CLASS AND WOMAN

The title 'woman' as against 'lady' and the positive inflection given to the idea of 'cheap' literature signified the centrality of class to both the discourses of femininity and those of the new journalism. That country dance of meanings in which the words 'lady' and 'woman' changed places was in full swing in the feminine press of the 1880s and 1890s. Wilde's refusal to edit *Lady's World* unless Cassell's agreed to change its title to *Woman's World* was only the most famous example of a general movement by which 'woman' became a positive term for 'all classes', not least in the magazine entitled *Woman* (Nowell Smith 1958: 149ff, 253ff).

But *Woman* also wanted to capture the penny serial from its associations with the 'unwholesome appetites' of sensationalism and working-class female reading. It proclaimed itself as cheap but stressed that it was 'healthy'. At least one early reviewer hoped 'it would supersede in many households some of those pernicious ones that are now taken by the fair sex' (*W.* 11 Jan. 1890: 2). One writer assured readers that 'a well-written periodical provided for the maid will prevent indulgence in trashy novelettes' (*W.* 18 Jan. 1893: 5). *Woman* itself might have fulfilled this function.

Despite maintaining its price at a penny throughout the decade, *Woman* assumed its readers were not female domestic servants with their notoriously unhealthy taste for trashy serials. Yet early editorials and advertisements stressed that it was for 'all classes of women who want something more than the "lady's" or "society" paper or cookery book and something less than the ponderous daily leader . . . or the academic weekly or monthly review' (*W.* 3 Jan. 1890: 1). Another reviewer was quoted approvingly in an early number as saying it would be 'as much appreciated by the well to do as by those to whom the low price offers a special attraction' (*W.* 15 March 1890: 2). Its first sub-title defined it as '[For] all sorts and conditions of women'.

This sub-title itself warns against taking at face value these claims to address a classless womanhood. It obviously recalled the title of Walter Besant's popular novel of 1882, *All Sorts and Conditions of Men*, which came second in a competition among readers of *Woman* to name the 'work of modern fiction which has made the most lasting and healthy impression on my mind' (*W.* 5 April 1890: 3). It was the story of an aristocratic heiress who proclaimed her sisterhood with the working-class seamstresses of East London by leaving the West End to live among them and help set up a model work-shop. Besant's heroine represented not merely a rejection of women's rights but a positively Ruskinian model of the lady which made the working-class woman the object of feminine benevolence rather than the subject of a shared gender identity.

Though the sub-title disappeared in 1891, the first of a number the magazine ran through in the decade, this particular version of the class/gender construction remained important in the paper. In 1895, in its only attempt to mobilise the readers as a group, the magazine suggested:

> an organisation for women akin to Freemasonry . . . . The Women's Guild of Sympathy . . . [to enable] women of the upper and middle classes who are anxious to contribute to the happiness of the world and in particular of womankind on non-sectarian lines . . . to unite all women . . . and to show what earnest-minded Englishwomen can do in the way of organising themselves on methodical lines and of working for good in a Christian spirit.
>
> (*W.* 3 April 1895: iii)

The editors' early construction of their readers as mainly middle and upper class was regularly recalled in articles which assumed that readers would enjoy a middle- or upper middle-class income and would employ a servant who had to be kept 'happy, comfortable and contented without detriment to her duties' (*W.* 18 Jan. 1893: 1).[5] The various changes in sub-title which indicated the magazine's struggle to define its readership in its early years ended in 1895 when it settled on 'A Paper for Gentlewomen', which it retained for the rest of the century. This suggests the consolidation of its target readership as solidly middle class, as indeed was almost certainly the case.[6] However, locating modern woman in class terms was only part of the problem of the new magazine.

Its project was a complex one, since it defined itself simultaneously as cheap-but-healthy and progressive-but-not-strong-minded. In the mid-1890s, the new giants of periodical publishing joined battle over the market for the penny weekly which they successfully re-made as 'healthy reading' (see Ch. 13). None of their multiple titles made claims to be 'advanced' and their task of redefining the femininity of the penny public was therefore comparatively easy. By contrast, *Woman* and its femininity were particularly fractured and constantly in process of reconstruction.

That fragmentation was evident at every level. Despite its insistence that it was 'not a class paper', *Woman's* 28 pages reproduced in a truncated and cheaper format many of the qualities of *Queen*; fashion news and patterns, illustrated lives and interviews, reviews, gossip about royalty and women in the news and illustrations – though, not surprisingly, these were less well-produced than *Queen's*. Display and other advertisements increasingly dominated the magazine on full-page spreads inside the covers and interleaved with editorial copy, taking up 11–14 of *Woman's* 28 pages in the mid-1890s, proportionally almost as much space as in the sixpenny ladies' papers. Like the ladies' papers and unlike Annie Swan, it did not locate the truth of its readers in an inner self explored through the confessional letter. However, the femininity it produced located these qualities of the lady in the practical domesticity of menu preparation, sewing and household tips. Although it assumed servants, it assumed also that the reader was engaged in the work of running the house, making her own clothes and managing the shopping as well as the moral economy of the family.

THE RETURN OF THE DOMESTIC IDEAL

Woman thus returned again and again to articulate domesticity as the natural expression of the female self. This aspect of its self-definition was clearly signalled in the very first number where the editor placed on the first page an article on the 'ideal' woman by Eliza Lynn Linton, by now notorious for her equally fierce attacks on women's rightists on one hand and the fashion-conscious woman on the other.

Linton's article was an uncompromising restatement of the dual theme of women's moral superiority and social subordination to 'the men with whom they are connected and . . . the children who are one day to be men and women, citizens of the state and mothers of the world' (*W.* 3 Jan. 1890: 2). She thus re-inscribed the absolute equation of women and maternity not only back into the

1890s but into the foreseeable future, where women's highest aim in life would always be 'to be able to merge themselves in others' (ibid.). She acknowledged that the modern woman wanted to be 'independent, active, self-supporting, individualised' and argued that she could be all this *as long as* she also remained 'essentially womanly in all the tenderness of love and recognition of differences which go to form the womanly character' (ibid.).

This abstract moralising, harking back as it did to the early nineteenth-century domestic writers, was not the usual mode in which the domestic appeared in *Woman*. Far more pervasive was the 'Wrinkle', a colloquialism equivalent to 'Tips' or 'Handy Hints', which embodied specific advice on a problem to do with housework. However, the 'wrinkle', with its address to practical economics, was linked with the rhetoric of moral management in the discourse of the domestic which circulated through the editorial copy and reader's contributions. A typical competition run in 1894 invited readers to submit essays on one of two topics which were equally weighted: 'When is a girl child closest to her mother?' and 'How can I cut down on household expenses?' (*W.* 3 Jan. 1894). In a similar competition to define what was 'unwomanly' most of the entries printed reproduced Linton's argument and her rhetoric; the neglect of home was absolutely unwomanly, the ultimate betrayal of womanliness was to forget that woman is only womanly when she sets herself to man 'like perfect music unto noble words' (*W.* 15 Nov. 1893: 7).

As with the earlier formulations of domestic ideology, the identification of 'womanhood' with the domestic and specifically the maternal was represented as universal. However, it assumed as norm the paradigmatic middle-class family of husband, wife, children and servants. In one of its characteristic bits of royal gossip in the 'D'You Know?' column *Woman* revealed that the Princess Christian was so anxious about the health of her son on his return from abroad that she had 'stood by while housemaids made the bed' so she could check the number of blankets. The point of the story was to show that 'All mothers [are] akin whatever their position may be' (*W.* 1 April 1896: 3). In this scenario the maid making the bed is not part of that kinship which links readers with royalty; she is neither motherly, nor – by extension – womanly.

An analogous process was at work in Linton's article which re-worked the earlier relationship of nation and race to femininity. What is remarkable about this 1890s version, is how explicit Linton made the nationalist and racist elements endemic in this model of femininity. The earlier *Englishwoman's Domestic Magazine* subsumed national identity into a classed femininity. In this later version, written as Britain's imperial role was being redefined, class was subsumed in a racialised and nationalist version of gender. The passage is worth quoting at length:

Englishwomen have always held a prominent place in English life. Without direct political power they have unbounded personal influence and by that influence they have greatly helped to form the national character. A breath of the strong old Norse life still lingers about them and makes them

181

emphatically the fit companions and worthy mothers of men. Less vivacious than the French, they are less petulant and more steadfast; less sensuous than the Italians, they are better educated and more cleanly minded; more independent and refined than the Germans, they are not the mere household drudges to which Teutonic women have sunk. They move on grander, more heroic lines than any of these; and the ideal Englishwoman stands among those white-armed daughters of the gods who know how to command respect while giving love.

(*W.* 3 Jan. 1890: 1)

The comparison is only with Britain's European rivals, but the apotheosis of the English woman reveals its inherent racism. As with the hierarchies of European nations invoked in the male imperialist romances like *She*, the superiority of Britain to Italy or France is set in a larger world order where the 'white-armed' rulers of the world inspire respect among those implicitly darker and lesser. Just as masculinity was redefined during this period in terms of Britain's imperial power, so the concept of the 'Englishwoman' was given a Social Darwinist inflection.

The centrality of race and nation to the 'womanliness' constructed by the magazine was less coherent than this article suggested. It veered between relatively serious articles on Chinese women and footbinding and Indian women and suttee and more frivolous 'Letters from Abroad'. What united these was the assumption of the view from an 'English set', in which the 'natives' are viewed as exotic, victimised and childish but always as 'other' (*W.* 31 Jan. 1900: 11 and 13; 2 March 1892: 5; 18 Jan. 1890: 11). What was crucial here was not the construction of the 'other woman' but the model of a self which the magazine offered its readers, a true femininity produced as always white and British as well as middle class.

Like *Woman at Home*, this magazine was a metropolitan publication with a readership across Britain but also 'throughout the English-speaking world' and especially in the 'Indian Empire' (*W.* 1 Jan. 1891: 3). What distinguished it from Annie Swan's *Woman at Home* was the complete absence of any space in the magazine for such readers to explore their relationship with the imperial 'homeland'.

The absolute hegemony of London in terms of dress and furniture but also in reading, ideas and attitudes was everywhere apparent. The shops, theatres and concerts it recommended or reviewed were in London, the gossip columns – which became increasingly important – dealt largely with London, or even more narrowly with New Grub Street and Clubland. The assumption that the magazine existed to make all its readers into Londoners was embodied in its 'Factotum Agency', an arrangement whereby 'country subscribers' could use the good offices of the magazine to buy items from London shops and conduct business with London agencies (see e.g. *W.* 3 Jan. 1890: 16).

AN ADVANCED PAPER?

Despite insisting that it was not a 'class paper', *Woman* made an interest in female royalty and aristocracy as well as a commitment to fashion as important as they were in the papers it deplored. For most of the decade its opening article was a gossip column called 'D'You Know?' which routinely began with information about Victoria.

As for appearance, as Bennett later confessed, *Woman* assumed: 'that the chief interest of the educated woman was with her personal appearance and articles and news and drawings intended to help her constituted the main part of the paper' (Hepburn 1979: 34). It always included several pages of illustrated fashion news and paper patterns, ran special fashion issues and maintained 'Answers to Correspondents' which dealt with health, appearance and dress. As a penny paper, it never attempted to provide the elaborate engravings or high quality photographs characteristic of *Queen* and the other sixpenny papers. Its fashion was illustrated with sketches embedded in the text. These, as Bennett rightly pointed out, were poorly drawn but had what were by now essential characteristics, female figures

> either solitary or in a universe peopled solely by women [all of which were] taller than life and slimmer than life with hand and fingers longer than life; and [with] . . . their lips parted in an everlasting simper.
>
> (Hepburn 1979: 33)

Woman thus re-made the traditions of middle-class domestic journalism by drawing specifically on the genres and ideology of the ladies' illustrated newspapers to create a new kind of cheap but healthy journal.

Such an account brings into question the magazine's claims to be 'advanced'. Since it refused the feminist analysis of women's rights, *Woman* rejected the journalistic models offered by the small feminist press. Instead it drew on the contradictions endemic in the periodical discourses of ladyship to construct its version of the 'intelligent but womanly woman'. In its claim to be all things to all women, *Woman* never explored its own ideological inconsistencies. Instead it exploited to the full the heterogeneity of the magazine formula which allowed different models of the self to sit side by side on the page without interrogating each other.

In the tradition of the feminine journal, it made girls' education central to its project but it treated women's demand for higher education simply as an unproblematic extension of the old rather than a contentious demand for the new. In 1893 it ran a series of articles called 'Where Girls Grow Wise' which dealt equally sympathetically with middle-class girls' schools, a French convent, Somerville Hall at Oxford and the London School of Medicine (*W.* 29 March 1893: 3; 12 April 1893: 3–4; 26 April 1893: 3). This last article was signed 'Aesculapia Victrix' (The Woman Doctor Triumphant), but this was the only acknowledgement that the entry of women into medicine was a highly contentious issue.

In 1898 *Woman* began to offer 'scholarships' of £25 to young women nominated by readers who wished to pursue an educational course (e.g. *W.* 5 Jan. 1898: 9). These were competitive and success depended on the number of voucher-votes from readers each candidate secured. A similar scheme run in 1899/1900 was aimed specifically at those wishing to pursue a Course of Commercial Training (see e.g. 8 Feb. 1899: 1). As I suggested in Chapter 8, this competition was neither original nor entirely disinterested. It was part of a more general competition between girls' and women's magazines in which such 'scholarships' played an important part rather than a radical intervention into the campaign for women's education (see p. 138).

The second-round scholarship, which was for commercial training, entered that other area into which the middle-class girl had 'advanced' by the 1890s, namely paid employment outside the home. Throughout the decade *Woman* included articles acknowledging that many women were in 'The World of Breadwinners', as one series was entitled. The case was made in its second number in a lively attack on an article by Lady Cowper in the *Nineteenth Century*:

> [Her] idea seems to be the highly original one that women should stay at home and mind the baby and be generally happy with their more or less cosy surroundings instead of going forth into the world with the view of earning their own livings, if single or, if married, (as of course they all ought to be) of helping their poor husband to keep the family pot boiling. Very good, my dear Lady Cowper . . . but how about the few thousand women and girls who have to get their own living, not having the good fortune, like yourself, to be born in the lap of luxury.
>
> (*W.* 11 Jan. 1890: 5)

It was typical of the fractured nature of *Woman*, especially in its early days, that this was followed eight pages later by a review supporting Lady C. and labelling the working woman as a manifestation of the general 'crisis in the life of women' (*W.* 11 Jan. 1890: 11). Though there was never any explicit acknowledgement that its position was contradictory, the 'Breadwinners' series gave way to alternating 'Chats with Young Mothers' and 'Chats with Young Housewives'. Though it resisted talk of rights, an early editorial had argued for women's trades unions and given space to Clementina Black to write on women's work (*W.* 18 Jan. 1890: 4). It continued throughout the decade to give brief but sympathetic notices of campaigns around such issues as the Shop Hours bill which specifically affected working women, the Conference of Women Workers and women's work on Poor Law Boards and School Boards (e.g. *W.* 18 Jan. 1890: 3 and 9; 15 Nov. 1893: 7).

It was in relation to the market in print that *Woman* was most consistently favourable to women's demands for access to public discourses and economic rights and it is no surprise that Bennett used his experience as editor to write a book on *Journalism for Women*. Journalism as a potential job appeared again and again in articles on women's work, in interviews with writers, in short stories and in the by-lined articles carrying women's names.

From its inception *Woman* had followed the tradition of using the magazine to encourage women to write for public print. Though it had no space for the confessional letter, it ran regular essay competitions, from which men were explicitly barred, and it published the winning entries. The competition titles assumed a narrow definition of women's interests but these contradictions had been endemic in the competition since Beeton. *Woman* strengthened the radical elements of the genre by using it to encourage women readers to submit articles for inclusion in the body of the paper. These would be accepted if sufficiently 'short and smartly written'. Like the late eighteenth- and early nineteenth-century magazines, it blurred the divide between the writer and reader, but in the new situation of the 1890s, with journalism now a profession which women could enter, *Woman*, unlike those early papers, offered to pay for such pieces at the commercial rate of 1 guinea per 800 words (*W.* 3/1/1890: 8).

These different elements scattered through its pages left open to readers the possibility of constructing a radical agenda in terms of education and access to paid work. But *Woman* never systematically exploited even these potential ruptures in the discourse of the lady. When it did attempt an overview, what became evident was the difficulty of constructing any definition of femininity which did not depend upon an understanding of the female body as 'less robust' than the male and as essentially maternal. Richard Le Galienne went as far as it was possible to go in redefining that relationship when he suggested in a special Literary Supplement on 'The New Womanhood' in 1894 'Let women become senior wranglers, lawyers, doctors, anything they please as long as they remain mothers' ('New Womanhood', *W.* Lit. Supp. 1894: 1).

An overview on women and work in the editor's 'Preliminary Observations' to a series on 'How Women May Make Money' promised 'merely sound practical information and advice on what has been done and may be done and how those who are fitted to work should set about it' (*W.* 23 Oct. 1893: 8). But the 'Observations' stressed that women's unequal position in the job market was a condition of their physical inferiority to men and their lack of 'the business instinct' which men had developed over generations.

> The robust body of the man has gradually developed a robust mind, a mind that can calculate, can grasp the situation and come to a prompt conclusion with little effort; the robust physique accounts for the pluck which enables him to go through with what he has started upon. Woman often has the temerity to begin but wants the pluck to overcome obstacles.
>
> (ibid.)

He acknowledged that:

> There are women who never have headaches and never feel inclined to sit down and have a good cry, who can work uniformly well throughout fifty of the fifty-two weeks of the year.
>
> (ibid.)

But these remained 'exceptions' that proved the general rule. The article deployed a muddled Social Darwinism to draw a deeply pessimistic view of women's current position in the market. It left undeveloped, but explicit, the argument that New Womanhood could only come about in some indefinite future when women might have evolved the more robust physique needed for business success.

The inescapable constraints of the female body were evident also in the advertisements, which came to occupy 11–14 of the magazine's 28 pages. These usually included publishers' notices of novels and other magazines, full-pages for well-known department stores like D.H. Evans or Maple and Co., proprietary foods and baby foods, domestic cleaning materials and carpet sweepers, knick-knacks and furniture, and bicycles. A substantial proportion were always addressed to and featured the female body; its need for fashionable clothes, a better complexion and a good corset and also its tendencies to illness. Beetham's Glycerine and Cucumber, the arsenic wafers, the Beecham's Powders and Mother Siegel's Syrup which appeared regularly in the advertisements were recommended also in the advertorials and answers to correspondents.

Here under various pen-names, including 'Medica', writers dispensed advice to readers along lines which would not alienate advertisers. The increasingly close relationship between advertising and editorial copy in women's magazines in general was flagged for months in 1895 when one of the advertisements on the front cover of *Woman* carried a recommendation for shoes from 'Butterfly' who wrote the advertorials in the *Lady's Pictorial* (e.g. 13 Nov. 1895).

Woman learned much from such up-market papers about the ways in which advertising and women's journalism worked together. In 1894 when a letter to *The Times* accused the ladies' papers of recommending items on the basis of hand-outs and free gifts from advertisers, *Woman* distanced itself from such devious financial dealings (*W.* 17 Jan. 1894: 5). But its claim only to accept advertising for products which it had tested rings hollow – especially given the extent of advertising it carried. If it is to be believed, *Woman* was even more dependent on advertising than the ladies' papers. In its third year, it told readers that it 'enables us to give every week for one penny what without advertising would cost five pence to produce' (*W.* 6 Jan. 1892: 2). As with the ladies' papers, so in *Woman* the visible and growing importance of advertising in its pages not only created specific named goods as desirable but also constructed for the reader a feminine self in which the female body was reproduced ideologically in terms of reproduction and economically in terms of consumption.

NEW JOURNALISM AND FEMININITY

Despite all this, *Woman* established a reputation for being 'advanced' (Hepburn 1979: 34). This may have been due to the motto 'Forward but not too fast' which it carried either on its title page or cover or both from its launch in 1890 until March 1899. This slangy pun with its hint of sexual daring was 'an incitement to lively comment in the bars and clubs' of masculine London when the magazine appeared (Pound 1952: 96). In this, as in much else, *Woman* was to prove a sheep in wolf's clothing and any gentleman buying it in the hopes of something saucy must have been disappointed.

The catchy motto was significant not because of its sexual politics but because it was characteristic of the New Journalism, where indeed *Woman* was systematically and unambiguously in the vanguard. The personalised tone and stress on personalities in its reporting, the illustrated interview, the use of the 'tit-bit' rather than the sustained argument, the competitions for readers, the reliance on advertisements and the steady increase in the importance of illustration as against letter press, all were there in *Woman*.

The magazine deployed these devices to create a feminised space of a particular kind in the magazine. Its most striking stylistic feature throughout the decade was its relentlessly chatty tone which insisted that it was the reader's friend rather than an authority figure or mentor. This effect was created first by the titles of the regular articles: 'Snuggery Small Talk', 'D'You Know?' and 'This and That'. Even the weekly music and book reviews were 'Music and Mummery' and 'Book Chat', later 'Barbara's Book Chat'. Advice on domestic and dress matters became 'Wrinkles'. The articles under these colloquial headings consisted of short discrete items, each barely more than a sentence or two long, with no apparent connection between them beyond their existence on the page, tit-bitty journalism in its purest form. 'D'You Know?' consisted of snippets of gossip usually beginning with the Queen or some other royal. 'This and That' dealt with dress and fashion. This kind of writing became more important over the 1890s; the editorial, 'Woman to Women' which appeared in the first few numbers with longer serious articles disappeared and was replaced with the 'D'You Know?' column.

Both subject and tone of these features was feminised. They were domestic, intimate and related to gossip, a form of speech associated particularly with women. This feminine inflection was emphasised by a number of devices, including the illustrated headings. 'Snuggery Small talk', for example, was illustrated with a vignette of women leaning towards each other as they talked or sat in relaxed poses round a table. The visuals thus reinforced the feminine connotations of the title.

This feminised space differed from that in *Woman at Home*, where Annie Swan's 'Over the Teacups' used a similar device to very different effect. For Annie Swan 'woman talk' could be serious. In *Woman* this was impossible. In this magazine to feminise was to belittle; the talk might be intimate but it must also be 'small', 'snug' and cosy. Annie Swan's moral economy depended on the circulation of feelings. *Woman* never defined womanliness in terms of the soul or the heart. 'Gossip' or 'wrinkles' were the currency which its writers and readers shared as women. There was no place in *Woman* for the letter about personal situations, love or romance. Correspondence was limited to questions of dress, appearance or household matters. Despite the rhetoric which placed woman as the moral centre of the home as well as the nation and the empire, moral issues were never discussed. Woman's important choices were of bonnet style and dinner menu.

This may account for an absence even more remarkable than that of the 'Love and Romance' letters column. For most of the 1890s *Woman* gave little space to fiction and virtually none at all to romantic fiction. The paper began to carry serials late in the century but the kind of fiction found in other penny magazines was never important to it. Its short stories in the early days were often ghost stories or depended on a plot twist; in Bennett's period as editor he contributed some lively squibs under the pen-name of Sal Volatile but no long or serious works of fiction. However Bennett continued the magazine's tradition of giving short but lively book reviews. In these he stressed that fiction and life must not be confused. It was on aesthetic criteria, not truth to life or having a 'good purpose', that a novel must be judged (*W.* 4 April 1894: 2). The novel and especially the romance, traditionally so important to women's reading, was therefore represented in *Woman* as a matter of opinion, of 'chats about books' or 'chats with authors', rather than of emotional involvement.

The most important single elements in the feminisation of the magazine's journalistic space was the editorial use of female pseudonyms. Unlike those magazines created round a single female persona ('Myra', 'Isabel' or 'Annie Swan'), *Woman* used a range of editorial names, beginning with Marjorie and Marguerite, to which were added Barbara and Sal or Sal Volatile, Hermione and 'Medica'. The journalistic use of first names only was a radical departure from contemporary social practice, which was much more formal than in the late twentieth century. The meaning of a name like 'Marjorie' as a by-line was at once to introduce a note of almost aggressive intimacy and to signal that this was the world of journalism. There was no serious attempt in *Woman* to develop any of these personae. The device was used with little attempt to conceal that it was simply a journalistic game. When Bennett devised the name Sal Volatile he was clearly parodying the convention as he used it. Readers were, therefore, invited to take pleasure in their own knowingness as readers of the New Journalism, while they enjoyed what the magazine offered.

In one important respect, however, readers were not invited to share the editorial strategy. These female pen-names concealed a series of male editors whose identity and, more important, gender were never revealed in the pages of the magazine.[7] While it might be acceptable for more sophisticated readers to enjoy the knowledge that 'Sal' was not a 'real' person, it would not do to reveal that she was not a woman at all. This silence is telling. In the 1850s Beeton as a matter of course conducted the *EDM* with a masculine persona and the female identity of his co-editor remained almost invisible. In the 1890s the situation had apparently reversed itself. The male editor entered the feminised space of the journal disguised as a woman.

For Bennett, his time on the editorial staff of *Woman* was crucial to his progression from provincial clerk to metropolitan journalist and then to internationally famous author. He had persuaded his father to put up the substantial sum of £300 for the shares in the company which he had to buy to secure the job. It launched him into a writing career. Looking back on his period on the paper, however, it was not this material and intellectual advantage which Bennett represented as important.

Instead, he was at pains to show himself as a more 'advanced woman' than any of his readers. Indeed his reviews of books, theatre and music written under various female pseudonyms, especially 'Barbara', were he claimed 'of so advanced a kind that they might . . . have ruined the paper had they been read' (Hepburn 1979: 35). His biographer, Margaret Drabble, follows Bennett in this estimate of his position on the magazine (Drabble 1975: 59). Yet the tradition of such reviews was well established in the lady's magazine and could be accommodated within its discourses of education and leisure. Though Bennett did welcome the *Yellow Book* and treat new fiction seriously, Barbara and her 'Chats about Books' were not the disruptive presence he describes.

Even more significantly, Bennett represented himself as the only truly advanced woman on the staff of the paper. It is appropriate that this truth manifested itself in relation to that crucial signifier of traditional femininity, the corset. Bennett wrote:

> I recall remarking to a circle of regular contributors that corsets as then worn were unhealthy, unhygienic and indefensible. Nobody could honestly deny the truth of the statement but if I had asserted that the Ten Commandments were indefensible I could not have produced a greater horror on sweet earnest countenances. I was made to understand that if my opinion got about . . . the paper would be utterly ruined. Therefore my opinion was not permitted to get about.
>
> (Hepburn 1979: 35)

This story is more interesting for what it denies than for what it asserts. Bennett conceals the paper's dependence on advertising, including advertising for corsets, for its financial viability. Even more significantly, he denies his economic and cultural power over the women contributors and instead invests them with the power he holds himself, as editor and shareholder. The gender dynamics of this encounter are significant since they were invisible in, yet structured the magazine.

Cross-dressing was a theme of 1880s and 1890s Advanced Fiction, notably Sarah Grand's *Heavenly Twins* voted best novel of 1893 in *Woman* and Olive Schreiner's *Story of an African Farm* (*W.* 4 April 1894: Comp.). In these novels cross-dressing was used to explore the possibility of new gender formations, both masculine and feminine, as Wilde had done in his editorship of *Woman's World* (Brake 1994: 127–47). Cross-dressing in other magazine stories of the 1890s was a device for tricking the innocent onlookers, as in Conan Doyle's 'Man with the Watches' (*Strand* XVI 1898: 33–43).[8]

The game of disguise played by the male editors in *Woman* partakes more of the trickery of the detective story than the serious exploration of gender identity in advanced fiction or in Wilde's model of editorship. It was an element of that New Journalistic feminisation of the press which I have described, a symptom not only of the struggle over the meaning of the feminine but also over who had access to its power.

13

WOMAN-TALK AS COMMODITY: THE PENNY DOMESTIC MAGAZINE

This page will be devoted to that most fascinating subject for women – shopping. What should we do without that occupation, that solemn business of our days, that gives us such joy and such head-aches, mental confusion, dizziness and causes our respective men . . . such veiled amusement when we cite a day's shopping as infinitely more fatiguing than a day in the City or law courts.

('Lady Veritas', *Woman's Life* I, i, 1895: 3)

My editorial experience has left me impressed with one thing in particular, and that is the need for what is called the 'personal note' in journalism . . . I believe in human nature . . . . And so, recognising that any paper or writer that is to attract and touch human nature has to rely on the 'personal note', I will write weekly notes of an intimate kind, treating my readers as friends.

('Come In!', *My Weekly* I, i, 1910: 1)

The most important journalistic development of the 1890s in terms of women's reading was the cheap, that is the penny, domestic weekly. By 1910 it had established that dominance in the market which it was to retain unbroken for the rest of the twentieth century. Simultaneously cheap and 'respectable', these magazines used the well-established formula of the genre to revitalise the tradition of the English domestic woman's journal which stretched back to Beeton in mid-century.

The 1890s even more than the 1880s was marked by a proliferation of new kinds of cheap periodical for women which addressed very different groups of readers and stressed different aspects of femininity. In some the female reader was assumed to be interested only in fashion and dress-making (*Butterick's* or *Isobel's Dressmaking at Home*); in some she was immersed in domesticity and mothering (*Home Sweet Home, Household Hints and Mother's Handbook*). In contrast to these were the girls' magazines (*Girls' Own Paper, Young Ladies' Journal* and *Girls' Realm*) and those which addressed women simultaneously in various domestic and familial roles (*Mothers and Daughters*). The long-established link between fiction, femininity and cheap print was re-forged in new magazines like *Forget-Me-Not* and *Lily* but also in the dozens of titles sold at a penny or a halfpenny which perpetuated the tradition of the 'mill-girl' serial with titles like *My Lady's Novelette* and the *Lady's Own Novelette*.

The penny domestic magazines specifically repudiated the taint of sensationalism which still attached to such serials. They insisted that their fiction was 'healthy' and mixed it with other, specifically didactic, kinds of writing. On the other hand, they made no pretensions to be 'advanced' but situated their readers in the domestic and the familial, a location often made explicit in their titles: *Home Notes, Home Chat, Home Sweet Home*.

They deployed the by now familiar ingredients of women's journalism. Unlike earlier publishers who attempted cheap domestic papers, notably Beeton, the new publishing houses of the 1890s were not forced to go up-market. The massive increase in the number of titles sold for a penny was, therefore, matched by a huge increase in the circulation figures for individual titles – at least by the standards of the previous century. *Home Chat* claimed the 200,000 of its first print run had to be topped up with a further 35,000 and that tens of thousands soon became regular subscribers (*HC* 26 March 1898: 95). *Woman's Life* carried 'Lady Veritas's' views on shopping first to the 200,000 readers who bought the magazine and then to the several hundred thousand beyond who had access to it through the processes of borrowing and sharing which still ensured every copy had multiple readers (Altick 1957: 396).

The penny domestic magazines addressed not just a larger readership but a very different one from earlier magazines and from more up-market journals. The magazines continued to assume that the reader was likely to employ a servant, rather than be one herself, but *Home Chat's* weekly column of recipes for 'Tired House-wives' and other regular features assumed that she was involved in the practical work of running the home rather than simply supervising others (*HC* 14 Sept. 1895: 65).

Yet *Home Chat* and *Home Notes* drew explicitly on recent developments in the expensive ladies' papers, claiming to offer for a penny everything offered by the sixpennies and there was some justice in this claim (*HC* I 1890: 1). Though they used a small page size (*Home Chat* was typical at 6½ × 9¼ inches) and were printed on poor quality paper, they were as thick as much more expensive magazines, as lavishly illustrated and employed some of the same journalists.[1] Certain meanings of the feminine likewise persisted across the price range. The idea of the 'lady', the struggle to close the gap between a femininity defined by domestic labour and one defined by appearance, the centrality of the commodity to both the journal and the woman, all appeared in the penny papers.

The fragmentation of the woman reader into different target groups was echoed in the cheap, as in the expensive journals, by the representations of the feminine self as fragmented, dispersed through the journal in its various constituent genres and in the advertisements. These increasingly dominated the pages of the penny, as they did the up-market press, with visual representations of bits of bodies and scattered domestic objects. The meaning of this fragmented femininity, however, was radically re-worked in these cheap journals and the various strategies for re-creating a coherent model of the feminine self were not identical to *Queen's* or even those of *Woman at Home*. In this chapter I trace the process of re-creating the domestic woman for the twentieth century, focusing mainly on Harmsworth's hugely successful *Home Chat* and on *My Weekly*, which is still being produced from the same firm which launched it in 1910.

THE BATTLE FOR THE MARKET

The rise of the penny domestic magazine in the 1890s was mainly the work of the new-style publishing houses of Newnes, Harmsworth and Pearson with their multiple publications and aggressive marketing. Harmsworth was the first of the three to realise the potential of mass produced magazines for women. His *Forget-Me-Not* (1891) included general articles on dress and fashion but was mainly given over to the traditional female diet of romantic fiction (12 out of 16 pages of an average number). It offered 'healthy' reading and targeted 'the engaged girl' rather than the mill-girl. Two years later Harmsworth launched another penny weekly, *Home Sweet Home*, which, as its title indicated, was more determinedly domestic. These magazines were illustrated and subsidised by advertising but they were printed on poor quality paper and looked cheap. In January 1894 Pearson launched *his* bid for the penny market with *Home Notes*. This was a monthly but it was better produced and thicker than its rivals and as well as the domestic advice which its name suggested, it carried news of Paris fashions and a free dress pattern with each issue. With this, the struggle for this new market intensified and further penny publications from both Harmsworth and Newnes followed.

Other publishers also produced penny magazines for women and some, like the publisher of *Woman*, sustained successful single titles throughout the decade. However, the dominance of the new publishing barons was established by 1895 and confirmed by the fate of three publications launched within a year of each other.

The first of these was Cassell's *Paris Mode*. Cassells had, since its founding in 1848, been one of the most successful publishers of the Victorian era, with multiple periodical titles on its list including the very popular *Cassell's Family Magazine*. It had ventured into women's journalism before with the *Ladies' Treasury* in the 1860s and with the *Lady's (Woman's) World*, which Wilde had edited, in the 1880s (Nowell-Smith 1958: 76, 180, 115, 147–51). Now it decided to launch its own penny weekly, with all the usual ingredients (fiction, fashion, domestic advice) but in a large (quarto) size, printed on good quality paper and with a coloured front page. Despite all this, *Paris Mode* did not, as Cassells had hoped, bring in 'a new era in the annals of popular fashion papers'. Instead it lost the firm £8,000 in nine months before they abandoned the experiment (Nowell-Smith 1958: 181–2).

By contrast, not only did Pearson's *Home Notes* continue to flourish but in the next year Harmsworth and Newnes both launched even more successful penny domestic weeklies. *Home Chat*, which started just three months after *Paris Mode*, was to prove 'a gold mine' for Harmsworth both in terms of advertising and sales until the 1950s (ibid.). Newnes's *Woman's Life*, also launched in 1895, rapidly reached a circulation figure of 200,000 and continued publication until 1934 when it was revamped as *Woman's Own*, one of the titles which was to dominate the mid-twentieth-century market. The collapse of *Paris Mode* just as *Home Chat* was taking off may be directly related, as the historian of Cassells argues (ibid.).[2] It was certainly symptomatic. Though fashion was an essential ingredient, the successful new magazines were those which proclaimed themselves as domestic and which were the products of the new publishing houses epitomised by Harmsworth.

Unlike the ladies' journals, the penny magazines spurned the small advertiser and concentrated on wooing commercial buyers of their space with promises of 'results'. In the press directories they stressed that advertisements always faced reading matter and were completely integrated into the copy unless they were on the cover, the best place of all. They offered special positions related to editorial material and assured potential buyers that attention was given to display, that crucial visibility of the desirable commodity.[3]

All these methods were evident in *Home Chat*. Full-page advertisements remained an important element but they were dispersed through the text and in addition many were on the same page as editorial copy, which was similarly broken up so that the two were visually indistinguishable. Because the magazine adopted the double column format it was easy to divide the page and give one column to advertising and one to editorial copy and this contributed to the difficulty of distinguishing between them. What looked like a short story might turn into an account of 'Dr. William's Pink Pills for Pale People', which carried the tradition of medical advertising into the new journals with its offer to cure 'all the troubles of the female' *and* 'effects of worry and overwork' in men (*HC* 28 March 1896: 97) (Figure 13.1).

Physical and visual blurring of the boundaries thus went with a more systemic confusion of the work of adman and editor. Advertisements began to be placed strategically in relation to the editorial matter so that puffs for wools and patterns appeared on the page facing the last of 'Fashion Talk' (*HC* 14 Sept. 1895: 634–5). The 'advertorial' in which specific named shops or brands were recommended in the editorial pages was taken up from journals like *Myra's* and extended. Instead of relating only to the topic of dress and fashion, as in *Myra's Journal*, or being located in one section of the paper as in *Woman at Home*, the advertorial could appear anywhere in *Home Chat* even in the editorial and was as likely to feature 'Bovril' as it was the latest fashion novelty (*HC* 29 Feb. 1896: 512).

The woman reader, in a now familiar double movement, therefore became identified with the commodity. In the first instance this was the magazine. Proprietors described their publications as though they were women. *Home Notes*, for example, according to Pearson was the 'daintiest' of the ladies' weeklies (see Mitchell's *Press Directory* for 1900). *Forget-Me-Not* 'In a wrapper of delicate forget-me-not blue' was 'as bright and pure as the flower from which it gets its name' (Pound 1959: 129).

The second stage in this process was that the female reader's identification with the magazine became the signifier of that more general identification of the woman with commodities which I described in Chapter 10. The representation of the commodified female body, which by the mid-1890s had become so dominant in the ladies' papers, was taken up and re-worked for the very different readership of *Home Chat* and the other penny papers. This was an important part of a general translation of 'ladyship' from the expensive into the penny papers.

LADYSHIP AT PENNY PRICES

The concept of 'the lady' had been central to cheap reading for women throughout the century. The mill-girl fiction serials like the *Lady's Own Novelette* and *My Lady's Novelette* continued in the 1890s to offer stories centred on 'true-born ladies'. These aristocratic maidens, whether they lived in the great houses of London Society or the country mansions of a timeless England, were the 'personi-fication of maiden purity and sweetness'. This and their beauty ensured them heartbreak and trial before they were won by the hero's 'straightforward manly sincerity and intense passion' (*Lady's Own Novelette* I: 2, 18).

Even though they claimed to reject the values of this kind of writing, much of the fiction in *Home Chat* and the other domestic weeklies worked with the same formulae and settings. The fiction serial which ran in *Home Chat* in 1896 called 'The Theft of the Duchess of Datchett's Diamonds' promised the double plea-sures of a thriller and a glimpse into high Society. 'Which Loved her Best?' by Jean Middlemas in Volume I featured high Society murder, intrigue and romance, with a convent and bags of money thrown in (*HC* 14 Sept. 1895: 641–6).

Competing with this figure from formulaic fiction was the figure of the 'lady', not as tormented heroine but as knowledgeable woman, a model and source of instruction to the reader. *Home Chat* signalled its debt to the sixpenny papers by making its lead item 'Chit-chat' or 'Society Small Talk' 'by Lady Greville' which mimicked such gossip columns as the *Queen's* 'Upper Ten Thousand'. This was 'tit-bits' journalism in its purest form, a disparate collection of information and opinion, each item just four or five lines long, arranged without any apparent connection or any sense of their relative importance. It could include discussion of the latest fashion in hats, novel-reading, the Bible or cycling as a sport for women, all treated as equally important. However, as its by-line suggested, the emphasis was on 'Society', which meant the 'Upper Ten Thousand' and other celebrities (actresses, writers and clerics). Above all it meant royalty and this now included not just the British royal family but all the minor royalties of Europe.

In Lady Greville's regular column, which became 'Boudoir Chat' in the new century, the contradictory meanings of 'the lady' were given a new resonance. The chatty tone of the column, its designation as 'Chit-chat' or 'Small Talk' assumed the intimate conversation of equals. Its stress on the personal implied a common womanhood. So did other elements of the magazine which dealt with ladies, especially the inevitable 'Chat with Celebrities' where readers were 'invited into the homes' of Society ladies and famous writers. But, of course, the whole point of such features and of the aristocratic by-line was that they suggested a world to which readers could only have access in fantasy or in print. It was precisely the distance of 'Lady Buxton' from the reader of *Home Chat* which made a visit to her home interesting (*HC* 5 Oct. 1895: 109–10).

All these papers promised

> [to] provide in crystallised form news of the doings of Ladies in Society and the World, whose position, character and endowments make their lives interesting to their less distinguished sisters.
>
> (*Home Life* I 1890, quoted in Davidoff 1986: 75)

Like the format of the periodical itself, which both rooted the reader in the here-and-now and pointed her towards a potentially different future, so the concept of the lady simultaneously offered itself as an image of radical equality and a mark of hierarchy. This double definition not only informed the gossip column. It shaped much of the material in the magazine, whether articles on model mothers featuring aristocratic ladies or notes on 'etiquette'. Above all it was enacted in the fashion pages.

FASHION AND SHOPPING

Dress and fashion were, of course, central to the construction of the Society Lady in the periodical press. Oscar Wilde was only expressing a truism when he observed that the 'lady's world' ('the *mundus muliebris*') was defined by papers like the *Queen* and the *Lady's Pictorial* exclusively in terms of 'mere millinery and trimmings' (Nowell-Smith 1958: 253). But whereas Wilde sought to change the definition of 'the lady's world' in terms of dress, Harmsworth and Pearson encouraged their editors to exploit it. In simply commercial terms, it made sense to exploit the established relationship between the periodical which had to offer each number as 'new' and up to date and the fashion industry with all its attendant advertising, which likewise depended on novelty as the ultimate value.

The linked discourses of 'the lady' and 'fashion' confirmed both that femininity was about appearance and that this visibility was produced through commodities. *Home Chat* assumed that physical appearance was central to femininity and that in this respect at least women were not born but made and made themselves. Even 'the plain girl' could make herself 'as popular and charming as her Beautiful Sister' (*HC* XV 29 Feb. 1896: 501). Central to that making was 'fashion' which was explicitly linked to the ideal of the Lady. *Home Chat's* 'Dress and Fashion' article therefore regularly appeared over another aristocratic-sounding by-line, 'Camilla and Lady Betty'. This occupied a central place in the magazine, with 2½–3 pages each week, inset illustrations and offers of patterns in the well-established tradition of fashion journalism.

Home Chat thus assumed that now familiar definition of femininity as vested in the clothed female body and therefore constantly in process of construction through the work of fashion. Although the pages were smaller than in the ladies' papers, the paper cheaper, and the quality of illustration less good, the penny papers reproduced the image of the constructed female body which was so dominant in the ladies' papers. This extended beyond the fashion pages to the rest of the magazine, carried mainly by the advertisements, which also assumed that the female body was constantly in need of correction and reconstruction: by various scientific and electric corsets for the body shape, 'Koko', 'Harlene' and 'Alexander' for hair colour, Pears or Beethams for the skin and Beechams for general health (Figures 13.1, 13.2).

The promise of transformation of the female body through the purchase of commodities was implicit in all these advertisements. Equally, the impossibility of ever arriving at perfect femininity was evident in the contradictory claims they made. Sometimes on the same page those who were 'Too Stout' were recommended to take 'Dr. Grey's Fat Reducing Pills for either Sex' while those with 'Thin Busts' were promised that they could be 'quickly transformed' (*HC* 14 Sept. 1895: 653; 24 Oct. 1896: 314). The ideal female body regulated in the interests of appearance was always still to be made.

The construction of this feminine self as spectacle and as commodity could not be simply carried over from the ladies' papers with its meaning unchanged, even where the same products were advertised. However well produced for the price, the cheap domestic magazine could not compete with *Queen* visually or as a signifier of the commodity. Moreover, it clearly situated its readers in the world of household work and family relationships. The magical transformation promised by the advertisers contradicted that powerful ideology which made women's love and labour the agents of social transformation. It was also contradicted by the material circumstances which made it unlikely that most readers would have unlimited access to the commodities it advertised. In these magazines, then, a femininity of the commodity had to be linked back to domestic work.

The complexities of this process can be traced in the opening number of Newnes's successful *Woman's Life*, which promised its readers a column on 'that most fascinating subject for women', shops and shopping. Attributed to another aristocratic persona, 'Lady Veritas', this article defined 'shopping' as women's work. Transposed from the more expensive papers, this 'truth' made invisible the shop girls for whom shopping was indeed weary labour. It denied the differences of income which separated women from each other and gave some easier access to 'shopping' than others. It even implicitly excluded all those kinds of shopping which were not related to looking and to a femininity defined by appearance. No reader would have made the mistake of thinking that she referred to buying the family groceries.

Shopping was defined here as both 'a solemn business' and a pleasure. It 'gives us such joy and such head-aches, mental confusion, [and] dizziness' (*WL* I 1895: 3). Men failed to recognise this. Women, however, recognised that constantly

Two widths of forty-four inch molleton flannel, or flannelette, will make the gown, which is fixed to a circular yoke piece.

Modelled for children from two to eight. Quantity for the largest size, two yards and a-half.

Design No. 525.—Little Girl's Zouave Frock. —The frock is complete in itself in Empire style. The fastening is at the back. Two crossway bands of velveteen, to match the zouave, take away the severely plain appearance.

The frock is modelled in three sizes, for girls from six to twelve years of age.

Design No. 525.—Flat paper pattern, 6½d.; or, tucked up, including flat, 1s. 3½d. Cut-to-measure pattern, 3s. 1d.

Quantity of double width material for girls of twelve, three yards; and of velveteen, three-quarters of a yard.

Design No. 525. - Little Lad's Highwayman Coat.—This miniature Claude Duval has his coat so arranged that the triple capes are removable, and he is then transformed into a sporting-looking gentleman in a sacque coaching coat of more modern cut.

Modelled for children from four to eight years.

Quantity of cloth for the largest size, two yards and a-quarter.

Page 13.1 Page of *Home Chat* (28 March 1896: 125) © Manchester City Art Galleries

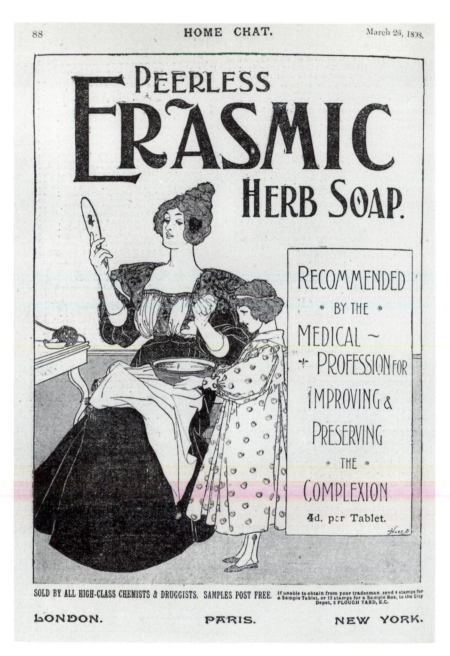

Figure 13.2 Advertisement from *Home Chat* (26 March 1898: 88)
© Manchester City Art Galleries

re-making one's femininity through shopping was painful work as well as plea-sure. The ambiguous status of shopping was indeed familiar, since it reproduced the confusion which had characterised the construction of domestic labour throughout the century. Home was still both the site of woman's pleasure and of her work. Defining femininity in terms of 'shopping' was new, but its characterisa-tion followed an old ideological pattern.

That pattern was also still embodied in the magazine's doubled definition as entertainment and instruction. These domestic magazines with their illustrations and easy-to-read format offered themselves primarily as entertainment but they also fulfilled their traditional role as instructor of the female reader. Like Beeton's *EDM* in the 1850s, *Home Chat* in the 1890s had not only to reconcile a femi-ninity defined by appearance and one defined by the invisible work of domes-ticity, it had to hold women's work and pleasure together on the telos of 'home'.

Beeton had deployed a doubled discourse of female subjectivity to solve this problem; his reader was defined simultaneously as the desirable woman of the fashion-plate and the domestic woman whose skills brought her fashionable self into being. So in *Home Chat*, the commodified and fashionable body was brought into being through the distinctively feminine skills of shopping, making and making do, of sewing, re-dyeing and altering.

In this process the advertorial and the advice column were crucial. Like the advertisement, the advertorial mediated a femininity in which image, desire and shopping were linked (Smith 1990: 190). It offered commodities to close the gap between the female reader and the models of fashionable beauty offered in the magazine. However, the advertorial recognised that buying the right products was a necessary but not sufficient condition. 'Feminine' skills were also needed. In the first instance this might mean being a skilful shopper but this was always specifi-cally related to other kinds of competence – those of application, of sewing and re-making.

Advertorials thus blended imperceptibly into that staple genre of all these papers, the advice column. The 'Hints on Health and Beauty' (*Woman's Life*) or 'Dress and Fashion' (*Home Chat*) both acknowledged and addressed the difficul-ties of constructing the 'natural' female body. The task of making that body, through shopping, sewing and the application of the appropriate ointments, pills or lotions was recognised as demanding work and as requiring practice and instruction. Like their twentieth-century descendants, these magazines not only 'tie[d] the ideality of image to information about how to rectify bodily deficien-cies'. They assumed that the work of creating the female self 'is consciously planned, takes time and involves the use of tools and materials and the acquired skills of its practitioners' (Smith 1990: 197).

The advertorials and advice columns overtly employed the discourse of fashion and beauty which produced 'woman' as the passive object of the male gaze; covertly they assumed the reader was an agent, who could enjoy deploying her skills and knowledge in self-creation. Dorothy Smith argues that such acknowl-edgement of the work of femininity must be both pleasurable and empowering for women (Smith 1990). For readers of the penny papers this may well have been true. But we should be cautious about unreservedly celebrating it. This work of femininity was not recognised as labour or skill either culturally or materially. It could not be acknowledged outside the woman's world of 'chat' and 'gossip' without endangering the dominant definition of natural femininity.

Economically, these developments in women's magazines locked the feminine even more firmly into the purchase of commodities. The skills of shopping, the pleasures of creating a self through consumption, must always be constrained both by what the shopper can afford and by what the capitalist system offers as choice. Discursively, the writings of 'Lady Betty' as of 'Myra' locked women more firmly into definitions as objects not subjects of desire. Feminine desire was the desire to be desired (by the man) and it was to create this self that the magazines instructed their readers.

THE RE-CREATION OF THE 'TIRED HOUSEWIFE'

The constant creation of the regulated and beautiful body was not, however, the only – or even the most important – way the advertorials and advice columns defined the work of femininity. Though the female body continued to remain a dominant visual motif, advertisements were as likely to be for domestic goods – convenience foods or cleaning materials – as for beauty products and dresses. Between the full-page display advertisements for Harlene hair-care products and one for Beecham's pills would be a page given to the virtues of Chivers Jelly, Borwick's Baking Powder, Cerebos Salt, DCL Yeast and – inevitably – yet another cure for those who were 'Too Stout' (*HC* 14 Sept. 1895: 662–4). The letter press, too, was full of domestic and familial advice.

All the penny domestic magazines ran columns of 'Hints', 'Wrinkles' or 'Tips' which engaged with feminine skills not in terms of making the desirable female body but in relation to the care of the home and the reproduction of the family. The skills involved overlapped; both included shopping and sewing, but they were directed towards the production of a very different kind of femininity. This ubiquitous address to the problems of 'the Busy Housewife' was one of the major differences between these papers and up-market journals like *Queen*.

Unlike the work involved in the fashionable body, domestic labour in *Home Chat* was constantly named not as pleasurable but as difficult and demanding, indeed exhausting. The housewife was likely to be both 'Busy' and 'Tired'. 'Tired housekeepers' were told 'we have arranged all your meals for you' complete with recipes (*HC* 14 Sept. 1895: 655–6). A series for those embarking on the career of home-making was called 'The Difficulties of a Young Housekeeper (and how they were overcome)' (*HC* 12 March 1898: 593). Like much of the advice in these magazines, this addressed the practical skills needed to cook, keep a house clean and manage a budget.

The last of these was crucial. The magazine recognised that the difficulties of domestic work were often economic. It ran advice on shopping which was far

removed from the pleasures suggested by Lady Veritas (*HC* 2 Nov. 1895: 277).
Advice series on the management of consumption were sometimes disguised as
fiction, like one serial called 'A Successful Love Match' which offered to show
'How a Young Couple got Together a Pretty Home at a Very Small Cost' (*HC* 17
April 1897: 237). Whether disguised as 'Tips' or exemplified in a didactic tale, the
difficulties – as against the pleasures – of consumption were defined as central to
this femininity.

Such articles insisted that domestic labour was indeed time-consuming and
required a range of skills. Moreover it was central to the readers' femininity and
was likely to colour every aspect of the magazine, except – an important exception
– the serialised fiction. Even articles which seemed to offer a respite were caught
up in the truism that women's work was never done. 'Glimpses into a Thousand
Homes' which promised the treat of a view of aristocratic high life, proved to be 'A
Series of Articles which will give every woman many hints of Decoration and
Furnishing' (*HC* 26 March 1898: 62).

The difficulties involved in the reproduction of the family were also emotional
and the skills required went beyond the economic and the practical. Caring for
children was demanding and the maternal self was constructed in the magazines
as no more 'natural' than the perfect body. As well as running occasional features
on making children's clothes and didactic tales on the difficulties of child-care,
Home Chat ran a regular column of more general advice for mothers and provided
a feature specially to teach and entertain children (e.g. *HC* 12 March 1898:
617ff). 'Cheery Corner for the Chicks', like the cookery and sewing columns,
both provided an example for readers and entered directly into their lives to relieve
the emotional labour of child-care. This project was taken up in the 1890s in
specific magazines like *Baby* and *Babyland* but it entered into all the penny
domestic journals.

On marital difficulties, the magazines were more discreet. However, articles by
the Rev. E.J. Hardy, author of the popular *How to be Happy Though Married*
appeared occasionally and some of these directly addressed the problem of what to
do 'When Marriage is a Failure' (*HC* 30 May 1896: 548–9). Not surprisingly the
only solution was for women to work harder at making it succeed (*HC* 12 March
1898: 590, etc.). The tasks of emotional maintenance were addressed briskly and
all these magazines were more comfortable with a model of the domestic woman
as practical manager than as the regulator of domestic morals and emotions.

Unlike *Woman at Home* these penny magazines did not encourage readers to
write in to discuss their romantic, emotional or spiritual problems. The confessional letter was not an acceptable genre here. The magazine's long-running series
called 'In the Shadow of the Cross' (which ran into the late twentieth century)
provided a spiritual gloss on the 'Every Day Difficulties of Women' but it offered
spirituality as another 'wrinkle' or 'tip' on how to deal with family life (*HC* 29 Feb.
1896: 515–16). The seriousness with which Annie Swan addressed the moral and
emotional life of her readers did not fit with the determinedly chatty and cheerful
tone of *Home Chat* and its stress on what readers could *do*.

It is here in the domestic advice, as much as in the fashion and beauty pages, that we should look if we want to find a celebration of feminine skills and an empowering of female readers. Such titles as 'Dainty Work for Clever Fingers' specifically named the knowledge embodied in the domestic woman's practised hand. *Home Chat*, like its rivals, re-worked and spread to a wider readership than ever before the discourses of domestic labour as management and competence. Indeed the magazine sometimes seemed to suggest that the powers of this femininity bordered on the miraculous, as was suggested by one series entitled 'Something out of Nothing' (e.g. *HC* 14 Sept. 1895: 629). However, the sub-title, 'Tips for Economical Knick-knacks' made clear the limitations of the domestic woman's powers. Her economic management and 'clever fingers' might almost literally bring something out of nothing but the products of these capacities were likely to be 'knick-knacks'. The advice circulated in the magazines was merely 'tips', 'hints' or even 'wrinkles', the contrivances of accommodation.

Nevertheless, these 'hints' on domestic labour in the advice columns and advertorials must have offered readers pleasure both in their possession of skills and in enabling their development. They confirmed and validated the unremitting difficulty of women's labour in the home, offering a secularised version of the sanctification of daily life in the mothers' magazines of the 1830s and 1840s. These were significant but ambiguous pleasures.

Selling themselves with the double agenda of instruction and amusement, these magazines reproduced the ambiguous status of feminine skills and feminine power. By addressing her domestic skills and promising to return her re-created to her domestic labour, the magazines legitimated the pleasures readers gained from them as well as the expenditure of money and time. In this, they were reproducing familiar patterns of feminine reading in the new context of mass journalism.

THE PLEASURES OF 'CHAT'

The least ambiguous of the pleasures they offered was invested in the idea of 'chat' and in their offer of intimacy. The title '*Home Chat*' brilliantly summed up their characteristic gossipiness. The very different discourses of the commodified body and of household management were bound together by the intimacy of tone which marked not only this magazine but this kind of journalism. Fashion, domestic advice, mini-biographies of the Royal Family, interviews with celebrities, all were subsumed into the general category of 'chat'. This confidential tone was created by all those devices I have already described: the breaking up of the text into snippets or snatches, the colloquialisms and the creation of journalistic and editorial personae who addressed the reader as an intimate. The absence of the voice of the reader in the confessional letter in no way detracted from the magazine's insistence that it was involved in an exchange of views and that the reader was 'a friend'.

A crucial mechanism here was the development of a range of personae identified with different elements of the paper. Unlike the 'Lady Bettys' or the 'Lady

Grenvilles' of the fashion pages and the Boudoir Chats, the by-lines of the domestic columns were identified with an intimacy which suggested a close family member. 'Isobel', for example, who worked for Pearson and appeared in *Home Notes* as well as editing 'her own' sewing and cooking magazine, was simply identified by her first name, in the tradition of 'Myra' and the plethora of 'Barbaras' and 'Marjories' in *Woman*. 'Sister Rachel' took over the advice to young mothers in *Home Chat*, her name simultaneously suggesting one of the family and the expertise associated with the nursing orders. All these figures addressed the reader as friend, and their columns suggested an intimate exchange between women about those skills which pertained to femininity.

The magazine therefore represented itself not only as a repository of womanly wisdom, which it passed on to 'Young Mothers and New Housewives', but also as the place in which women shared with each other the secrets of their femininity. This was a truly 'new journalistic' pleasure and one which was taken up immediately and carried into the twentieth century by new kinds of penny domestic weekly.

MY WEEKLY:
THE PENNY MAGAZINE MOVES
INTO THE TWENTIETH CENTURY

Unlike all the other periodicals I have discussed so far, *My Weekly* was not produced by a London-based publisher but by the Dundee firm of D.C. Thomson. In 1910, this firm decided to launch a new title which would incorporate an older one (*People's (Penny) Stories*) and draw on their long experience in producing cheap periodicals. Their success is still evident, for whereas *Home Chat* and *Home Notes* lasted until the 1950s, *My Weekly* is still a bestseller in the 1990s and is still produced by the same publishers in Dundee. Moreover, its immediate success was such that in 1911, the year after it appeared, another paper with a very similar format, *Woman's Weekly* was launched which has also successfully continued until the 1990s, when it was the top-selling weekly in Britain for some years (Braithwaite and Barrell 1988: 193, 210).

At first sight it is difficult to explain this success. Though it deployed all the selling devices associated with the New Journalism, advertising and giving away free samples of scent and other goods with copies, *My Weekly* differed from the other penny weeklies most obviously in that it looked old-fashioned and less exciting (e.g. scent sachet with *MW* 127, 7 Sept. 1912). It was larger than *Home Chat* (8½ × 12 inches) and its lay-out in three columns of type seemed to hark back to the newspaper style of the older ladies' journals, like the early *Queen*. However, unlike the ladies' papers, *My Weekly's* early numbers were visually conservative. Though it carried some display advertising – including full-page – there were few large illustrations and above all there was no fashion-plate. In fact little attention was paid to fashionable dress in its pages and there was no aristocratic by-line. Unlike the other penny papers, *My Weekly* was not affected either by the tradition of ladies' publishing or by its definitions of femininity in terms of appearance and dress.

This may be explained in part because when it first appeared, the new penny weekly did not announce itself as a women's paper at all. Though it was almost immediately revamped as a magazine addressed to women, the opening editorial proclaimed that it would embody not the 'feminine' but 'the personal note in journalism'. This editorial was a manifesto both of the new paper and of the new journalism of which it was the purest example.

Under the large heading 'COME IN! The Editor and His Friends', the full-page three-column spread began:

> I'm glad to see you. This is a real pleasure! And I hope that this home of mine in 'My Weekly' will be a pleasant meeting place where we shall enjoy many an entertaining and useful talk . . . Let us be friends . . .
>
> (*MW* I, i, 1910: 1)

The use of personal pronouns, the direct address, the construction of the magazine as itself a 'home' in which readers could meet friends were all laid out here with as much subtlety as a quack doctor's advertisement. The editor went on, in characteristic fashion, to reveal the secret of the paper's policy, its commitment to the 'personal note' which it enacted so energetically:

> Let me give you a little of my confidence. It is this. My editorial experience has left me impressed with one thing in particular, and that is the need for what is called the 'personal note' in journalism . . . . I will try to select subjects which will appeal to readers through their human nature and their understanding of everyday joys and sorrows . . . . None knows better than I how at heart human nature is eternally kind . . . and none knows better how that human nature's charity and sentiment are ever associated with a longing that . . . itself may be encouraged on the long thorny road it has to go.
>
> (ibid.)

What is significant here is not so much that 'human nature' was assumed to be trans-historical and unaffected by such accidents as class, but that it was feminised. The qualities associated with human nature were those of the affections; they were the 'feminine' characteristics usually positioned as 'other' to the rational masculine self. *Man's* true nature was implicitly defined here as domestic and at its best in enduring an everyday life assumed to be difficult. Elsewhere the editorial speaks of 'the divinely ordered round of labour, love, pain and pleasure'. This took up that sanctification of women's everyday life which – in its secularised form – was a recurring motif of the domestic magazines. Here it was divorced from the practicalities of domestic management and generalised as essentially and unchangeably 'human'.

This was made explicit in the visual representation of the title *My Weekly*, which was supported by two medallions of women reading and the motto 'What's

Mine's Thine', and was made verbally explicit as the editorial came towards its peroration:

> I believe in human nature. I am interested in human nature . . . . I like human nature . . . . And so, recognising that any paper or writer that is to attract and touch human nature has to rely on the 'personal note', I will write weekly notes of an intimate kind, treating my readers as friends . . . . Toiling, moiling mothers can unfold to me stories happy and melancholy; servant girls may confide to me their worries and longings; ladies may give me their views of everything from missions to politics; youths and girls may consult me about what might be done for themselves or for parents and friends . . .
>
> Next week I shall take for my subject 'Lonely Lives' . . .
>
> (ibid.)

In working out this philosophy the editor drew on the model provided by the penny domestic weeklies launched in the 1890s. *My Weekly* used the same ingredients: romantic fiction in serial and short-story form, chit-chats or gossip columns, children's pages and competitions, and it adopted the same gossipy tone. Like *Home Chat* and *Home Notes*, it assumed that the reader was defined by the domestic. It gave even less attention than they did to employment for women, and excluded comments on the world of politics or public affairs. *My Weekly* thus located its reader firmly in the feminised world of the private, redefined through the new journalism.

It gave that location a rather different significance, however, from the other domestic weeklies. It is true that from the first it ran a regular feature on domestic matters under the name 'Mrs Help-at-Home'. But this jokey by-line was symptomatic of a general displacement of domestic labour onto the margins of its interest. *My Weekly* assumed that its readers were in the home, but feminine skills – whether of re-creating the fashionable body or of reproducing the family – were not at the centre of the magazine. As a result, the female body, whether as erotic surface or as work-machine, was notably absent, a crucial absence to which I return in a moment.

Instead of the blurring of the boundaries of entertainment and instruction which made the other domestic magazines return insistently to women's work, *My Weekly* offered itself primarily as entertainment and solace. Narrative was central to this persona and *My Weekly* carried both domestic and sensational romance in short-story and serialised form: 'You simply must read the sensational new serial by Mrs. Wentworth-Jones. It is a Novel throbbing with human interest' was a typical flyer (*MW* Front Cover no. 25: 1910). Here, as in the editorial, the magazine made an appeal not to a gendered readership but to a common human nature, symbolised by the metaphor of the heart which represented humanity but was also a symbol of the emotions and, therefore, of femininity.

The domestic, therefore, was constructed in this magazine not as the site of women's work and the product of her skills, but as the theatre of human nature, defined in terms of the feelings – or the heart. That home was a feminised space but it included, of course, not only children but also men. Masculinity here was re-cast in terms of its 'human' that is its affective or feminine elements. Or rather, femininity becomes an attribute of men.

The magazine by analogy was also represented as a 'home', a feminised space into which the readers were welcomed. In this *My Weekly* was following the other penny domestics which claimed that they were addressing not women, but 'homes' and families. *Home Chat*, for example, claimed that it was read by men, an assertion underpinned not by modern techniques of market research but by the argument, 'Does not Home include the husband, the father, the sons and the brothers as well as the mothers?' (*HC* II 1895: 607).

In this respect *My Weekly* made explicit the assumptions at the heart of the New Journalism. Harmsworth had said privately that woman was at its centre and the stress on tit-bits, visual attractiveness and gossipy tone were part of that general feminisation which I have already discussed. Central to these changes in journalism was the 'human interest' story, a story which appealed to a human nature defined – as *My Weekly* did – in terms of feeling, domestic relations and the similarities rather than the differences between human beings.

My Weekly expressed in its purest form the intimate address which was the hallmark of New Journalism and which has become more insistent with the increasing scale of the mass media. This rhetorical strategy mystified the commercial processes of publication, the position of the reader as purchaser and the status of the magazine as commodity. The editorial claim of equality with the reader and the invitation to readers to confide in him mystified the power of the producers in an increasingly professionalised media industry. This is a significantly different editorial strategy from that of Annie Swan, who simultaneously emphasised the common womanhood which joined her to her readers and the gap which separated them from her, as professional writer and media personality.

What does all this mean for the negotiation over the meaning of femininity in this period of the suffragettes and the 'strange death of Liberal England'?[4] The definition of human nature in terms of likeness rather than difference is the classic liberal move, though here it is the 'feminine' heart rather than the 'masculine' head which is the privileged organ.[5] It was a move into abstraction, a move which made invisible the technological and market mechanisms which created the magazine and brought the reader into being. It was a move which made invisible the female body, the material body of the woman who produced material effects on and for other bodies and the maternal body which produced other bodies. This body was there, in however shadowy a form, in *Home Chat*, but is hard to find in *My Weekly* where 'human interest' was defined in completely non-material terms. The editor of this magazine did not feel the need to conceal his male identity, as did the male editors of *Woman* or *Woman at Home*. And why should he? Given a definition of human beings as essentially alike in terms of heart, differences of gender and class – let alone economic power or the power to make your meanings stick – become unimportant.

Throughout this book I have argued that the relationship between the femininity of the magazines and the material bodies and constructed selves of women readers was fractured, fraught and constantly being re-made. One aspect of the New Journalism was its representation of femininity as powerful and the appropriation of feminised spaces and feminine qualities by male journalists like Bennett.

The identification not only of 'the personal note' in the New Journalism but of the whole of human nature with femininity seems a triumph for that femininity, and its attraction for women readers is understandable. However, the feminisation of the human self implicit in *My Weekly* did not act simply to empower women, either as writers or readers. Instead it confirmed the absolute divide of public from private, asserted the unimportance of the masculine worlds of economic and political power and so rendered attempts by New Women to enter these worlds pointless and self-defeating.

The opening editorial which I have quoted at length surrounded an inset poem which made this clear. Specifically taking up the terminology of separate spheres it was titled, 'Woman's Sphere'; it read:

> They talk about a woman's sphere,
>   As though it had no limit.
> There's not a place in earth or heaven,
> There's not a task to mankind given,
> There's not a blessing or a woe,
> There's not a whispered yes or no
> There's not a life, or death, or birth,
> That has a feather's weight of worth,
>   Without a woman in it.
> (*MWI* 1910: 1)

If woman's sphere, the private world of love and emotion, really constituted all that was worth while, why bother to have the vote, or struggle to be an editor of a penny weekly? The discourse which made femininity the signifier of the true, that is the inner self, of course had political implications which extended beyond the specific battles around suffrage or equality in the work-place. It made any kind of definition of the self as part of a group other than the biological family, any politics of solidarity, not just marginal to true humanity but actually counter to it.

THE PLEASURES OF *MY WEEKLY*

The continued popularity of *My Weekly* and *Woman's Weekly* suggests at the least that they produced for their (female) readers versions of femininity which they found desirable and were prepared to pay for week after week. James Joyce, that acute observer of the popular culture of the period, in his Gerty MacDowell created a character who produced herself and her desire entirely in terms of the magazines. For Joyce that femininity was to do with the visibility of

207

the commodified body, with 'looking, looking' and with the way 'she saw that he saw' (Joyce 1960: 477). But it was also to do with narrative, with the mastering narrative of romance which privileged the heart:

> Heart of mine! She would follow her dream of love, the dictates of her heart that told her he was her all in all, the only man in all the world for her for love was the master guide.

> (Joyce 1960: 475)

Joyce's juxtaposition of the masturbating Bloom and the romancing Gerty prefigures arguments by late twentieth-century feminists that romance constitutes a form of female pornography.[6] The pleasures these magazines offered certainly included those of fantasy and specifically sexual fantasy. *My Weekly* did not speak female sexual desire in terms of physical appearance and the fashionable lady but it did address it through narratives of erotic satisfaction and its appeal to the heart. The heart was simultaneously signifier of the physical (throbbing) and of the inner life of the emotions – a double meaning most clearly evident in the maidenly blush which had been the central trope of nineteenth-century debates around reading and female sexuality, and which Joyce brilliantly re-used in Gerty MacDowell's blush at the 'unladylike' reference to 'beetoteetom' (Joyce 1960: 459).

However, to understand fully the particular appeal of this magazine and its close rivals we have to return to their address to the reader as friend, and to their personal tone, the representation of print as direct and intimate speech. The relationship between writing and speech has not only been historically complex but has also generated fierce critical differences in the late twentieth century which are beyond the scope of this argument.[7] However, despite the critical debates which position speech and writing as opposites, they are in our culture intertwined and complement each other.

Women's magazines have historically produced – and still produce – their femininities out of a particular tangle of the oral and literary. The processes which made housework, recipes, dress-making or beauty tips the subject (and product) of print were never absolute. They have been embedded in a culture of oral transmission and demonstration in which readers have shared not only copies but chat. The move into print of recipes and household hints was complicated and its meanings were multiple. It could signal 'progress', that the old ways of doing things were no longer good enough. Print made, and makes, claims for domestic labour as skilled work, like other skilled jobs in a print-based culture. Fashion recreated the idea of progress as constant change, hence the link between the fashion industry and print culture.

Print might signify a range of options beyond those of the immediate family circle. But it also and always signifies loss of face-to-face contact, loss of community, loss of voice. The personal note in journalism addressed that loss. Ironically it addressed it precisely through that move into abstraction which I have discussed. Every reader was the same and could be addressed in an undifferentiated way as 'friend', but the tone of that address promised to make good the loss which was its premise.

One of the attractions of *My Weekly* was, as its title indicated, that it first addressed the privatised individual woman at home, offering something for herself alone. However, it also identified her isolation at home as a problem and offered its intimate address as a consolation. It was not accidental that the second editorial specifically addressed those who led 'Lonely Lives'. The magazine offered this isolated reader what Benedict Anderson has called an 'imagined community' (Anderson 1983). First, this community was the (imagined) writer and then that of other potential readers. *My Weekly* dramatised this by inviting readers to comment on and offer advice to each other, a device rediscovered in the 1990s by a new generation of cheap domestic weeklies (see *Bella*).

The woman's magazine, by addressing the reader 'as woman', always creates the potential for an imagined community of women, or for women as an imagined community. This book has amply demonstrated that the meaning of that community was never simple nor static but nevertheless it was there. The cheap domestic weeklies turned women's 'chat' into the signifier simultaneously of 'human nature' and 'the New Journalism'. Just as the female body had become commodified, so woman-talk was what these magazines sold. But these other meanings still crucially depended on the idea of a shared femininity.

The imagined community of women was both the premise on which the woman's magazine rested and a promise. Like the magazine itself, which endlessly pointed – and still points – towards the next number, next week or next month, that promise was and is always displaced away from the present into an ever-receding future, in which 'women's chat' will be realised not as commodity but as the sign of utopian community. The debasement of this idea in magazines like *My Weekly* does not mean that it is without meaning or value. Meanwhile women readers, like Mrs Smith of Kent with whom I began this book, have always used the magazine in their own way – swapping copies, patterns, recipes and 'chat' in other kinds of exchange than those of the market in print.

NOTES

PREFACE

1 The discussion as to whether 'woman' is a universal or even a useful category has been at the centre of feminist debate and politics, addressed from positions as different as those of Audre Lorde (1984) and post-structuralist theorists like Diana Fuss (1989); see also Spelman (1988), Weedon (1987). The idea of 'strategic essentialism' is a potentially useful one but see Spivak (1995: 1–23) for a discussion of this formulation with which she is associated.

1 INTRODUCTION

1 This remains true, even though in the 1990s some magazines are appearing which claim to address men in terms of their masculinity rather than simply in terms of male sexuality.

2 Like the argument about the category 'woman' to which it is connected (see Preface note 1), this debate is central to contemporary feminism, and to gay, lesbian and queer studies. I have found Eve Kosofsky Sedgewick's chapter 'Axiomatic' in *Epistemology of the Closet* useful (Sedgewick 1991: 1–63); see also Haraway (1991), Jacobus *et al.* (1990) and Jordanova (1989).

3 As well as extensive sampling among a range of other journals, I read the magazines chosen for case study at three- or six-monthly intervals, depending on their frequency and length of publication. As always, this was contingent on finding whole runs.

4 The Research Society for Victorian Periodicals and its Review has provided a focus for such work. For a full discussion of the various methodological approaches to this kind of study see Chapter 1, 'Theories of Text and Culture' in the history I wrote with Ros Ballaster, Elizabeth Frazer and Sandra Hebron (Ballaster *et al.* 1991: 8–42).

5 Work on identifying editors and journalists and on codifying the mass of periodicals has been undertaken in the *Wellesley Index* and the *Waterloo Directory* but detailed historical and bibliographical work on the magazines discussed in this book has hardly begun. The difficulty of finding even one complete copy of a single magazine was made clear in the course of joint research for the Victorial Periodicals Hypertext Project. In order to find the covers and all the advertisements for one copy of the *Queen* we had to approach four libraries (Beetham *et al.* 1994).

6 Contemporary discussion of reading by the working class (usually assumed to be male) and by women (usually assumed to be middle class) was endemic in the periodical press of the nineteenth century. Some key articles are listed in the Bibliography and include: Ackland (1894), Bosanquet (1901), Gattie (1889), Hitchman (1880–1) and (1890), Leigh (1904), Salmon (1886a and b).

7 For an elaboration of the argument summarised here see Beetham (1990).

2 THE 'FAIR SEX' AND THE MAGAZINE: THE EARLY LADIES' JOURNALS

1 This connection has been discussed by many scholars including: Terry Lovell (1987), Janet Todd (1989), Dale Spender (1986) for pre-1800 and Kate Flint (1993 esp. 253ff).

2 On popular periodical and romance narratives for women, see Mitchell (1981).

3 One called itself briefly the *Englishwoman's Magazine* (1844–5), then added *and Christian Mothers' Miscellany* (–1854) before becoming the *Christian Lady's Magazine* (–1857).

4 Palmegiano argues that the evidence from a range of mid-century general periodicals shows women were almost universally named in terms of their familial and domestic roles (as wives, mothers or daughters) or their failure to achieve such roles (as spinsters or old maids) (Palmegiano 1976: 5).

3 THE QUEEN, THE BEAUTY AND THE WOMAN WRITER

1 Homans discusses the extent to which Victoria controlled her own representation as domestic woman in Homans (1993).

2 For example *LM&M* VI(1835) endpapers; 20 pages of advertisements included eight coronets or royal arms. These stand out visually, since at this period advertisements in these magazines seemed to have consisted almost entirely of written text. Because advertisements were habitually stripped out with the covers when magazines were bound, it is often impossible to find complete copies. Generalising about advertising is, therefore, fraught with difficulties.

3 I take up the question of the relationship between being looked at and femininity in later chapters, see Chapter 7.

4 Other magazines for ladies from this period included several which sustained publication for years. Among them were the *Ladies' Pocket Magazine* (1825–39), *Blackwood's Lady's Magazine and Gazette of the Fashionable World* (1836–60) and the *Ladies' Companion* (1849–52). Other fashion magazines from the 1820s which persisted into mid-century included the *World of Fashion and Continental Feuilletons* (1824–51). Two of the new fashion magazines from the 1830s and 1840s lasted throughout the century. They were the *Ladies' Gazette of Fashion* (1834–94) and *Le Follet: le Journal du Grande Monde, Fashion and Polite Literature* (1846–1900).

4 FAMILY AND MOTHERS' MAGAZINES: THE 1830s AND 1840s

1 Scott Bennett has argued for the *Penny Magazine* as the first mass magazine, Sally Mitchell for the *Family Herald*, which was the first to be composed and printed by machine (Bennett 1982; Mitchell 1981: 7). The question of who actually read these journals is a vexed one. The nature of the readership for particular periodicals – or even categories of periodical – throughout the nineteenth century is deeply problematic, even more difficult to be sure of than circulation figures. Evidence includes general discussions of reading, correspondence columns in periodicals themselves, autobiographies.

2 I differ in this from Dancyger, who includes such magazines in her pictorial history (Dancyger 1978: 34).

3 They were the *Mother's Magazine* (1834–49, –1869), the *British Mothers' Journal*

(1845–55), the *Englishwoman's Magazine and Christian Mother's Miscellany* (1846–54) and the *Mother's Friend* (1848–95).

4 Thanks to Ken Roberts for access to these. None of the volumes I have consulted had volume numbers.

5 She had also written under her first husband's name, Phelan.

5 THE BEETONS AND THE *ENGLISHWOMAN'S DOMESTIC MAGAZINE*, 1852–60

1 Claims about readership in the magazine which are the source of my figures do not make clear whether they are for copies sold or readers.

2 Isabella never claimed originality for her recipes and was indebted to Eliza Acton among others (Freeman 1977: 149–50).

3 Hood's poem became a central referent in the iconography of suffering womanhood. It deeply influenced the representation of the needlewoman as prostitute and victim which I discuss in later chapters (Nead 1988).

6 THE FEMALE BODY AND THE DOMESTIC WOMAN, 1860–80

1 Beeton pre-empted the actual repeal and then complained that delay in passing the legislation had cost £1,000 in tax by 1861 (Preface, *EDM* N.S. III 1861).

2 Discussion of the tight-lacing controversy in the *EDM* has been extensive; see Beetham (1991), Kunzle (1980), Roberts (1977), Steele (1985 esp. Appendix: 249–52).

3 For example, 1862 saw the launch of Dick's down-market *Bow Bells* with 'Madame Elise' as fashion adviser.

4 Out of seventeen titles listed by Ellegard in this category, twelve were a shilling in 1870 (Ellegard 1957: 32).

5 Ellegard asserts that all these fiction magazines had a large female readership but cites no external evidence (ibid.: 32ff).

6 For example, the *Sunday School Times and Home Educator* (Jan. 1860–Mar. 1925) edited by Mary Anne Hearne and the *Monthly Packet* edited by Charlotte Yonge (1851–98); see *Monthly Packet* I 1851: 'Introductory Letter' for the address to a specifically female readership (Drotner 1988: 118).

7 This may have been because lack of American copyright made it relatively cheap.

8 For example, the *Lady's Treasury* serial, *The Elopement* (1871 XI: esp. 50–6), Gaskell (1866).

9 The following serial in the *EDM* dealt with bigamy and infanticide; *Beechwood Manor* by the author of *Greyhills* and *Meredith Chichester*, serialised in *EDM* 1863–4.

10 I am indebted to Louis James for drawing my attention to this story in an unpublished paper 'Things Unattempted Yet: An Examination of the *EDM*, New Series Vol. I' given to the Research Society for Victorian Periodicals Conference at Waco in 1990.

11 Thanks to Anne Humphreys for permission to refer to her unpublished article 'Nature, Fiction and the *EDM*' also given at the Waco conference (see note 10).

12 Steel provided a very sharp definition and a high-quality picture.

13 The whole dress pattern cost 5*s.* 6*d.* in 1861, a pattern for the body alone, 2*s.* (*EDM* N.S. III 1861: 143).

14 Browne may also have written as 'A Woman'; Freeman attributes these articles to her on internal evidence (Freeman 1977: 259).

15 Beeton had advertised for advertisers in the very first number of the magazine (*EDM* I 1852: 125).

16 The most famous of these is Walter's *My Secret Life*. Judith Walkowitz points out how such

pornographic tropes were mobilised by the radical journalist, W.T. Stead, in the 1880s (Walkowitz 1993: 97ff).

17 Irigaray argues that 'Woman finds pleasure more in touch than in sight and her entrance into the dominant scopic economy signifies, once again, her relegation to passivity; she will be the beautiful object' (Marks and de Cortivron 1981: 101).

7 RE-MAKING THE LADY: THE *QUEEN*

1 E.W. Cox bought *Queen* from Beeton. Freeman gives the date of the sale to the proprietors of the *Lady's Newspaper* as July 1863 (Freeman 1977: 184). However, there was clearly some interim arrangement. Vol. I was published by Beeton at his office, 248 The Strand; Vol. II by Beeton 'at the office of Cox and Wyman', 346 The Strand, printed by John Wyman'; Vol. III from 346 The Strand with no named publisher, 'printed by John Crockford'.

2 For various meanings of 'Not at home' see Beeton (1861: 11).

3 For example 28 March 1885, 15⅓ pages of text; 10⅔ of illustration and 39 pages of advertising.

4 Typical costs in 1885 were 3s. 1d. for a skirt pattern, 2s. 7d. for a bodice and full dress pattern from 4s. 7d. to 5s. 7d. (*Q.* LXXVII 1885: 318).

5 Contemporary discussion on the relationship between gender, sexuality and the 'gaze' has been deeply influenced by film theory and especially by Laura Mulvey's 'Visual Pleasure and Narrative Cinema' (Mulvey 1975). That debate is useful for reading the kind of texts I consider here in that it links pleasure, sexuality and the visual aspects of popular culture. It does not however, address the specifics of how these work in terms of the materiality of print and the very different visual culture of the late nineteenth century. See also Gamman and Marshment (1988).

8 THE NEW WOMAN AND THE NEW JOURNALISM

1 For the debate about when new woman became The New Woman see Ardis (1990: 10), Jordan (1983), Rubenstein (1986: 16–23).

2 Books which deal with the *fin-de-siècle* in cultural politics include: Ledger and McCracken (1995), Showalter (1991), Stokes (1992).

3 There were campaigners who related gender inequality and sexuality and who developed positive models of same-sex desire for women but these were not public discourses (see Smith-Rosenberg 1991; Vicinus 1985). Henry James's *Bostonians* typically portrayed Olive's desire for Verbena as life-denying (James 1886).

4 Sexologists included Carpenter, Krafft-Ebing and Freud, whose *Studies on Hysteria* were published with Bauer in 1895 (Strachey 1986b: 6); on state legislation, see Smart (1992) and Weeks (1981); on social purity see Jeffreys (1985) and Bland (1995); for other writing see Engels (1884), Grand (1894) and contemporary work by Showalter (1991: 39 and passim), Walkowitz (1994).

5 New Woman fiction has been discussed by recent scholars in books which include: Ardis (1990), Boumelha (1982), Cunningham (1978), Flint (1993), Gilbert and Gubar (1989), Pykett (1992), Stubbs (1979).

6 Quoted by Ardis (1990: 11), Jordan (1983: 252) and Rubenstein (1986: 22); also in *Punch* again (21 Sept. 1895: 136).

7 Articles from this period on working-class reading include: Ackland (1894), Bosanquet (1901), Gattie (1889), Hitchman (1880–1), Humphries (1893), Lang (1901), Low (1906), Phillips (1900), Salmon (1886c). Articles specifically on girls'

and women's reading include: Low (1906), March-Phillips (1894), Moore (1885), Ridding (1896), Salmon (1886b).

8 *The Times* had installed the first Hoe press in Britain in 1857 but in the 1880s and 1890s improved versions could print on up to three reels of paper simultaneously on both sides.

9 Newnes's original flotation was in 1891 with capital at £400,000. The company was worth £1,000,000 by 1897 (Friederichs 1911: 134); Harmsworth Brothers Limited was established in 1896 with 500,000 ordinary shares at £1 for the Harmsworth brothers and the same number of preference shares for the public ((Pound 1959: 63).

10 The argument that mass culture is associated with the feminine is made by Huyssen who associates it with the emergence of modernism (Huyssen 1986). I disagree with this periodisation but find much of the rest of the argument useful.

9 REVOLTING DAUGHTERS, GIRTON GIRLS AND ADVANCED WOMEN

1 I am not here considering magazines addressed specifically to girls; on these see Drotner (1988) and Sally Mitchell's forthcoming book.

2 Mona Caird's question 'Is Marriage a Failure?' was taken up in the *Daily Telegraph* where it provoked 2,700 letters, many of them arguing that it was. They were collected in a volume by Henry Quilter (Bland 1995; Showalter 1991: 44; Stokes 1989: 23).

3 Walter Crane argued in *Woman* that the Revolting Daughter was 'a middle and upper middle class question' and of little wider relevance (*W.* 28 Feb. 1894: 5).

10 ADVANCING INTO COMMODITY CULTURE

1 The tax was 3s. per advertisement in 1789 and 3s. 6d. in 1815 (Wiener 1969: 9).

2 The cultural history of advertising is still woefully inadequate but see Richards (1990).

3 As researchers of nineteenth-century periodicals know, finding copies with advertisements in place is extremely difficult, sometimes impossible. This chapter is perhaps the most contingent of all as I have had to extrapolate from such evidence as I could find.

4 Rates were relatively cheap at a penny for ten words in the Exchange and for two words in the Mart section (*E&M* I 1868: 1).

5 The volume for 28 March 1885 had 30 full pages of advertisements including the covers, to 15.3 of text, including some classified ads and 11.6 of illustrations (*Q.* LXXVII 1885).

11 *WOMAN AT HOME*: THE MIDDLE-CLASS DOMESTIC MAGAZINE AND THE AGONY AUNT

1 She was the daughter-in-law of Sam and Isabella Beeton.

2 The magazine ran other royal biographies, including 'The Daughters of Queen Victoria' by Katherine Lee (*W. at H.* VII 1897: 161–203; see also 'Portraits of Queen Victoria', *W. at H.* VII 1897: 801–12).

3 The *Waterloo Directory* assumes this. Jane T. Stoddart also worked in an editorial capacity on the magazine, probably first under Nicoll and then as editor (see Nicoll 1945: 20).

4 In a six-month sample, out of 73 correspondents named, only 4 were named as men, with 7 whose gender was unspecified; whereas in the 'Love, Courtship and Marriage' column, out of 67 correspondents, 15 were men, 5 unspecified (*W. at H.* V 1895–6).

5 There were 3 who identified themselves as working class in a six-month sample of 73, ibid.
6 See *W. at H.* VII (1897–8: 603–6) for article on Annie S. Swan.
7 The first Elizabeth Glen series appeared in *W. at H.* I (1892–3: 11, 91, 179, 254, etc.; II, 21, 124, 175, etc.); the Margaret Grainger series was in *W. at H.* III (1894–5: 24, 92, 345, 481, etc.). The second Elizabeth Glen series appeared in *W. at H.* V (1895-6: 1, 81, 321, 401, 481, 585, etc.).

12 'FORWARD BUT NOT TOO FAST': THE ADVANCED MAGAZINE?

1 It was 'the first British periodical devoted to feminist issues' (Doughan 1987: 266).
2 *A Journal of Women's Work* until 1869 then title changed to *Englishwoman's Review of Social and Industrial Questions*.
3 The *Waterloo Directory* assumes, wrongly, that the *Woman's Suffrage Journal* was edited in London.
4 The collapse of such different ventures as *Women's Review* and *Spare Rib* in the late twentieth century indicates the difficulties which persist.
5 See e.g. articles on how to live on £550 or £450 a year 'without feeling poverty stricken' (*W.* 1 March 1890: 6; 3 Jan. 1894: 10).
6 I am grateful to Lynne Warren of John Moores' University, Liverpool, for allowing me to draw on her unpublished paper given at the RSVP Conference in Tampa, Florida, Sept. 1994 which confirms the generally middle-class nature of, at least the prize winners, in *Woman*.
7 When Gardner left the editorship, his male identity was revealed. Though the new editor was given a male title, there was no hint that he used the magazine's female names. In the new century, the magazine did acquire a woman editor.
8 This story and others from the 1890s involving cross-dressing were brought to my attention by Peter Farrar's *In Female Disguise* (1992).

13 WOMAN-TALK AS COMMODITY: THE PENNY DOMESTIC MAGAZINE

1 *Woman's Life* began with 62 pages a week; *Home Chat* had 58. The boast that they employed the same writers as the sixpennies was often true; Mrs Talbot Cooke, L.T. Meade and others wrote for both.
2 Nowell-Smith argues that Cassells over-estimated the new reading public ('[*Paris Mode*] died of ambition') but he attributes its demise directly to Harmsworth's success (Nowell-Smith 1958: 182).
3 See e.g. Pearson's claim that 'All advertisements face reading matter, unless specifically ordered for front or back page, thus considerably enhancing their value. The page devoted to the Home each week is very helpful to advertisers of Household Requisites etc. Special Attention given to display' (Mitchell 1900: 265).
4 The title of George Dangerfield's now old and rather outdated book still conveys that sense of the collapse of the Victorian which dominated the period.
5 Regina Gagnier's discussion on the liberal turn in the construction of nineteenth-century subjects has influenced my thinking here (Gagnier 1991).
6 Snitow (1983) is the key text in this debate but see also articles in Gamman and Marshment (1988 esp. Lewallen, '*Lace*, Pornography for Women?').
7 The key figure in this debate has been Derrida and in particular *Of Grammatology* (1976). However Bakhtin's very different approach to the relationship of speech to written text is another important locus of discussion.

SELECT BIBLIOGRAPHY
OF MAGAZINES CONSULTED

This is a list of some of the titles consulted in the process of writing this book. It is not a full bibliography.

KEY

Titles are listed in chronological order of their launch. Relaunches follow semi-colons (;)
N.S. means New Series
N.S. 2 means second New Series
I.S. means Improved Series
qv means look at the title indicated
(W) means weekly publication
(M) means monthly publication
(A) means annual publication

1770   The *Lady's Magazine* (M)–1832; merged with the *Lady's Museum* as the *Lady's Magazine and Museum* (M)–1837; merged with the *Court Magazine and Monthly Critic* as the *Court Magazine and Monthly Critic and Lady's Magazine and Museum* (M)–1847.

1798   The *Lady's Monthly Museum* (M)–1829; the *Lady's Museum* (M) 1829–31; N.S.–1832; merged with the *Lady's Magazine qv*.

1806   *La Belle Assemblée* (M)–1810; N.S.–1824; N.S.–1829; N.S.–1832; the *Court Magazine and Belle Assemblée* (M)–1836; the *Court Magazine and Monthly Critic* (M)–1838; merged with the *Lady's Magazine and Museum* as the *Court Magazine and Monthly Critic and Lady's Magazine and Museum* (M)–1847.

1813   The *Female Preceptor* (M), dedicated to Hannah More.

1832   *Maids', Wives' and Widows' Penny Magazine and Gazette of Fashion* (W)–1832; *Maids', Wives' and Widows' Penny Magazine* (W)–1833. The *Weekly Belle Assemblée* (W)–1834; the *New Monthly Belle Assemblée* (M)–1870.

1833   *Heath's Book of Beauty* (A)–1847; the *Book of Beauty or Royal Gallery* (A) 1848 only.

1834   The *Christian Lady's Magazine* (M)–1849.

1834   The *Mother's Magazine* (M)–1849; N.S.–1862.

1836   The *Magazine of Domestic Economy* (M)–1841; the *Magazine of Domestic Economy and Family Review* (M) 1842–4.

1844   The *Christian Mother's Miscellany* (M)–1845; the *Englishwoman's Magazine and Christian Mother's Miscellany* (M) 1846–54; the *Christian Lady's Magazine* (M) 1855–7.

1845   The *British Mother's Magazine* (M)–1855; the *British Mother's Journal* (M) 1856–63; the *British Mother's Family Magazine for 1864* (M) 1864 only.

1847   The *Lady's Newspaper and Pictorial Times* (W)–1863; merged with the *Queen* qv.

1848   The *Family Economist* (?)–1860.

1848   The *Mother's Friend* (M)–1859; N.S. 1869–87.

1849   The *Family Friend* (W)–1867; N.S. 1869–87.

1852   The *Englishwoman's Domestic Magazine* (M)–1859, published and edited by S. Beeton; N.S. 1860–4; N.S. 1865–77; absorbed by the *Milliner and Dressmaker and Warehouseman's Gazette* 1877.

1858   The *English Woman's Journal* (M)–1864; the *Alexandra Magazine* (M)–1865; the *Englishwoman's Review of Social and Industrial Questions* (M) 1866–1910.

1861   The *Queen* (W)–1863, published by S. Beeton; the *Queen, The Ladies' Newspaper* (W)–1970, published by Cox, 1970 merged with *Harper's Bazaar* as *Harper's and Queen* (M)–present.

1863   The *Victoria Magazine* (M)–1880, published by Victoria Press.

1864   The *Young Englishwoman* (M)–1877, published by S. Beeton then by Ward, Lock & Co.; *Sylvia's Home Journal* (M) 1878–91; *Sylvia's Journal* (M) 1892–1894.

1875   *Myra's Journal of Dress and Fashion* (W and M)–1912, published by Weldon; 1897 absorbed the *Lady's Magazine* qv.

1880   The *Girls' Own Paper* (W)–1927, published by the Religious Tract Society; *Woman's Magazine and Girls' Own Paper* (W)–1930.

1881   The *Lady's Pictorial* (W)–1921 (absorbed by *Eve*).

1885   *The Lady* (M)–present.

1886   The *Lady's World* (M)–1887, published by Cassells; *Woman's World* (M) 1888–1890.

1888   *Women's Penny Paper* (W)–1890; *Women's Herald* (W)–1893.

1890   *My Lady's Novelette* (W)–??

1890   *Woman* (W)–1912.

1891   *Forget-Me-Not* (W)–1918, published by Harmsworth.

1891   *Hearth and Home* (W)–1914, published by Beeton; absorbed by *Vanity Fair*.

1893   *Woman at Home* (M)–1920 subtitled 'Annie S. Swan's Magazine'; absorbed *The Girl's Realm* (est. 1898) in 1915.

1894   *Home Notes* (M until 1900, W thereafter)–1957, published by Pearsons; *Woman's Own* (W)–present.

1895   *Home Chat* (W)–1958, published by Harmsworth.

BIBLIOGRAPHY

PRE-1914 NON-FICTION

Ackland, J. (1894) 'Elementary education and the decay of literature', *Nineteenth Century* XXXV: 412–23.

Anon. (1867) 'The trade of journalism', *St Paul's Magazine* I: 306–18.

Anon. (1874) [The Author of 'Authors at Work'], 'The L.S.D. of literature', *Gentlemen's Magazine* N.S. XIII: 713–21.

Anon. (1897) 'The Old Journalists and the New', *Saturday Review* LXIII: 578–9.

Anon. (1898) 'Penny fiction', *Blackwood's Edinburgh Magazine* CLXIV 801–11.

Arnold, Matthew (1869) *Culture and Anarchy: An Essay in Political and Social Criticism*, London: Smith Elder.

—— (1887) 'Up to Easter', *Nineteenth Century* XXI: 629–43.

Author of 'The heavenward path' (n.d.) *Heroines of the Household*, London: James Hogg & Sons.

Beeton, Isabella (1861) *Beeton's Book of Household Management*, London: S.O. Beeton.

Bell, Lady (Mrs Hugh Bell) (1907) *At the Works; A Study of a Manufacturing Town* (2nd edition 1911), London: Nelson.

—— (1905) 'What People Read', *Independent Review* VII: 27.

Besant, Walter (1899) *The Pen and the Book*, London: Thomas Burleigh.

Billington, M.F. (1891) 'Women in journalism', pp. 58–62 in *Sell's Directory*, London: Sell's.

Black, Helen (1906) *Notable Women Authors of the Day*, London: McClaren & Co.

Bosanquet, Helen (1901) 'Cheap literature', *Contemporary Review* LXXIX: 671–81.

Carlyle, Thomas (1843) 'Morrison's pill', *Past and Present*, repr. 1893, London: Chapman and Hall.

Collins, W. (1858) 'The unknown public', *Household Words* XVIII: 217–22.

Crackenthorpe, Mrs B.A. (1894) 'The revolt of the daughters', *Nineteenth Century* XXXV: 23–5, 424–6.

—— (1895) 'Sex in modern literature', *Nineteenth Century* XXXI: 607–16.

—— (1839) *The Women of England, Their Social Duties and Domestic Habits*, London: Fisher, Son & Co.

—— (1843) *The Wives of England*, London: Fisher, Son & Co.

Ellis, Sarah Strickney (1893) *The Home Life and Letters of Mrs. Ellis*, compiled by her nieces, London: Nisbet.

Engels, Frederick (1884/1972) *The Origin of the Family, Private Property and the State*, London: Lawrence & Wishart.

Friederichs, Hulda (1911) *The Life of Sir George Newnes*, London: Hodder & Stoughton.

Gattie, W.M. (1889) 'What English people read', *Fortnightly Review* XLVI: 307–21.

Greg, W.R. (1862) 'Why are women redundant?', *National Review* XIV: 434–60.

Hitchman, F. (1880–1) 'The penny press', *Macmillan's* XLIII: 285–398.

—— (Anon) (1890) 'Penny fiction', *Quarterly Review* CLXXI: 151–71.

Hood, Thomas (1843) 'The song of the shirt', *Punch* V: 260.

Humphries, George (1893) 'The reading of the working classes', *Nineteenth Century* XXXIII: 690–701.

Jackson, Holbrook (1913) *The Eighteen Nineties*, London: Grant Richards; re-issued (1976) Brighton: Harvester.

Jeune, Lady (1895) 'The ethics of shopping', *Fortnightly Review* LVII: 122–32.

Johnson, Joseph (n.d.) *Clever Girls of our Time and How they Became Famous Women*, Edinburgh and London: Gall & Inglis.

Kirton, Dr J.W. (1882) *Happy Homes and How to Make Them*, London: Kempster & Co. and W. Swan Sonnenschein.

Lang, Andrew and X, A Working Man (1901) 'The reading public', *Cornhill Magazine* N.S. XI: 783–95.

Leigh, John G. (1904) 'What do the masses read?', *Economic Review* XIV (2): 166–77.

Linton, Eliza Lynn (1868) 'The girl of the period', *Saturday Review* XXV: 339–41.

Low, Florence B. (1906) 'The reading of the modern girl', *Nineteenth Century* LIX: 278–80.

March-Phillips, Evelyn (1894) 'Women's newspapers', *Fortnightly Review* N.S. LVI: 661–9.

—— (1895) 'The new journalism', *The New Review* XIII: 182–9.

Mill, John Stuart (1869) *The Subjection of Women*. Repr. 1912 *On Liberty, Representative Government, and The Subjection of Women: Three Essays by John Stuart Mill*, Oxford: Oxford University Press.

Moore, George (1885) *Literature at Nurse, or Circulating Morals*, edited by P. Coustillas, London: Cornhill.

More, Hannah (1834) 'Strictures on the modern system of female education', in *The Works of Hannah More, Volume III*, London: Fisher, Fisher & Jackson.

O'Connor, T.P. (1889) 'The new journalism', *New Review* I: 423–34.

Perkins, Jane Gray (1910) *The Life of Mrs Caroline Norton*, London: Murray.

Phillips, T.C. (1900) 'The reading of the working class', *Literature* VI: 359.

Ridding, Lady Laura *et al.* (1896) 'What should women read?' *Woman at Home* VI: 932–4.

Ruskin, J. (1865/1905) *Sesame and Lilies*, in E.T. Cook and S. Wedderburn (eds) *Works of Ruskin, XVIII*, London: George Allen.

Salmon, Edward (1886a) 'What boys read', *Fortnightly Review* N.S. XXXIX: 248–59.

—— (1886b) 'What girls read', *Nineteenth Century* CXV: 515–29.

—— (1886c) 'What the working classes read', *Nineteenth Century* CXV: 108–17.

Shorter, C.K. (1899) 'Illustrated journalism: its past and future', *Contemporary Review* LXXV: 481ff.

Smiles, Samuel (1859) *Self Help*, London: John Murray.

Smith, Laura Alex (1900) 'Women's work on the press: editorial and journalistic', *Mitchell's Press Directory*, London: Mitchell's.

Stanley, Maude (ed.) (1890) *Clubs for Working Girls*, London: Macmillan.

Trollope, A. (1867) 'Introduction', *St Paul's Magazine* I: 2–7.

Veblen, Thorstein (1899/1970) *The Theory of the Leisure Class; An Economic Study of Institutions*, London: Allen & Unwin.

Weisse, H.V. (1901) 'Reading for the young', *Contemporary Review* LXXIX: 829–38.

Wollstonecraft, Mary (1792/1975) *A Vindication of the Rights of Woman*, Harmondsworth: Penguin.

PRE-1914 FICTION

(Short title; year of first volume publication only.)

Allen, Grant (1895) *The Woman Who Did.*
Barrett Browning, Elizabeth (1857) *Aurora Leigh.*
Besant, Walter (1882a) *All Sorts and Conditions of Men.*
—— (1882b) *The Revolt of Man.*
Braddon, Mary (1862) *Lady Audley's Secret.*
Bronte, Charlotte (1849) *Shirley.*
Cross, Victoria (1895) *The Women Who Didn't.*
Dickens, Charles (1853) *Bleak House.*
Egerton, George (1893) *Keynotes.*
Gaskell, Elizabeth (1848) *Mary Barton.*
—— (1855) *North and South.*
—— (1866) *Wives and Daughters.*
Gissing, George (1891) *New Grub Street* (repr. 1968, Harmondsworth: Penguin).
—— (1893) *The Odd Women.*
Grand, Sarah (1888) *Ideala.*
—— (1894) *The Heavenly Twins.*
Grossmith, W. (1892) *The Diary of a Nobody*, (repr. 1962, London: Everyman).
Haggard, Rider (1887) *She.*
Haggard, Rider and Lang, Andrew (1890) *The World's Desire.*
Hardy, Thomas (1891) *Tess of the D'Urbervilles.*
—— (1896) *Jude the Obscure.*
James, Henry (1886) *The Bostonians.*
Paston, George (1898) *A Writer of Books.*
Schreiner, Olive (Ralph Iron) (1883) *The Story of an African Farm.*
—— (1891) *Dreams.*
Stoker, Bram (1897) *Dracula.*
Wilde, Oscar (1891) *The Picture of Dorian Gray.*

POST-1914

Adburgham, Alison (1964) *Shops and Shopping; Where, and in What Manner the Well-dressed Englishwoman Bought her Clothes,* London: Allen & Unwin.
—— (1972) *Women in Print: Writing Women and Women's Magazines from the Restoration to the Accession of Queen Victoria,* London: Allen & Unwin.
Adorno, T.W. and Horkheimer, M. (1977) 'The culture industry: enlightenment as mass deception', in James Curran, Michael Gurevitch and Janet Woollacott (eds) *Mass Communication and Society,* London: Edward Arnold.
Althusser, Louis (1971) 'Ideology and ideological state apparatuses', in *Lenin and Philosophy and Other Essays,* trans. Ben Brewster, London: New Left Books.
Altick, Richard D. (1957) *The English Common Reader: A Social History of the Mass Reading Public, 1800–1900,* Chicago: Chicago University Press.
Anderson, Benedict (1983) *Imagined Communities: Reflections on the Origin and Spread of Nationalism,* London: Verso.
Anderson, Patricia (1991) *The Printed Image and the Transformation of Popular Culture, 1790–1860,* Oxford: Clarendon Press.
Anderson, Paul (1931) 'The History and Authorship of Mrs Crackenthorpe's Female Tatler', *Modern Philology* 27: 354–60.
Ardis, Ann (1990) *New Women; New Novels: Feminism and Early Modernism,* New Brunswick: Rutgers University Press.

Armstrong, Nancy (1985) *Desire and Domestic Fiction: A Political History of the Novel*, Oxford: Oxford University Press.

Asquith, Margot (1920) *The Autobiography of Margot Asquith*, London: Butterworth.

Ballaster, R., Beetham, M., Frazer, E. and Hebron, S. (1991) *Women's Worlds; Ideology, Femininity and the Woman's Magazine*, London: Macmillan.

Barnard, M. (1991) *Introduction to Printing Processes*, London: Chapman and Hall.

Barret-Ducrocq, Françoise (1991) *Love in the Time of Victoria: Sexuality, Class and Gender in Nineteenth-Century London*, trans. John Howe, London: Verso.

Barthes, Roland (1972) 'Myth today', in *Mythologies* trans. Annette Lavers, London: Jonathan Cape.

—— (1976) *The Pleasure of the Text*, trans. Richard Miller, London: Jonathan Cape.

Beetham, Margaret (1985) '"Healthy reading"; the periodical press in late Victorian Manchester', in A. Kidd and R. Roberts (eds) *City, Class and Culture: Studies of Cultural Production and Social Policy in Victorian Manchester*, Manchester: Manchester University Press.

—— (1990) 'Towards a theory of the periodical as a publishing genre', in L. Brake, A. Jones and L. Madden (eds) *Investigating Victorian Journalism*, London: Macmillan.

—— (1991) '"Natural but firm": the corset correspondence in the *Englishwoman's Domestic Magazine*', *Women: A Cultural Review* 2 (2): 163–7.

—— (1994) with A. Bowers, D. Fuller, L. Hunter *et al. Victorian Periodicals Hypertext Project*, Oxford: C.T.I. Centre for Textual Studies.

Benjamin, Walter (1968) 'The work of art in the age of mechanical reproduction', in *Illuminations*, edited by Hannah Arendt, New York: Harcourt Brace & World Inc.

Bennett, Scott (1982) 'Revolutions in thought: serial publication and the mass market for reading', in J. Shattock and M. Wolff *The Victorian Periodical Press: Samplings and Soundings*, Leicester: Leicester University Press.

Bennett, Tony (1982) 'Theories of the media, theories of society', in Michael Gurevitch, Tony Bennett, James Curran and Janet Woollacott (eds) *Culture, Society and the Media*, London: Methuen.

—— (1986) 'The politics of the "popular" and popular culture', in Tony Bennett, Colin Mercer and Janet Woollacott (eds) *Popular Culture and Social Relations*, Milton Keynes and Philadelphia: Open University Press.

Best, G. (1982) *Mid-Victorian Britain, 1851–70*, Glasgow: Fontana/Collins.

Betterton, Rosemary (ed.) (1987) *Looking On: Images of Femininity in the Visual Arts and Media*, London: Pandora Press.

Berger, John (1972) *Ways of Seeing*, London: BBC.

Bland, Lucy (1992) 'Feminist vigilantes of late-Victorian England', in C. Smart (ed.) *Regulating Womanhood*, London: Routledge.

—— (1995) *Banishing the Beast: English Feminism and Sexual Morality, 1885–1914*, Harmondsworth: Penguin.

Bostick, T. (1980) 'The press and the launch of the Women's Suffrage Movement, 1866–7', *Victorian Periodical Review* 13: 125–31.

Boumelha, Penny (1982) *Thomas Hardy and Women: Sexual Ideology and Narrative Form*, Brighton: Harvester.

Bowlby, Rachel (1985) *Just Looking: Consumer Culture in Dreiser, Gissing, and Zola*, London: Methuen.

Boyce, G., Curran, J. and Wingate, P. (eds) (1978) *Newspaper History from the Seventeenth Century to the Present Day*, London: Constable.

Braithwaite, Brian and Barrell, Joan (1988) *The Business of Women's Magazines*, 2nd edn. London: Associated Business Press.

Brake, Laurel (1994) *Subjugated Knowledges: Journalism, Gender and Literature in the Nineteenth Century*, London: Macmillan.

Bristow, Joseph (1991) *Empire Boys: Adventures in a Man's World,* London: HarperCollins.

Brown, Lucy (1985) *Victorian News and Newspapers,* Oxford: Clavendon.

Butler, Judith (1990) *Gender Trouble,* New York: Routledge.

—— (1993) *Bodies that Matter: On the Discursive Limits of Sex,* New York: Routledge.

Cameron, Deborah (1986) *Feminism and Linguistic Theory,* London: Macmillan.

Cannadine, David (1983) 'The context, performance and meaning of ritual: the British monarchy and the "Invention of Tradition"', in E. Hobsbawm and T. Ranger (eds) *The Invention of Tradition,* Cambridge: Cambridge University Press.

Clarke, Tom (1950) *Northcliffe in History: An Intimate Study of Press Power,* London: Hutchinson.

Colby, Veneta (1970) *The Singular Anomaly: Women Novelists of the Nineteenth Century,* New York: New York University Press.

Cole, G.D.R. and Postgate, R. (1938/1946) *The Common People; 1746–1946,* London: Methuen.

Corrigan, Phillip and Gillespie, Val (1977) *Class Struggle, Idle Time and Social Literacy,* Brighton: John Noyce.

Craik, Jennifer (1994) *The Face of Fashion: Cultural Studies in Fashion,* London: Routledge.

Cross, Nigel (1985) *The Common Writer: Life in Nineteenth-century Grub Street,* Cambridge: Cambridge University Press.

Cruse, Amy (1930) *The Englishman and His Books in the Early Nineteenth Century,* London: Harrap.

Culler, Jonathan (1982) *On Deconstruction: Theory and Criticism after Structuralism,* Ithaca: Cornell University Press.

Cunningham, Gail (1978) *The New Woman and the Victorian Novel,* London: Macmillan.

Dalziel, Margaret (1957) *Popular Fiction a Hundred Years Ago: An Unexplored Tract of Literary History,* London: Cohen & West.

Dancyger, Irene (1978) *A World of Women: Illustrated History of Women's Magazines,* Dublin: Gill & Macmillan.

Dark, Sidney (1922) *The Life of Sir Arthur Pearson,* London: Hodder & Stoughton.

Darlow, T.H. (1925) *William Robertson Nicholl: Life and Letters,* London: Hodder & Stoughton.

Davidoff, Leonore (1986) *The Best Circles: Society, Etiquette and the Season,* London: Croom Helm.

Davidoff, Leonore and Hall, Catherine (1987) *Family Fortunes: Men and Women of the English Middle Class 1780–1850,* London: Hutchinson.

Davies, Tony (1983) 'Transports of pleasure', in *Formations of Pleasure,* London: Routledge & Kegan Paul.

de Marly, Diana (1980) *Worth, Father of Haute Couture,* London: Elm Tree Books.

de Vries, Leonard and Laver, James (1968) *Victorian Advertising,* London: John Murray.

Dollimore, Jonathan (1991) *Sexual Dissidence: Augustine to Wilde; Freud to Foucault,* Oxford: Clarendon Press.

Dorson, R. (1968) *The British Folklorists: A History,* London: Routledge & Kegan Paul.

Doughan, David (1987) 'Periodicals by, for and about women in Britain', *Women's Studies International Forum* 3: 261–73.

Doughan, David and Sanchez, Denise (1987) *Feminist Periodicals, 1855–1984; An Annotated Bibliography of British, Irish and Commonwealth Titles,* Brighton: Harvester.

Douglas, Ann (1977) *The Feminisation of American Culture,* New York: Alfred Knopf.

Drabble, Margaret (1975) *Arnold Bennett: A Biography,* London: Futura.

Driver, Elizabeth (1989) *A Bibliography of Cookery Books Published in Britain, 1875–1914,* London: Prospect.

Drotner, Kristen (1988) *English Children and their Magazines, 1751–1945,* New Haven and London: Yale University Press.

Ellman, Richard (1988) *Oscar Wilde*, Harmondsworth: Penguin.

Ellegard, Alvar (1957) *The Readership of the Periodical Press in Mid-Victorian Britain*, Goteburg: Goteburg University Press.

Farrer, Peter (ed.) (1992) *In Female Disguise*, Garston: Karn.

Fergus, Jan (1986) 'Women, class and the growth of magazine readership in the provinces', *Eighteenth-Century Culture* 16: 41–56.

Ferguson, M. (1983) *Forever Feminine: Women's Magazines and the Cult of Femininity*, London: Heinemann.

Fetterley, Judith (1978) *The Resisting Reader: A Feminist Approach to American Fiction*, Bloomington: Indiana University Press.

Flint, Kate (1986) 'Fictional suburbia', in P. Humm, P. Stigant and P. Widdowson (eds) *Popular Fictions: Essays in Literature and History*, London: Methuen.

—— (1993) *The Woman Reader, 1837–1914*, Oxford: Oxford University Press.

Forrester, Wendy (1980) *Great Grandmother's Weekly: A Celebration of the Girls' Own Paper*, London: Lutterworth.

Foucault, Michel (1979) *Discipline and Punish*, New York: Vintage.

—— (1980) *Power/Knowledge: Selected Interviews and Other Writings, 1972–1977*, Brighton: Harvester.

—— (1981) *The History of Sexuality: An Introduction*, Harmondsworth: Pelican.

Freeman, Sarah (1977) *Isabella and Sam; The Story of Mrs. Beeton*, London: Victor Gollancz.

Fried, A. and Elman, R. (eds) (1969) *Charles Booth's London*, Harmondsworth: Penguin.

Friedan, Betty (1965) *The Feminine Mystique*, Harmondsworth: Penguin.

Fuss, Diana (1989) *Essentially Speaking: Feminism, Nature and Difference*, New York: Routledge.

Gagnier, Regina (1986) *Idylls of the Market Place: Oscar Wilde and the Victorian Public*, Aldershot: Scolar Press.

—— (1991) *Subjectivities: A History of Self-Representations in Britain, 1832–1920*, Oxford: Oxford University Press.

Gaines, Jane and Herzog, Charlotte (eds) (1990) *Fabrications: Costume and the Female Body*, New York and London: Routledge.

Gamman, Lorraine and Marshment, Margaret (eds) (1988) *The Female Gaze: Women as Viewers of Popular Culture*, London: Women's Press.

Gardner, V. and Rutherford, S. (eds) (1992) *The New Woman and her Sisters: Feminism and Theatre, 1850–1914*, Hemel Hempstead: Harvester Wheatsheaf.

Gay, Peter (1984) *The Bourgeois Experience: Victoria to Freud* I and II, Oxford: Oxford University Press.

Gilbert, S. and Gubar, S. (1979) *The Madwoman in the Attic: The Woman Writer and the Nineteenth Century Literary Imagination*, New Haven and London: Yale University Press.

—— (1989) *No Man's Land II: Sexchanges*, New Haven and London: Yale University Press.

Gorham, Deborah (1976) 'The Maiden Tribute of Babylon Revisited', *Victorian Studies* (Spring): 353–79.

—— (1982) *The Victorian Girl and the Feminine Ideal*, London: Croom Helm.

Greer, Germaine (1971) *The Female Eunuch*, London: Paladin.

Grierst, G. (1970) *Mudie's Circulating Library and the Victorian Novel*, Indiana: Indiana University Press.

Gross, John (1969) *The Rise and Fall of the Man of Letters: English Literary Life since 1800*, Harmondsworth: Penguin.

Gurevitch, Michael, Bennett, Tony, Curran, James and Woollacott, Janet (eds) (1982) *Culture, Society and the Media*, London: Methuen.

Hall, Stuart (1980) 'Encoding/decoding', in Stuart Hall *et al.* (eds) *Culture, Media, Language: Working Papers in Cultural Studies*, London: Hutchinson, 972–9.

Haraway, Donna (1991) *Simians, Cyborgs and Women: The Reinvention of Nature*, London: Free Association Books.

Helsinger, E., Sheets R., and Veeder, W. (1983) *The Woman Question* I, II and III, Manchester: Manchester University Press.

Hepburn, James (ed.) (1979) *Arnold Bennett: Sketches for Autobiography*, London: Allen & Unwin.

Herstein, Sheila R. (1985) 'The *English Woman's Journal* and the Langham Place Circle: a feminist forum and its woman editors', in Joel Weiner (ed.) (1985) *Innovators and Preachers: The Role of the Editor in Victorian England*, Westport and London: Greenwood Press.

Hindley, Diana and Hindley, Geoffrey (1972) *Victorian Advertising, 1837–1901*, London: Wayland.

Hobsbawm, E.J. (1975) *The Age of Capital, 1848–1874*, London: Weidenfeld & Nicolson.

Hobsbawm E.J. and Ranger, T. (1983) *The Invention of Tradition*, Cambridge: Cambridge University Press.

Hollis, Patricia (1970) *The Pauper Press*, Clarendon Press: Oxford.

Homans, Margaret (1993) '"To the Queen's private apartments": Royal Family portraiture and the construction of Victoria's sovereign obedience', *Victorian Studies* 37: 92–3.

Houghton, Walter (ed.) (1966–87) *The Wellesley Index of Victorian Periodicals*, I, II, III and IV, Toronto: Toronto University Press.

Humphreys, Anne (1990) '*Englishwoman's Domestic Magazine*', paper presented at RSVP Conference, Waco, Texas.

Hunter, Jean (1977) '*The Lady's Magazine* and the study of Englishwomen in the eighteenth century', in Donovan H. Bond and W. Reynolds McLeod (eds) *Newsletters to Newspapers: Eighteenth-century Journalism*, Morgantown: School of Journalism, West Virginia University.

Huyssen, Andreas (1986) *After the Great Divide: Modernism, Mass Culture, Postmodernism*, Indiana: Indiana University Press.

Hyde, Montgomery (1951) *Mr. and Mrs. Beeton*, London: Harrap.

Jacobus, Mary (1986) *Reading Woman*, London: Methuen.

Jacobus, Mary, Fox Keller, Evelyn and Shuttleworth, Sally (eds) (1990) *Body/Politics; Women and the Discourses of Science*, New York and London: Routledge.

James, Louis (1982) 'The trouble with Betsy', in J. Shattock and M. Wolff (eds) *The Victorian Periodical Press: Samplings and Soundings*, Leicester: Leicester University Press.

Jameson, Frederic (1979) 'Reification and Utopia in mass culture', *Social Text* 1: 130–48.

Jeffreys, Sheila (1985) *The Spinster and her Enemies; Feminism and Sexuality, 1880–1930*, London: Pandora.

Jordan, Ellen (1983) 'The christening of the new woman: May 1894', *Victorian Newsletter* 48.

Jordanova, Ludmilla (1989) *Sexual Visions: Images of Gender in Science and Medicine*, New York: Harvester Wheatsheaf.

Joyce, James (1960) *Ulysses*, London: Bodley Head. (Orig. 1922.)

Kaplan, E. Ann (1984) 'Is the gaze male?', in Ann Snitow, Christine Stansell and Sharon Thompson (eds) *Desire: The Politics of Sexuality*, London: Virago.

Koon, Helene (1979) 'Eliza Haywood and the Female Spectator', *Huntingdon Library Quarterly* 42: 43–57.

Kovacevic, Ivanka (1975) *Fact into Fiction: English Literature and the Industrial Scene, 1750–1850*, Leicester: Leicester University Press.

Kristeva, Julia (1986) 'Women's time', pp. 187–213 in Toril Moi (ed.) *The Kristeva Reader*, Oxford: Basil Blackwell, 187–213.

Kunzle, David (1977) 'Dress reform as anti-feminism: a response to Helene E. Roberts's "The exquisite slave: the role of clothes in the making of the Victorian woman"', *Signs* 2 (3): 570–9.

—— (1980) *Fashion and Fetishism: A Social History of the Corset, Tight-lacing and Other Forms of Body Sculpture*, New Jersey: Rowman & Littlefield.

Leavy, Barbara Fass (1980) 'Fathering and *The British Mother's Magazine, 1845–1864*', *Victorian Periodical Review* 13: 10–17.

Lee, Alan J. (1973) 'The management of a Victorian local newspaper: "The Manchester City News" 1864–1900', *Business History* 15: 139–47.

—— (1976) *The Origins of the Popular Press, 1855–1914*, London: Croom Helm.

Lee, Amice (1955) *Laurels and Rosemary: The Life of William and Mary Howitt*, London: Oxford University Press.

Levine, Philippa (1987) *Victorian Feminism*, London: Hutchinson.

—— (1990) '"The humanising influence of five o'clock tea": Victorian feminist periodicals', *Victorian Studies* 33: 293–306.

Lewis, Jane (1986) *Labour and Love: Women's Experience of Home and Family, 1850–1940*, Oxford: Basil Blackwell.

Lorde, Audre (1984) *Sister Outsider*, Freedom, CA: The Crossing Press.

Lovell, Terry (1987) *Consuming Fiction*, London: Verso.

McCracken, E. (1993) *Decoding Women's Magazines*, Basingstoke: Macmillan.

MacDonnell, Diane (1986) *Theories of Discourse: An Introduction*, Oxford: Basil Blackwell.

McRobbie, Angela (1978a) 'Working-class girls and the culture of femininity', in CCCS Women's Studies Group, *Women Take Issue*, London: Hutchinson.

—— (1978b) '*Jackie*: an ideology of adolescent femininity', University of Birmingham: CCCS Occasional Paper.

McRobbie, Angela and Nava, M. (eds) (1984) *Gender and Generation*, London: Macmillan.

Madden, L. and Dixon, D. (1975) *The Nineteenth-century Periodical Press in Britain: A Bibliography of Modern Studies, 1900–1971*, Toronto: Toronto University Press.

Maidment, Brian (1987) *The Poor House Fugitives: Self-taught Poets and Poetry in Victorian England*, Manchester: Carcanet.

Maine, G.F. (ed.) (1948/1961) *The Works of Oscar Wilde*, London: Collins.

Marks, I. and de Cortivron, I. (1981) *New French Feminisms: An Anthology*, Brighton: Harvester.

Mattelart, Michèle (1986) *Women, Media, Crisis: Femininity and Disorder*, London: Comedia.

Mayo, Robert (1962) *The English Novel in the Magazines, 1740–1815*, London: Oxford University Press.

Meech, Tricia (1986) *The Development of Women's Magazines, 1799–1945*, Catalogue of Exhibition and Account of Manchester Polytechnic's Collection: Manchester Polytechnic.

Mercer, Colin (1986) 'Complicit pleasures', in Tony Bennett, Colin Mercer and Janet Woollacott (eds) *Popular Culture and Social Relations*, Milton Keynes and Philadelphia: Open University Press.

Mills, Sarah (ed.) (1994) *Gendering the Reader*, Hemel Hempstead: Harvester Wheatsheaf.

Millum, T. (1975) *Images of Women: Advertising in Women's Magazines*, London: Chatto & Windus.

Mintel Market Intelligence (1986) 'Magazines', *Mintel* 75–88.

Mitchell, Sally (1977) 'The forgotten woman of the period: penny weekly family magazines of the 1840s and 1850s', in Martha Vicinus (ed.) *A Widening Sphere: Changing Roles of Victorian Women*, Indiana: Indiana University Press.

—— (1981) *The Fallen Angel: Chastity, Class and Women's Reading, 1835–1880*, Ohio: Bowling Green University Popular Press.

Mix, K. (1960) *A Study in Yellow: The Yellow Book and its Contributors*, London: Constable.

Modleski, Tania (1982) *Loving with a Vengeance: Mass Produced Fantasies for Women*, New York and London: Methuen.

—— (1991) *Feminism without Women; Culture and Criticism in a 'Post-Feminist Age'*, New York: Routledge.

Morris, Meaghan (1988) *The Pirate's Fiancée: Feminism Reading Post-modernism*, London: Verso.

Mulvey, Laura (1975) 'Visual pleasure and narrative cinema', *Screen* 16 (3): 6–16.

Mumby, F.A. (1930, revised edition with Norrie 1954) *Publishing and Book Selling: A History from the Earliest Times to the Present Day*, London: Cape.

Mumm, S.D. (1990) 'Writing for their lives: women applicants to the Royal Literary Life Fund, 1840–1880', *Publishing History* 27: 27–47.

Murray, Janet H. (ed.) (1982) *Strong-minded Women and Other Lost Voices from Nineteenth-Century England*, Harmondsworth: Penguin.

—— (1985) 'Class versus gender identification in *The Englishwoman's Review* of the 1880s', *Victorian Periodical Review* 18(4): 138–42.

Nead, Lynda (1988) *Myths of Sexuality: Representations of Women in Victorian Britain*, Oxford: Blackwell.

Nestor, Pauline (1982) 'A new departure in women's publishing; *The English Woman's Journal* and the *Victoria Magazine*', *Victorian Periodical Review* 15(3): 93–106.

Nicoll, M.R. (ed.) (1945) *The Letters of Annie S. Swan*, London: Hodder & Stoughton.

Nowell-Smith, Simon (1958) *The House of Cassell, 1848–1958*, London: Cassell.

Palmegiano, E.M. (1976) *Women and British Periodicals, 1832–1876*, Toronto: Victorian Periodical Newsletter, University of Toronto.

Parker, Rozsika (1984) *The Subversive Stitch: Embroidery and the Making of the Feminine*, London: Women's Press.

Pateman, Trevor (1983) 'How is understanding an advertisement possible?' in Howard Davis and Paul Walton (eds) *Language, Image, Media*, Oxford: Basil Blackwell.

Plant, Marjorie (1974) *The English Book Trade*, 3rd edn, London: Allen & Unwin.

Pollock, Griselda (1988) *Vision and Difference: Femininity, Feminism and the Histories of Art*, London: Routledge.

Poovey, Mary (1989) *Uneven Developments: The Ideological Work of Gender in Mid-Victorian Britain*, London: Virago.

Pound, Reginald (1952) *Arnold Bennett: A Biography*, London: Heinemann.

Pound, R. (1966) *The Strand Magazine, 1891–1950*, London: Heinemann.

Pound, R. and Harmsworth, G. (1959) *Northcliffe*, London: Cassell.

Pykett, Lyn (1992) *The Improper Feminine: The Woman's Sensation Novel and the New Woman Writing*, London: Routledge.

Radway, Janice (1987) *Reading the Romance: Women, Patriarchy and Popular Literature*, London: Verso.

Raymond, Janice (1986) *A Passion for Friends: Towards a Philosophy of Female Affection*, London: Women's Press.

Read, Donald (1979) *England, 1868–1914*, London: Longman.

Rendall, Jane (1987) '"A moral engine"? Feminism, liberalism and the *English Woman's Journal*', in Jane Rendall (ed.) *Equal or Different? Women's Politics, 1800–1914*, Oxford: Basil Blackwell.

Richards, Thomas (1990) *The Commodity Culture of Victorian England: Advertising and Spectacle, 1851–1914*, London: Verso.

Rinehart, Nan (1980) '"The girl of the period" controversy', *Victorian Periodical Review* 13 (1–2): 3–9.

Roberts, Helene E. (1977) 'The exquisite slave: the role of clothes in the making of the Victorian woman', *Signs* 2(3): 555–69.

Roman, Leslie, Christian-Smith, Linda and Ellsworth, Elizabeth (1988) *Becoming Feminine: The Politics of Popular Culture*, Lewes: Falmer Press.

Rubenstein, David (1986) *Before the Suffragettes: Women's Emancipation in the 1890s*, New York: St Martin's Press.

Schults, R.L. (1972) *Crusader in Babylon: W.T. Stead and the Pall Mall Gazette*, Nebraska: Lincoln.

Schuwer, P. (1966) *History of Advertising*, London: Leisure Arts Ltd.

Sedgewick, Eve Kosofsky (1991) *The Epistemology of the Closet*, London: Hamish Hamilton.

Sharpe, Sue (1976) *Just Like a Girl: How Girls Learn to be Women*, Harmondsworth: Penguin.

Shattock, Joanne and Wolff, Michael (1982) *The Victorian Periodical Press: Samplings and Soundings*, Leicester: Leicester University Press.

Shevelow, Kathryn (1989) *Women and Print Culture: The Construction of Femininity in the Early Periodical*, New York: Routledge.

Shires, Linda (ed.) (1992) *Rewriting the Victorians: Theory, History and the Politics of Gender*, New York: Routledge.

Showalter, Elaine (1982) *A Literature of Their Own: From Charlotte Bronte to Doris Lessing*, revised edn, London: Virago. (Orig. 1977.)

—— (1991) *Sexual Anarchy: Gender and Culture at the Fin de Siècle*, London: Bloomsbury.

Shuttleworth, Sally (1990) 'Female circulation: medical discourse and popular advertising in the mid-Victorian era', in Mary Jacobus, Evelyn Fox Keller and Sally Shuttleworth (eds) *Body/Politics: Women and the Discourses of Science*, New York and London: Routledge.

Smart, Carol (1992) 'Disruptive bodies and unruly sex: the regulation of reproduction and sexuality in the nineteenth century', in Carol Smart (ed.) *Regulating Womanhood: Historical Essays on Marriage, Motherhood and Sexuality*, London: Routledge.

Smith, Dorothy (1988) 'Femininity as discourse', in Leslie Roman, Linda Christian Smith and Elizabeth Ellsworth (eds) *Becoming Feminine: The Politics of Popular Culture*, Lewes: Falmer Press.

—— (1990) *Texts, Facts and Femininity*, London: Routledge.

Smith-Rosenberg, C. (1991) 'Discourses of sexuality and subjectivity: the New Woman 1870–1936', in M. Duberman, M. Vicinus and G. Chauncey (eds) *Hidden from History: Reclaiming the Gay and Lesbian Past*, Harmondsworth: Penguin.

Snitow, Ann (1983) 'Mass market romance: pornography for women is different', in Christine Stansell and Sharon Thompson (eds) (1983) *Desire: The Politics of Sexuality*, London: Virago.

Spain, Nancy (1956) *The Beeton Story*, London: Ward Lock.

Spelman, Elizabeth (1988) *Inessential Woman: Problems of Exclusion in Feminist Thought*, London: Women's Press.

Spender, Dale (1986) *Mothers of the Novel*, London: Pandora.

Spivak, Gayatri (1995) *Outside in the Teaching Machine*, New York: Routledge.

Stearns, Bertha Monica (1930) 'The first English periodical for women', *Modern Philology* 28: 45–59.

—— (1933) 'Early English periodicals for ladies', *Proceedings of the Modern Languages Association* 48: 38–60.

Steele, Valerie (1985) *Fashion and Eroticism: Ideals of Feminine Beauty from the Victorian Era to the Jazz Age*, New York: Oxford University Press.

Stokes, John (1989) *In the Nineties*, Hemel Hempstead: Harvester Wheatsheaf.

—— (1992) *Fin de Siècle, Fin du Globe: Fears and Fantasies of the Late Nineteenth Century*, Basingstoke: Macmillan.

Strachey, James (ed.) (1986a) *Sigmund Freud VI: Jokes and their Relationship to the Unconscious*, re-edited by Angela Richards, Harmondsworth: Penguin.

—— (1986b) *Sigmund Freud VII: On Sexuality*, re-edited by Angela Richards, Harmondsworth: Penguin.

Strachey, Ray (1978) *The Cause: A Short History of the Women's Movement in Great Britain*, London: Virago.

Stubbs, Patricia (1979) *Women and Fiction: Feminism and the Novel 1880–1920*, Brighton: Harvester.

Swinnerton, Frank (1969) *The Bookman's London*, revised edn, London: Allen Wingate. (Orig. 1952.)

Thompson, E.P. (1967) 'Time, work-discipline and industrial capitalism', *Past and Present* XXXVIII 56–97.

Thompson, Dorothy (1990) *Queen Victoria: Gender and Power*, London: Virago.

Todd, Janet (1989) *The Sign of Angelica: Women, Writing and Fiction, 1660–1800*, London: Virago.

Tuchman, Gaye, Daniels, A.K. and Benet, J. (eds) (1978) *Hearth and Home: Images of Women in the Mass Media*, New York: Oxford University Press.

Tuchman, Gaye and Fortin, N. (1989) *Edging Women Out: Victorian Novelists, Publishers and Social Change*, New Haven: Yale University Press.

Turner, E.A. (1965) *The Shocking History of Advertising*, Harmondsworth: Penguin.

Uffelman, Larry (1992) *The Nineteenth-century Periodical Press in Britain: A Bibliography of Modern Studies, 1972–1987*, Edwardsville: Victorian Periodical Review.

Van Arsdel, Rosemary (1978) 'Mrs Florence Fenwick-Miller and the *Woman's Signal, 1895–1899*', *Victorian Periodical Review* XI (2): 107–17.

Van Thal, H. (1979) *Eliza Lynn Linton*, London: Allen & Unwin.

Vicinus, Martha (1985) *Independent Women: Work and Community for Single Women, 1850–1920*, London: Virago.

—— (1991) 'Distance and desire: English boarding school friendships, 1870–1920', in M. Duberman, M. Vicinus and G. Chauncey (eds) *Reclaiming the Gay and Lesbian Past*, Harmondsworth: Penguin.

Vincent, David (1989) *Literacy and Popular Culture: England, 1750–1914*, Cambridge: Cambridge University Press.

Walker, Linda E. (1974) 'Employment questions and the women's movement in late Victorian and Edwardian society with particular reference to *The Englishwoman's Review*', unpublished MA dissertation, Victoria University, Manchester.

Walkowitz, Judith (1994) *City of Dreadful Delight: Narratives of Sexual Danger in Late Victorian London*, London: Virago.

Warren, Lynne (1974) '*Woman*' paper presented at the RSVP Conference, Tampa, Florida.

Watkins, Charlotte C. (1985) 'Editing a "class journal": four decades of the *Queen*', in Joel Wiener (ed.) *Innovators and Preachers: The Role of the Editor in Victorian England*, Westport and London: Greenwood Press.

Watson, Melvin R. (1956) *Magazine Serials and the Essay Tradition, 1746–1820*, Louisiana State University Studies, Humanities Series number 6, Baton Rouge: Louisiana State University Press.

Watt, Ian (1957) *The Rise of the Novel: Studies in Defoe, Richardson and Fielding*, London: Chatto & Windus.

Weedon, Chris (1988) *Feminist Practice and Postructuralist Theory*, Oxford: Basil Blackwell.

Weeks, Jeffrey (1981) *Sexuality and its Discontents: Meanings Myths and Modern Sexualities*, London: Routledge & Kegan Paul.

Whipp, Richard (1987) 'A time to every purpose; an essay on time and work', in P. Joyce (ed.) *The Historical Meanings of Work*, Cambridge: Cambridge University Press.

White, Cynthia L. (1970) *Women's Magazines, 1693–1968*, London: Michael Joseph.

Wiener, Joel (1969) *The War of the Unstamped: The Movement to Repeal the British Newspaper Tax*, Ithaca and London: Cornell University Press.

—— (ed.) (1985) *Innovators and Preachers: The Role of the Editor in Victorian England*, Westport and London: Greenwood Press.

Williams, Raymond (1961) *The Long Revolution*, London: Chatto & Windus.

—— (1966) *Communications*, London: Chatto & Windus.

—— (1977) *Marxism and Literature*, Oxford: Oxford University Press.

Williamson, Judith (1978) *Decoding Advertisements: Ideology and Meaning in Advertising*, London: Marion Boyars.

—— (1986) *Consuming Passions: The Dynamics of Popular Culture*, London: Marion Boyars.

Wilson, Elizabeth (1985) *Adorned in Dreams: Fashion and Modernity*, London: Virago Press.

Wilson, E. and Taylor, E. (1989) *Through the Looking Glass: A History of Dress from 1860 to the Present Day*, London: BBC Books.

Winship, Janice (1978) 'A woman's world: *Woman* – an ideology of femininity', in CCCS Women's Group (eds) *Women Take Issue*, London: Hutchinson.

—— (1987) *Inside Women's Magazines*, London and New York: Pandora Press.

Wolf, Naomi (1990) *The Beauty Myth*, London: Vintage.

Wolff, M., North, J. and Deering, D. (eds) (1976) *The Waterloo Directory of Victorian Periodicals, 1824–1900* I, Ontario: Waterloo.

INDEX

World of Fashion and Continental Feuilletons 211
Worth, 76, 105
writer(s) 2, 19–21, 127; men as 21, 86, 207; women as 21, 39, 42–4 *passim*, 50, 64–6, 70, 79–81, 89, 96, 111, 125, 127, 128–9, 132, 165, 170, 172–3, 177, 184, 189
writing 172–3; as domestic activity 42; *écriture feminine* 13; as a

profession 127, 128, 140, 170–1, 173, 206
Yellow Book 121, 189
Yonge, Charlotte 212
Young Englishwoman 71, 138, 141; *see also Sylvia's Journal*
Young Gentlewoman 138
Young Ladies' Journal 190
Young Man 138
Young Woman 138, 141